Wood Turning in North America Since 1930

Artists in the Exhibition:

Joyce Anderson
Derek A. Bencomo
Edward J. Bosley
Michael J. Brolly
Jacob E. Brubaker
Christian Burchard
Arthur Espenet Carpenter
M. Dale Chase
Michael Chinn
Fletcher Cox
Frank E. Cummings III
John Diamond-Nigh
Virginia Dotson
Addie Draper
David Ellsworth
Paul W. Eshelman
Ron Fleming
Giles Gilson
Jerry Glaser
Michael N. Graham
Stephen Hogbin
Michelle Holzapfel
Robyn Horn
Michael Hosaluk
Todd Hoyer
William Hunter
Carl Huskey
C. R. (Skip) Johnson
John Jordan
Ron Kent
Frank Knox
Max Krimmel
Dan Kvitka
Stoney Lamar

Bud Latven
Mark Lindquist
Melvin Lindquist
Steve Loar
John (Jake) May
Hugh E. McKay
Connie Mississippi
Bruce Mitchell
Ed Moulthrop
Philip C. Moulthrop
Thomas Nicosia
Dale L. Nish
Harry Nohr
Craig Nutt
Rude Osolnik
Stephen Mark Paulsen
Gord Peteran
Michael James Peterson
James Prestini
H. Wayne Raab
Hap Sakwa
Norm Sartorius
Jon Sauer
Merryll Saylan
Betty J. Scarpino
Lincoln Seitzman
David Sengel
Mark Sfirri
Michael Shuler
Alan Stirt
Bob Stocksdale
Jack Straka
Del Stubbs
Robert Trout
Howard Whipple

WO OD

TURNING

IN NORTH AMERICA

SINCE 1930

Wood Turning Center and Yale University Art Gallery

This book is published on the occasion of the exhibition *Wood Turning in North America Since 1930*, organized by the Wood Turning Center, Philadelphia, and the Yale University Art Gallery, New Haven.
The exhibition and publication have been made possible in part by the Windgate Charitable Foundation, the Barra Foundation, the Chipstone Foundation, and the National Endowment for the Arts, a Federal agency. Additional support has been provided by Robyn and John Horn, Jane and Arthur Mason, Ruth and David Waterbury, and the Wornick Family Foundation.

Exhibition Dates

The Minneapolis Institute of Arts
October 21–December 30, 2001

Renwick Gallery of the Smithsonian American Art Museum
March 15–July 21, 2002

Yale University Art Gallery
September 10–December 1, 2002

Designed by Nathan Garland, New Haven, Connecticut
Printed by Amilcare Pizzi, S.p.A., Milan, Italy

LCC 2001 132602
ISBN 0-89467-095-6 cloth
ISBN 0-89467-094-8 paper

Contents

Lenders

Louise Brown Albert
Arizona State University
    Art Museum
The Arkansas Arts Center
    Foundation Collection
Garry K. and Sylvia Bennett
Robert M. Bohlen
Fleur Bresler
Phyllis and Sidney Bresler
Jay Brubaker
Burton Creek Collection
Gayle and Andrew Camden
Arthur Espenet Carpenter
F. Hayden Cochran
Martha and Pat Connell
Virginia Dotson
Ann Draper
David Ellsworth
Elvehjem Museum of Art,
    University of
    Wisconsin-Madison
Julian H. Fisher
Samuel M. Freeman II
Jerry Glaser
Harland and Elizabeth Goldwater
High Museum of Art
Stephen Hogbin
John and Robyn Horn
Michael Hosaluk
Charles Ray Huskey
Hank and David Ingebretsen
C. R. (Skip) Johnson
Wendy Evans Joseph
Bruce and Marina Kaiser
Susan and Neil Kaye
Donald and Kate King
Victor and Helen Lenox
Drs. Claude Lieber and
    Ursula Seinige
Lindquist Studios Archive
    Collection
Dr. Irving Lipton

Joseph Mamone
Jane and Arthur Mason
Samuel May
Mayo Clinic Art Collection
Forest L. Merrill
The Metropolitan Museum of Art
Connie Mississippi
Mobile Museum of Art
Museum of Fine Arts, Boston
The Museum of Modern Art
Oakland Museum of California
Margaret A. Pennington
The Philadelphia Museum of Art
Renwick Gallery of the Smithsonian
    American Art Museum
Gloria Roby
Robert A. Roth
Schenectady Museum
The Society for Contemporary Crafts
Lynn Sommer
Southern Highland Craft Guild
The Speed Art Museum
Kenneth Spitzbard
Bob Stocksdale and Kay Sekimachi
David and Nancy Trautenberg
Robert Trout
West Virginia State Museum
Wood Turning Center
Ron and Anita Wornick
Yale University Art Gallery

Preface

This survey exhibition and publication of modern American wood turning, a joint venture of the Wood Turning Center and the Yale University Art Gallery, is testimony to the belief that lathe art has come of age. The idea for the exhibition arose from my own twenty-five-year involvement in this exciting field as a production turner, artist, and organizer of workshops and exhibitions. As the idea germinated in the late 1990s, it was natural to turn again to people who had helped the field gain recognition earlier in the decade. When I met Edward (Ned) Cooke, Jr., he was a young associate curator in the American Decorative Arts and Sculpture department under Jonathan Fairbanks at the Museum of Fine Arts, Boston. In 1991, I talked him into coming to Philadelphia to co-curate the Wood Turning Center's "Challenge IV" exhibition with Canadian sculptor Stephen Hogbin and Philadelphia ceramist Rudolf Staffel. Ned became entranced with lathe-turning, and our acquaintance grew.

In the early 1990s, I also met Charles Hummel. Having facilitated the research on and relocation and reconstruction of the Dominy Shops at the Winterthur Museum, Charles was knowledgeable about production lathe-turning. He contributed his insights and collegial guidance as the Wood Turning Center organized the 1993 "World Turning Conference" at the Hagley Museum in Wilmington. Soon recruited to serve on the Center's Board, he convinced the Trustees that the Center should co-organize a major exhibition of lathe art in America.

The original idea—an exhibition of "Beowulf to Virginia Woolf" scope—was fortunately scaled down after brainstorming with Ned Cooke, who is now the Charles F. Montgomery Professor of American Decorative Arts at Yale University. He broached the project to Patricia E. Kane, Curator of American Decorative Arts at the Yale University Art Gallery, and soon Charles Hummel and I were on the train to New Haven to present the concept to her. As this book shows, pictures of lathe-turned objects are worth a thousand words. Pat was intrigued by their beauty and went about selling the survey idea to crucial contacts at Yale. The curatorial team evolved as Charles Hummel and myself for the Wood Turning Center; and for Yale, Pat Kane, Ned Cooke, and Glenn Adamson, then a doctoral candidate in the Department of the History of Art. The exhibition, this publication, and the conferences are a tribute to finding good partners.

The curatorial team's early discussions and selections were informed by the Wood Turning Center's library and archives. Reviewing 500 turned objects, selected from over 20,000 slides, hundreds of artists' files, and original historical documents, led to many lively discussions. Artists' responses to the team's questionnaire contributed tremendous information and insights. Trips to study institutional and private collections added unique perspective to the search for information and representative objects for the exhibition.

This book reflects tremendous teamwork behind the scenes, and the curatorial team is indebted to everyone's assistance. Behind every curatorial team member stands a dedicated spouse. Sincere thanks to Walter Scott Braznell, Marlene Hummel, Tina LeCoff , Alicia Volk, and Carol Warner and for their unyielding patience and continuous support. I join Jock Reynolds, Henry J. Heinz II Director of the Yale University Art Gallery, in thanking the many individuals named in his acknowledgments for their efforts in realizing this tribute to twentieth-century lathe art. As the objects and this publication so clearly demonstrate, American lathe art has a distinctive history and is poised for a dynamic future.

Albert LeCoff
Executive Director,
Wood Turning Center

Acknowledgments

This publication records the history of wood turning in North America in the twentieth century and is the result of a collaborative effort among the staff of the Wood Turning Center, the Yale University Art Gallery, and the Department of the History of Art at Yale University. The Wood Turning Center brought to the project its archival resources and institutional experience pertaining to the evolution of the field of turned wood. Yale contributed the expertise of its Art Gallery staff at organizing publications and traveling exhibitions, and the scholarship of its faculty and graduate students. The collegial interchange has produced both a stunning exhibition and a publication whose pioneering history of this field will have lasting value.

  This project could not have been accomplished without the cooperation of the artists, institutions, collectors, gallery owners, and other colleagues who made their collections available for study and generously shared their knowledge with the curators. In particular we thank the lenders to the exhibition for parting with their works for the duration of the show. We appreciate the time the artists took to respond to questionnaires and to help locate examples of their work. A number of gallery owners helped facilitate access to collections, including Martha Connell, Ray Leier, and Mike Mendelson. For their assistance in numerous ways we thank our colleagues listed on these pages. The Minneapolis Institute of Arts emerged as the opening venue and conference site. Ruth and David Waterbury, BA 1958, of Minneapolis facilitated many interactions with the museum. The Renwick Gallery of the Smithsonian American Art Museum in Washington, D.C., provided the middle venue. Kenneth Trapp, Curator-in-Charge, and Jeremy Adamson, Senior Curator, facilitated internal arrangements. The project came full circle to the Yale University Art Gallery, from early meetings to the final exhibition venue and closing conference.

  Support for this publication, the exhibition, and its accompanying educational programs has come from many sources. Early in the history of the project the Windgate Charitable Foundation made a generous challenge grant was to the Wood Turning Center that provided the necessary basis for subsequent fund raising efforts. Additional funds came from the Art Gallery's endowed exhibition funds, the Center for the Study of American Art and Material Culture at Yale, and the McNeil Fund for Graduate Study at Yale. Kathleen Derringer and Dennis Danaher assisted in preparing grant applications to corporations and foundations. A generous grant was received from the National Endowment for the Arts, and the Chipstone Foundation underwrote the cost of the color printing in the publication. Grants from the Barra Foundation, Inc., to the Wood Turning Center underwrote the costs of the conferences in Minneapolis and at Yale. We are particularly appreciative of Ruth and David Waterbury, who not only contributed themselves but who solicited funds

For their assistance in numerous ways we thank our colleagues:

Ellen J. Landis, Albuquerque Museum, New Mexico; Walter A. Van Horn, Anchorage Museum of History and Art, Alaska; Michelle Povilaitis and Ann Sullivan, Arizona State University Art Museum, Tempe; Alan Du Bois, Arkansas Art Center, Little Rock; Jennifer M. Downs and Dr. Judith A. Barter, The Art Institute of Chicago; Michelle W. Locke, Art Museum of South Texas, Corpus Christi; Rebecca Moore, Atlanta History Center, Georgia; Kevin Montgomery, Bishop Museum, Honolulu; W. Scott Braznell; Meredith Cohen; Stephie L'Heureux, The Contemporary Museum, Honolulu; Todd Olson, Cooper-Hewitt, National Design Museum, Smithsonian Institution, New York; Melissa G. Post, The Corning Museum of Glass, New York; Phyllis Greenwood, Creators Equity Foundation, Berkeley, California; Cheryl Hartup and Charles Venable, Dallas Museum of Art; Dr. Mary F. Holahan, Delaware Art Museum, Wilmington; Bonita Fike, The Detroit Institute of Arts, Michigan; Pam Richardson, Elvehjem Museum of Art, Madison, Wisconsin; Martha R. Severens, Greenville County Museum of Art, South Carolina; Jody Cohen, Donald Peirce, and Margaret Reneke, High Museum of Art, Atlanta; Pauline Sugino, Honolulu Academy of Arts, Hawaii; Laura Vookies, Hudson River Museum, Yonkers; Theresa Slowikowski, Hunter Museum of American Art, Chattanooga; David Reyes, Huntsville Museum of Art, Alabama; Jeffrey Tenuth, Indiana State Museum and Historic Sites, Indianapolis; Jackie Wampler, James A. Michener Art Museum, Doylestown, Pennsylvania; Lynne Campbell, Kresge Art Museum, East Lansing, Michigan;

Ruth Resnicow, Marietta/Cobb Museum of Art, Georgia; Cynthia Nelson, Mayo Clinic, Rochester, Minnesota; Kip Peterson, Memphis Brooks Museum of Art, Tennessee; Jane Adlin, The Metropolitan Museum of Art, New York; Martha Tonissen Mayberry, Mint Museum, Charlotte, North Carolina; Rene Paul Barilleaux, Mississippi Museum of Art, Jackson; Paul W. Richelson and Rowena Van Hoof, Mobile Museum of Art, Alabama; Kim Pashko and Leah Ross, Museum of Fine Arts, Boston; Katherine S. Howe, The Museum of Fine Arts, Houston; Luisa Lorch and Terence Riley, The Museum of Modern Art, New York; Ulysses Grant Dietz, The Newark Museum, New Jersey; Joy Walker, The Oakland Museum, California; Michael S. Wright, Old Capitol Museum of Mississippi, Jackson; Mike Hammer, Philadelphia Museum of Art, Pennsylvania; Jeremy Adamson and Marguerite Hergesheimer, Renwick Gallery of the Smithsonian American Art Museum, Washington, D.C.; Thomas Michie, Rhode Island School of Design, Providence; Nancy Harm, Schenectady Museum, New York; Karen Baye, Sheldon Memorial Art Gallery and Sculpture Garden, Lincoln, Nebraska; Frances E. Kornacki, The Slater Memorial Museum, Norwich, Connecticut; Janet McCall, The Society for Contemporary Crafts, Pittsburgh; Laurey-Faye Long, Southern Highland Craft Guild, Asheville, North Carolina; Peter Morin, The Speed Art Museum, Louisville, Kentucky; Lindsay S. Suter; Lee Mooney, The Toledo Museum of Art, Ohio; David M. Carroll, Utah Museum of Fine Arts, Salt Lake City; Charles Morris, West Virginia State Museum, Charleston; and Dan Carver, Yeiser Art Center, Paducah, Kentucky.

to match the Windgate Charitable Foundation grant from collectors and others with an interest in craft. For their generous support we thank Judith and Martin Bloomfield, Fleur and Charles Bresler, Dain Rauscher Corporation, W. John Driscoll, Ruth C. Greenberg, Douglas and Michael Heller, Robyn and John Horn, Klemm Analysis Group, Inc., Jane and Arthur Mason, Jan Peters and Ray Leier, the T. Rowe Price Associates Foundation, Inc., Frances and George Reid, Norton Rockler, Kenneth Spitzbard, Jamienne S. Studley and Gary J. Smith, John G. Taft and Martha McPhee, F. T. Weyerhaeuser, and the Wornick Family Foundation, Inc. Without the support of these contributors, the project could not have been brought to completion.

Many individuals expended time and effort on behalf of this publication. We are grateful to Glenn Adamson, Graeme P. Berlyn, Edward S. Cooke, Jr., Patricia E. Kane, and Andrew D. Richardson for writing essays; Albert LeCoff and Glenn Adamson for composing entries on individual objects; Mary Cheek Mills for writing the biographical information; Susan Hagen for compiling the glossary; and Todd Hoyer and the American Association of Woodturners for providing illustrations of turned bowls in relation to the logs they are turned from. Nathan Garland brought his refined graphic design skills to the publication. John Carlano produced most of the transparencies for the dazzling colorplates, and Carl Kaufman produced a significant number as well. John Kelsey gave the manuscript an informed critical reading and Susan Hagen compiled the glossary. Lesley Baier applied her keen editing skills to the book. Harriet Hodges compiled the index.

Within the Art Gallery many individuals play a role in bringing exhibitions to fruition. I extend thanks to Susan Frankenbach and Lynne Addison of the Registrar's Office; Burrus Harlow, Clark Crolius, and the entire installation staff; Mary Kordak and Ellen Alvord of the Education Department; Louisa Cunningham and other administrators in the Business Office; Marie Weltzien in Public Relations who was assisted by Group M in development of the publicity materials; Richard Moore and Remo Capello in Facilities; and John Pfannenbecker in Security. From beginning to end Nancy Yates handled the myriad administrative details in the American Arts Office.

The pages of this book show a broad range of techniques and attitudes toward turned wooden objects. The strength of this field in the twentieth century is that it embraced so many different forms and attitudes toward turned wood. Here you will find small, delicate vessels of extreme refinement, as well as massive works with crude, aggressive surfaces. The range of the work presented here is a source of wonder and delight.

Jock Reynolds
The Henry J. Heinz II Director,
Yale University Art Gallery

Introduction

This publication celebrates the fabrication of wooden objects on the lathe at a time when wood is less and less a part of everyday life. Indeed, when one wants to affirm good luck now at the turn of the twentieth century by a "knock on wood," wood is often in short supply. It has been amalgamated and replaced by new materials and new processes. Yet imitations of wood surfaces in the form of coatings and plastic laminates often cover our surroundings and testify to the enduring value our society places on the warmth and graphic qualities of wood. Wood is a natural material of infinite variation in its color, figure, texture, and density. Among its remarkable properties is its ability to be bent, to be shaped easily with sharp-edge steel tools, to resist conducting electricity, and to insulate.

The history of wood turning in the first half of the twentieth century concerns in part the use of the lathe to produce multiples that had utilitarian value. The lathe allows an individual to shape materials more quickly than is possible with such tools as hammers or gouges, chisels, and scrapers. At mid-century, when society placed a very high value on objects made of organic materials, wooden vessels and other lathe-made implements enjoyed a heyday. Later in the century, with an aesthetic shift to bright colors and man-made materials, the production of wooden functional objects declined. The waning taste for everyday wares made of wood did not, however, mean the cessation of lathe-made objects. The character of the end product changed. In the latter part of the twentieth century, many wood turners used the lathe to create unique objects as well as those with sculptural as opposed to functional value.

A strange dichotomy runs through the history of twentieth-century wood turning in North America, in that the craft values equally woods with the most commercial value in the lumber industry and those with the least. This exhibition and publication abound in examples of rare, expensive woods with high intrinsic value, from the satinwood used by Bob Stocksdale in the 1950s to the cocobolo favored by William Hunter in the 1990s. From the early 1940s when Rude Osolnik first scavenged spurs discarded by a local veneer factory and from them turned imperfect shapes whose irregular forms were in keeping with contemporary aesthetics, many turners have utilized roots, as well as decayed and insect- and disease-infested wood, to produce objects of remarkable aesthetic beauty. Examples of this phenomenon also abound here, from Osolnik's spur bowls to the kamani pieces turned by Derek Bencomo in the 1990s.

Of all the crafts, wood turners would seem to be closest to gem cutters in their approach to materials. Just as a gem cutter analyzes an uncut stone to find within it and then reveal its most startling visual properties, so many wood turners approach a chunk of raw wood. Superb aesthetic judgment is required to perceive the potential for variations in figure, color, or texture in a block of wood and then expose those qualities and wed them with the turned form. Masterful examples are found in the work of Bob Stocksdale and Dan Kvitka. For those using decayed, insect-infested, or diseased wood this aesthetic ability must be linked with consummate craft skill to maintain the integrity of wood structure that has been violated. Awesome examples of this skill are found in the work of David Ellsworth and Todd Hoyer.

Another strong turning tradition that runs from the earliest to the latest examples in this publication is that of lamination—working from blocks made up of pieces of wood with contrasting color and figure. For these turners, strategy and planning rather than intuition and chance assume critical importance in the creative act. The work of Thomas Nicosia exemplifies this technique as expounded by manual training texts early in the century, and the works of Bud Latven and Virginia Dotson show its evolution in the 1990s. Variations in this tradition range widely from the use of commercial birch plywood by Osolnik, to the random patterns achieved by Max Krimmel, to the precise designs rendered by Lincoln Seitzman.

The diversity of approaches to this common material—wood— are almost as surprising as the diversity of wood itself. Some turners, especially those like M. Dale Chase who use ornamental lathes, produce work of exquisite refinement. Others, such as Mark Lindquist, leave evidence of wood structure brutally ripped apart and of the massiveness of the trees from which wood comes. Still others, as for example Giles Gilson and Michael Hosaluk, explore another traditional use of wood as an effective surface for painted decoration. The objects illustrated here demonstrate the many avenues of creativity followed by those who apply the power of the lathe to the world's foremost organic material.

Patricia E. Kane
Curator of American Decorative Arts,
Yale University Art Gallery

From Manual Training to Freewheeling Craft:
The Transformation of Wood Turning, 1900–76

Edward S. Cooke, Jr.

Within the past several decades, wood turning has experienced both a resurgence and a transformation. In explaining its evolution from a factory-based process that mass-produced great quantities of utilitarian objects or parts to a shop-based pursuit of an individual making unique design- and labor-intensive objects, many writers have focused on the brilliance of individuals who purportedly have single-handedly altered the field, especially James Prestini, Bob Stocksdale, Stephen Hogbin, Mark Lindquist, and David Ellsworth.[1] These canonized turners certainly exerted an influence, but they were part of a larger, century-long development that spawned a number of different practitioners. To understand fully the present fit of wood turning within the world of object making, it is important to look at the entire century and to recognize that turning was an integral part of industrial arts training in the first quarter of the century, the developing do-it-yourself hobbyist movement in the second quarter of the century, the soft modernism of design in the 1940s and 1950s, and the freewheeling crafts of the 1960s and early 1970s. The desire and ability to turn, as well as the favored forms and aesthetics, underwent a number of changes over the course of the past hundred years, and it is important to understand the contexts of these developments.

Manual Arts and Industrial Arts

In the last decades of the nineteenth century, many American manufacturing leaders recognized that the effectiveness of apprenticeship was declining under the pressure of increased mechanization, greater task specialization, and overall complexity of production. These men collaborated with educators to develop manual training, a new form of education that would not only provide basic skills in reading, writing, and arithmetic, but would also acquaint youth with industrial processes, develop tool skills, and provide a base of technical versatility. Manual training combined general exercises to develop complete understanding of tool properties and actions (referred to at the time as "Russian exercises") with practical projects in which the goal of a finished, usable product provided a high level of engagement and furthered the student's overall mental and physical development (the goal of the Sloyd system of training).[2] The manual training curriculum in high schools increasingly brought construction and decoration into a "natural relation" of interdependence and thus fostered a certain material literacy. Whether they became producers or consumers, students benefited from this broad approach: future industrial workers gained a greater sense of design issues—proportion, contour, balance, and unity—while future professionals acquired some sense of quality fabrication and materials.[3]

Turning was an ideal activity for manual training. With a single lathe and a handful of cutting tools, the student could quickly understand and master correct tool handling and techniques, gain experience with steel cutting tools and wooden forms, and develop a refined sense of shape and proportion through a number of different exercises such as cylinders, tapers, spindles with repeated beads and fillets, and rosettes. Once confident of his workmanship, the student could make a napkin ring or goblet following the dimensions given in a drawing, or even work out his own drawing for a vase or candlestick with pleasing compound curves. The first published texts to accompany such instruction, such as Fred Crawshaw's *Problems in Wood Turning*, appeared at this time and explicitly stated their intent to provide clear explanation of processes, demonstrate the reasons or principles underlying tool handling, and offer

Carl Huskey
1 *Compote*
ca. 1940s
Walnut, felt
H 7 $^1/_{16}$ × Diam 10 $^1/_2$
Collection of Charles Ray Huskey

Note to the Reader:
Throughout the publication
dimensions of works of art
are given in inches.
The numbers in parentheses
refer to the color illustrations.

Carl Huskey and his family were typical of early turners, in that they made work exclusively on a production basis. This compote shows the efficient piece-work system that the Huskeys applied to the construction of complex shapes. It is composed of three separate pieces: the faceplate-turned base and bowl, and the spindle-turned stem that joins them. Each element could be fashioned quite quickly, and each was shallow in dimension so that readily available, inexpensive milled stock could be used as the raw material. Though such early production work was humble in its technical and aesthetic pretensions, it was an important basis for the careers of the earliest studio turners such as Rude Osolnik (see 27–31).

Fig. 1. Advertisement from *Industrial-Arts Magazine* 11, no. 6 (June 1922): ix. The American Saw Mill Machinery Company was just one of several manfacturers who offered lathes specifically for school shops.

Fig. 2. Advertisement from *Industrial-Arts Magazine* 19, no. 1 (January 1930): inside of back cover. The illustration depicts a typical layout for turning instruction.

good measured drawings to follow. These manuals stated that spindle turning—shaping a piece of wood that was rotating while it was held between the headstock and tailstock—was educational in that it fostered proper handling of tools, while faceplate turning—shaping a piece of wood that was secured only to the headstock—was more vocational in that it fostered the manipulation of wood to produce required results. At this time, wood turning was felt to be both an art and a science.[4]

Nevertheless, critics of manual training and manual arts claimed that such education did not provide skilled workers. In 1906 the Massachusetts Commission on Industrial and Technical Education issued a report that pointed out the weaknesses of the developmental emphasis and warned that American industry would fall behind that of other countries if the schools did not provide skilled mechanics. That same year, the National Society for the Promotion of Industrial Education was founded and began to lobby the federal government for the national reform of manual training. Instead of providing general mechanical skills and inculcating aesthetic sensibility among all children, manual training gradually became a form of vocational shop work. The target students were disadvantaged urban or rural children. Funding for such pedagogical change was ensured with the passage of the Smith-Hughes Act in 1917, a bill that provided federal funding for shop equipment, improved facilities, and curriculum development. In the late teens specialized courses in cabinetmaking, carpentry, and patternmaking began to appear in which the commercial and vocational aims were explicit: the classroom was organized like a shop; students were treated like employees and expected to follow certain standardized procedures; and instructors were taught how to manage the tool room, organize their equipment, and plan the flow of student work. Educational reformers referred to the new approach as the industrial arts, although the term encompassed both manual training and vocational education during the 1920s.[5]

The influx of federal funds to purchase new equipment coincided with mechanical improvements in the lathe. Prior to the 1910s, the power system for lathes, consisting of overhead shafts and fly belts, made conditions dangerous, noisy, and unsanitary. It was hardly an environment conducive to learning. Around 1915, the first individual, variable speed, electric-head motors were adapted to lathes. At the same time, manufacturers began to enclose the drive belts and connections. The result was an improved, reworked power tool appropriate for use in the schools. Many scholastic shops used Smith-Hughes funding to acquire new "student-friendly" lathes, thereby spawning a healthy new lathe market. Companies such as Oliver, Greenfield Tap and Die, and American Saw Mill Machinery began to advertise school or manual arts lathes that were safe, rugged, and simple, yet could produce respectable and accurate work (Fig. 1). Many models permitted spindle turning between the headstock and the tailstock, as well as faceplate turning either over the ways or on the outboard end of the headstock. Period photographs reveal that many schools set up a half dozen or so lathes in their shops (Fig. 2).[6]

With an increase in the number of individual lathes and the efficiency of their operation, wood turning instruction blossomed. In many ways the 1920s were the golden years of lathe instruction in the schools. A number of guides were published, including Archie Milton and Otto Wohlers's *A Course in Wood Turning for High Schools* and William Klenke's *Art and Education in Wood Turning*. Through a progressive sequence of exercises and projects, these publications emphasized both the value

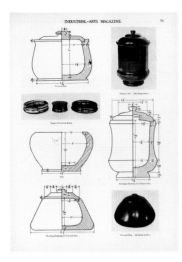

Fig. 3. Typical turning exercises for an industrial arts curriculum from *Industrial-Arts Magazine* 4, no. 2 (August 1915): 73. Measured drawings and thick bases of faceplate-turned elements are typical of this period.

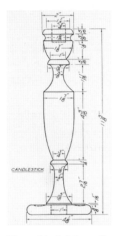

Fig. 4. "Artistic" candlestick from *Industrial-Arts Magazine* 14, no. 9 (September 1925): 356. Instructors of this period stressed the importance of detailed measured drawings and classically derived shapes and proportions.

Fig. 5. Inlaid turnings from *Industrial-Arts Magazine* 8, no. 6 (June 1919): 211. Turners in the late 1910s and 1920s used inlay or laminations to add color or decorative effect to their substantial turnings.

of complete tool control and the importance of graceful and artistic design. The mastery of cutting, in which a tool was applied to a rotating piece of wood, linked motor and mental activities, and the exposure to harmonious lines and flowing curves awakened the aesthetic sensibilities of the students. In both textbooks, the authors stressed the importance of mastery in cutting and shearing with the skew and gouge rather than scraping with round-nose or square chisels to develop shapes. For these writers, design was linked to form and profile, not the type of wood. In fact, instructors of this period made no explicit reference to the figure of the wood. The only decorative element in addition to shape was the use of inlaid stringing in the 1920s and polychrome laminations in the early 1930s, but such practices merely drew attention to form or transitions in profile. Although certain projects continued the earlier interest in spindle turning, the textbooks of the 1920s stated that faceplate work had greater practical and educational value and therefore developed a wider range of projects for such techniques, especially bowls and vases. Many of the projects included in these publications became the standard exercises for all subsequent guides. Basic projects included tool handles, mallets, rolling pins, Indian clubs, napkin rings, towel rings, and circular picture frames, while the most advanced forms of this period included covered boxes, nut bowls, vases, and candlesticks and lamps (which featured faceplate-turned bases and spindle-turned shafts).[7]

The new interest in form, shape, and feel of turned objects that emerged in the late 1910s and 1920s signaled a new focus upon wood turning as a design exercise that required a good eye and facile hands. Unity of lines and spaces, continuity of shape, and the classically inspired use of various convex and concave curves were stressed in the detailed measured drawings and the text describing the projects (Figs. 3–5). Many of the people who pioneered a revival of wood turning in the 1930s and 1940s, including James Prestini and Rude Osolnik, received their initial introduction to turning under the influence of this industrial arts curriculum, and their interest in faceplate turning is based in this experience.[8]

In rural areas, shop teachers in philanthropic programs used the same lathe curriculum to provide employment skills. The lathe was presented as an ideal tool for the limited production of marketable wood exports in the southern highlands of North Carolina, Kentucky, and Tennessee. For example, Carl Huskey, a student in Otto Mattil's woodworking class at the Settlement School in Gatlinburg, Tennessee, in the late 1920s, went on to become a woodworker and turner in that town. He ran a shop that catered to the tourist trade visiting Great Smoky Mountains National Park and used scrapers to make a line of faceplate work characterized by bulbous shapes and smooth transitions (1).[9]

Hobbyists

During the economic crises of the 1930s, industrial arts education became more vocational in purpose. Woodworking, which had been ideal for a balanced technical/cultural education in the first quarter of the century, became less integral to the new, practically oriented curriculum. Courses in mechanical drawing, graphic design and printing, dress design, automobile repair, electrical engineering, and metalworking rose to prominence as education leaders worked closely with industrial leaders to ensure a ready supply of mechanics with specific skills in the growing modern industries. Much of the coursework emphasized socialization and interaction on the shop floor. The focus was not so much on individual

Howard Whipple
2 *Intarsia Box #116*
1947
Mahogany and various inlaid woods
H 1 ½ × Diam 6
Inscribed on underside in black ink:
116/Howard Whipple [script]/June 8, 1947
Oakland Museum of California,
Lent by Mrs. Howard Whipple, A77.40.6

Howard Whipple developed a personal variation on an ancient woodworking technique called intarsia. Through this process, a variety of shaped pieces of veneer are inlaid into a solid piece of wood to achieve a pattern of color and figure. To create a piece like this box, Whipple cut the tiny slivers of his designs on a bandsaw and arranged them into a pattern face down. He then glued the bottom of the inlays and placed them into a recess that he turned into the box top. Whipple used only hardwoods and was unusual for his early interest in exotic woods; he reputedly used over 800 different imported and domestic varieties over the course of his wood-working career.

expression anymore, but rather on knowledge and experience with contemporary industrial practices. Students often visited local factories, attended lectures by industry experts, and gained experience working cooperatively. Teachers focused not so much on skill and design development but increasingly on shop management, the use of uniform instruction sheets, and flow of projects. Woodworking was divided up into specialties such as carpentry (house carpenters and form makers for concrete), millworkers (who used tablesaws and other large machines to produce large quantities of goods), cabinetmakers (who mastered joinery), and patternmakers (who used a lathe to scrape models for casting molds). Patternmakers continued to use wood lathes, and metalworkers used metal lathes, but the number of wood lathes in schools seemed to decline. Photographs of school interiors revealed far fewer lathes, sometimes only one per school. Fewer lathe manufacturers took out advertisements in the dominant magazine *Industrial Arts and Vocational Education*, a pattern that suggests a weakening market in the schools.[10]

As the school basis of wood turning declined, a new type of turner emerged—the hobbyist. In the 1920s, a dramatic increase in home ownership, particularly small-sized suburban homes, and the widening of electrical service to these houses spawned the growth of a do-it-yourself, home workshop movement. Appealing to both skilled blue-collar workers and white-collar professionals, this form of domestic masculinity evoked a preindustrial artisanal competence, one based on the knowledge of producing a finished product from raw material and on a task orientation rather than time orientation. In a modern economy, recreational craftwork was not important for its income or cost saving but rather for the satisfaction it provided the practitioner: it was both a pleasurable activity that was work-like as well as a task that was leisurely, a possible source of supplemental income, but more often a drain on time and money. The value placed on home shop work only intensified during the Depression as skill and self-sufficiency became more meaningful than financial wealth. As the home became the location for and object of useful leisure time activity, more men took up woodworking as a hobby (Fig. 6). In fact, more home craftsmen worked in wood than in any other medium: some focused on home improvement, others on making furniture.[11]

Turning became another favored woodworking activity because the home turner could make useful and beautiful items for his own home, for gifts, or for sale to earn some supplemental income. As electric tools were still relatively expensive in the 1920s and early 1930s, only the most dedicated and wealthy do-it-yourselfers purchased lathes, which cost about $20 to $40 without the motor. Early amateurs such as Howard Whipple of Berkeley, California, or Cecil Read of St. Paul, Minnesota, are good examples of professionals who turned objects later in life. The former was a retired banker who began in the late 1930s to make decorative round boxes with inlaid floral and geometric designs of exotic woods (2), the latter an insurance executive who turned simple bowls from local woods such as elm and walnut as well as olive (Fig. 7).[12]

Beginning in the early 1930s, lathe companies shifted their attention from the school market to the hobbyist, offering smaller, lighter versions of their equipment and printing instructional guides. American Saw Mill Machinery Company, Boice Crane, Walker-Turner Company, and Wallace & Company all began to offer cheaper bench lathes suitable for the home shop. By the mid-1930s, the lathe headed the list of home power tools. Delta Manufacturing Company's *Getting the Most Out of Your*

Fig. 6. Advertisement for Corby's whiskey from *Collier's* (October 1, 1954). Home workshops had become so prevalent by the 1950s that they were used as backdrops for advertisements that needed to evoke male social activities. Note the lathe in the right foreground.

Fig. 7. Olive wood bowl made by Cecil Read, ca. 1953, from *Designer-Craftsmen, U.S.A., 1953* (New York: American Craftsmen's Educational Council, 1953), 55.

Lathe (1935) was pitched to the home shop turner and emphasized that "wood turning is a fascinating art, and the lathe, more than any other tool in the shop, is in itself a complete unit capable of producing finished work."[13] Many articles claimed that the lathe was ideally suited to the recreational woodworker because it offered "the most excitement and the deepest gratification to the beginner."[14]

The shift from educational turning to recreational turning can also be found in a new edition of William Klenke's turning manual. Dropping the term educational from the original 1921 title, the 1937 edition explicitly noted that the changes in the book arose from the introduction of portable motorized lathes that permitted the establishment of thousands of well-equipped home shops in which hobbyists enjoyed making useful and beautiful objects. With this new audience in mind, Klenke offered more exercises for furniture projects so that Depression do-it-yourselfers could make more of their own furniture in colonial revival styles. He further emphasized that wood turning "allows for much artistic expression, and soon makes it possible for you to create your own designs."[15] And he expanded upon the previous notion of design by urging the recreational turner to pay attention not only to form and proportion, but also to the character of the wood. His volume was one of the first publications to emphasize that figure could be a decorative feature and that wood rich in figure often needed only a graceful outline to make a pleasing object.

During the 1930s and 1940s, the popular hobbyist magazines offered additional information on wood turning to the growing numbers of home shop woodworkers who used the lathe in combination with other tools and thus were not likely to buy a turning-specific volume such as Klenke's guide. *Popular Science*, which led the interest in recreational craft and sponsored the National Homeworkers Guild, published a two-part feature in 1931. Located in the "Ideas for the Handyman" section, these articles focused upon sharpening turning tools and spindle turning, suggesting that furniture legs were the most popular product of the home lathe. *Popular Mechanics* followed suit several years later, offering a brief overview of turning in 1935 and following up with an extensive four-part article entitled "Turn Right!" in late 1937 and early 1938.[16]

While these articles described and analyzed turning techniques, the emphasis was on "the correct method of working" rather than the "skill in the handling of the turning tools."[17] This switch from a focus on particular techniques to a concern with general approach can also be seen in the new emphasis on scraping, which was described as an "easier and more accurate" technique used by "amateur woodworkers," rather than cutting—"used by the last of the professional wood turners, who look upon the scraping methods with infinite contempt."[18] Cutting required skill, facilitated speed, and obviated the drudgery of sanding; scraping was easier, privileged safety and accuracy over speed, and necessitated considerable sanding to achieve an acceptable surface. Thus the shift to scraping signaled the decline of the professional turner and the prominence of the hobbyist. The expansion of the hobbyist turner can also be seen in the several articles that demonstrated how to make "homemade" lathes using old sewing machine heads, washing machine motors, and readily available hardware. *Popular Mechanics* in particular recognized that not everyone could afford a new lathe and thus offered alternative ways to get the do-it-yourselfer turning. The popular literature also encouraged the amateur turners to collect and season their own wood. The scavenging of local

Fig. 8. Maple and beech plates and bowls made by H. C. Dubuke, ca. 1943, from *Contemporary New England Handicrafts* (Worcester, Mass.: Worcester Art Museum, 1943), 21.

wood or cast-offs from the saw mill was seen as an important part of the recreational aspect of the craft. It reinforced the amateur's connection to the preindustrial woodworker who oversaw everything from start to finish.[19] One hobbyist, H. C. Dubuke of Florence, Vermont, gained a reputation as the leader in the revival of wood turning in New England. Using mainly Vermont maple, he made plates, bowls, and other tableware in which the figure was the main decorative element (Fig. 8). Another hobbyist, Fred Rossiter, drew inspiration from the rural environment of the historical turner. He worked in a bucolic setting in Redding Ridge, Connecticut, where he could easily look out of the many windows of his shop and see his gardens and orchards.[20]

Also linked to the hobbyist were a number of self-taught turners who sought to make a living from turning. On the West Coast, the declining lumber business and increased tourism made possible by the automobile inspired amateurs to take up turning as a vocation in the late 1920s. The best known of this group were the redwood turners in Eureka, California, and myrtlewood turners in Coos and Curry counties, Oregon, who began to offer salad bowls, plates, covered boxes, and a range of knickknacks for the emerging tourist market. Not linked to a tradition of professional turning, these turners used simple, expedient techniques. They relied solely on flat and round-nose scrapers and sandpaper in order to avoid the skill-dependent and riskier cutting; hired workers as scrapers, sanders, or finishers; mounted their faceplate work on a single screw chuck to reduce set-up time even though the base had to be thicker; and emphasized convenience over form or finish. Much of their marketing was linked to the indigenous nature and individuality of the wood: the depth of redwood burls and varying hue of silky myrtle were distinctive and spoke of a particular region. Bill Beaumont, who established the dominant shop in Coos Bay in 1929, took up turning to support his family at the beginning of the Depression. His ability to convert a hobby into a business, hire local men without previous experience, and concentrate on the tourist trade contrasts with turning firms such as John Grass in Philadelphia, which had a strong technological base sustained over generations of craftsmen who produced utilitarian objects and parts.[21]

The emergence of the home shop turner in the 1930s had a lasting effect on American turning just as the professional trade faced the challenges of competitive technology—new power tools such as the router and surfacer to shape wood—and competitive materials—fiberglass, aluminum, and plastic products replaced some products formerly made of turned wood. While demand for furniture parts (chair legs, table legs, and stretchers in particular) and architectural millwork (balusters and columns) continued, much of this work was produced in larger firms using complex replicating lathes rather than in smaller shops where turners worked at simple lathes. The number of turning mills and shops as well as the number of skilled all-around turners declined during the 1930s, and the transmission of skills suffered. Even in school shop classes, instructors began to argue for the elimination of dangerous skew chisels and cutting tools, whose very sharp edges could easily cut the inattentive student. They were also dangerous because in inexperienced hands, they could get caught in the rotating wood and either pry off a piece of wood that might strike an innocent bystander or be ripped out of the student's hands and transformed into a projectile. The safer scrapers were not as sharp and did not cut into the wood.[22]

One line of turning succession was carried on by Jake Brubaker, whose grandfather had learned the craft from Joseph Lehn, a prolific Lancaster County, Pennsylvania, maker of small saffron containers and covered containers that were turned and painted. In the early 1930s, Brubaker established Brubaker-Frank Novelty Company, a turning shop that specialized in polychromed laminations, which they labelled "ARTWOOD." From the 1930s until his death in 1981, he continued to make traditional Lehn forms, but instead of painting them relied on richly figured local woods such as walnut (3). He also continued his interest in polychrome laminations, incorporating non-wood materials such as pewter and plastic to provide additional color and pattern (4). Introduced to turning at age four by his grandfather, Brubaker also taught his son and grandsons. Nevertheless, he did not derive a full-time livelihood from turning. Employed as a designer and patternmaker for Hubley Manufacturing Company and as a Mennonite minister, he in fact gave most of his work away as presents.[23]

The legacy of the amateur, who brought total engagement, high aspirations, and a true passion to creation, was to reenergize the possibilities of turning in the middle of the century. Bill Frank, blinded in an industrial accident in 1947, took up woodworking and became a proficient turner who relied on touch, smell, and hearing to turn delicately thin bowls (Fig. 9). Harry Nohr, a postmaster from Mineral Point, Wisconsin, began to turn in 1959 and then made bowls full-time upon his retirement from the Postal Service in 1966. He earned fame for turning thin bowls of burls, pressing them into free-form shapes and finishing them with a rubbed epoxy surface (5). In Lancaster County, Pennsylvania, Paul Eshelman, a music teacher for twelve years, began to take industrial arts classes at Millersville Normal School in 1942. After completion of his degree, he remained at Millersville as a woodworking instructor and gained international recognition for his colonial-style furniture and bowls (6–7). It was amateurs such as Nohr and Eshelman who revitalized turning just as its professionals suffered significant setbacks.[24]

Fig. 9. Bill Frank of Chicago, with examples of his work, from *Popular Mechanics Magazine* 108, no. 6 (December 1957): 109.

Turning as Design

The "rediscovery" of the lathe coincided with a new perspective on lathe-made vessels as objects of design in the late 1940s. Beginning with the 1939 World's Fair, Americans had looked to Scandinavia for a new sort of soft modernism in which skilled craftsmen/designers worked closely with industry to make simple, affordable work that celebrated materials and craftsmanship. Reacting against overly stylized work of the 1930s or the industrial work promoted in fascist and communist countries, Americans of the post-World War II period gravitated towards the warm teak, natural upholstery, earthy stoneware, and reflective silver of functional objects produced in democratic industrialized countries. Among the champions of Scandinavian design was Edgar Kaufmann, Jr., curator of decorative arts at New York's Museum of Modern Art and one of the most authoritative writers on modern design in the 1940s and 1950s, who believed it was a modern, industrially produced applied art that could measure up to the quality of handcraft.

Fig. 10. Bowls designed in 1949 by Finn Juhl (1912–1989), from *Craft Horizons* 13, no. 4 (July/August 1953): 30.

One of Kaufmann's favorite Danish designers was Finn Juhl, who in 1949 designed very influential bird-mouth bowls of teakwood to be made by the Danish turner Magne Monsen and marketed by Kay Bojesen (Fig. 10). The strong formal qualities of Juhl's footed bowls with sagged rims appealed to the modern design aesthetic, and they were often placed as accent pieces on the furniture of Juhl and other Danish designers in

Jacob E. Brubaker
3 *Saffron Box*
1946
Mahogany
H 6 ⅝ × W 2 ¹⁵/₁₆ × D 2 ¹⁵/₁₆
Inscribed on underside in black ink:
J E Brubaker/1946; and in blue ink:
Born Oct 2 1897/Died June 5 1981
Collection of Jay Brubaker, grandson
of Jacob E. Brubaker

This humble lidded box is a rare
surviving example of production turner
Jake Brubaker's early output. He learned
the saffron container shape from his
grandfather and in turn handed it
down to his son and grandson. Brubaker
also turned weed pots and polychrome
bowls on a large-scale basis. The
mahogany used in this piece was
probably scavenged from his workplace,
Hubley Manufacturing Company,
a toymaker in Lancaster, Pennsylvania.

Jacob E. Brubaker
4 *Moon Container*
1969
Walnut, osage orange, pewter, bakelite
H 5 × Diam 6 ½
Incised in an arch: APOLLO II MOON
Jul 20 1969 J.E.B.
Collection of Lynn Sommer

This lidded dish, made to celebrate
the moon landing in 1969, combines
Brubaker's amateur interest in astrono-
my with an ingenious design. Each of
the circular inlays represents a phase
of the moon's cycle. They were made
by setting a row of circular pieces of
osage orange wood into a walnut board.
Brubaker then used a plug cutter to
remove circular sections from the board,
each one successively closer to the edge
of the osage orange inlays than the
last. He topped the dish with a lid of
handspun pewter and added a found
bakelite doorknob as a handle. Brubaker
made two versions of *Moon Container:*
he kept this one, and gave the other to
President Richard Nixon.

Harry Nohr
5 *Bowl*
ca. 1974
White birch burl
H 5 ⅛ × Diam 13 ¼
Inscribed on underside: HN
Elvehjem Museum of Art, University of
Wisconsin-Madison, Class of 1947
Gift Fund Purchase, 1974.25

Among studio turners, Harry Nohr was
ahead of his time in rediscovering
the use of turned green, or unseasoned,
wood. Typically he turned the piece
and then allowed it to deform into an
eccentric shape during the drying
process. Nohr preferred figured native
Wisconsin hardwoods and, characteristically for his generation, avoided
cracks, marks of decay or disease, and
other imperfections. He invented an
unusual method of stabilizing his
bowls, in which the pieces were put in
presses after being turned and then
dried quickly in his kitchen oven.

Paul W. Eshelman
7 *Punch Bowl*
ca. 1955
Walnut, silver
H 5 ⅝ × Diam 14 ⅜
Silver foot marked on underside:
SKINNER[incuse]; burned on underside
of bowl in script: Paul W. Eshelman/
Rohrerstown, Pa.
Collection of Victor and Helen Lenox

Like James Prestini and Bob Stocksdale,
Eshelman was influenced by the vogue
for Scandinavian design that swept
America in the 1940s and 1950s. In
1958, Eshelman's work was exhibited
alongside Stocksdale's at the Brussels
World's Fair, but his piece was unfortu-
nately stolen from the display. This
punch bowl shows the style and quality
of Eshelman's turnings at the time. It
was the result of a collaboration with
a dentist friend, who cast the base from
his supply of silver. The pair executed
two identical punch bowls, with each
collaborator receiving one. In addition
to this experiment with mixed media,
Eshelman was interested in working
with pewter inlay, paint, and ebonized
finishes.

Paul W. Eshelman
6 *Tilt-Top Table*
ca. 1955
Walnut
H 28 × W 30 × Diam 30
Burned on underside of top:
Paul Eshelman/Rohrerstown, Pa.
Collection of F. Hayden Cochran

Until the 1960s, lathe-turning in universities and secondary schools was primarily confined to the fabrication of furniture components. Paul Eshelman was a woodworking teacher whose lathe work ranged more widely than most, from traditional and contemporary furniture to vessels in varied materials.

Although Eshelman worked in a variety of styles, including classical, Scandinavian modern, and organic design, a high level of craftsmanship is common to all his work. He was particularly comfortable working with colonial forms, such as this reproduction tilt-top table with a turned top, pedestal, and "bird-cage."

Fig. 11. Double salad bowls designed by Kay Bojesen (1886–1958), from Eldon Rebhorn, *Woodturning* (Bloomington, Ind.: McKnight & McKnight, 1970), 25.

Fig. 12. Elephants and bears designed by Kay Bojesen, from Arne Karlsen, *Contemporary Danish Design* (Copenhagen: Danish Society of Arts and Crafts and Industrial Design, 1960), 76.

the early 1950s. Bojesen himself designed several other items made on a lathe, including teak salad bowls with fully rounded profiles (including a spherical double salad bowl) as well as toy animals (Figs. 11–12). This woodwork satisfied the modernist interest in form expressing function and in the tactile manipulation of materials whose inherent properties provided the decoration.[25] As the MOMA publication *How to Make Objects of Wood* explained, turning was more than good technique: ". . . the test and satisfaction of your craftsmanship will depend on your ability to design original and interesting forms."[26] For many interested in good design, the lathe was an ideal tool to explore the essence of shape in bowls and platters.

Kaufmann's interest in Scandinavian turning paralleled his interest in the work of James Prestini, an American designer. Prestini had been exposed to turning and metal spinning in industrial arts classes in the 1920s, enjoyed turning as an amateur who explored form and quiet figure while a teacher at Lake Forest Academy from 1933 to 1942, and incorporated turning in order to teach about form while an instructor at the Institute of Design in Illinois. Although Prestini experimented with a wide variety of forms including bracelets and cigarette cups (8–9), he paid particular attention to platters and bowls, forms that allowed him to accentuate graceful lines (10–13). Prestini employed scraping techniques to set new standards for thinness, sought smooth lacquered finishes, and favored evenly figured woods such as birch, cherry, walnut, and Mexican mahogany (although he experimented with sandblasted and ebonized finishes and did make a few examples of richly figured ebony, zeleny topal, and sycamore). Accepted as a designer who understood form, Prestini had his work validated by Kaufmann, who accessioned the turner's work into the permanent collection of the Museum of Modern Art in 1943 and 1945, included him in the 1947 exhibition "One Hundred Useful Objects of Fine Design," and wrote the lead essay for the influential 1950 book, *Prestini's Art in Wood*. In the latter, Kaufmann celebrated Prestini for his combination of science and art; as an engineer/designer and a maker of beautiful, pure shapes; and as lineal descendant, through László Moholy-Nagy with whom he taught at the Institute, of the idealism of the Bauhaus.[27]

Acceptance by Kaufmann and the Museum of Modern Art opened other doors for Prestini. In Boston, the Department of Design in Industry at the Institute of Contemporary Art, which hosted an annual "Design for Christmas" show beginning in 1949, featured turned bowls and platters by Prestini in the first two shows. And in such architectural magazines as *House Beautiful* and *Arts & Architecture*, Elodie Courter praised Prestini for subtle variations in depth and profiles and for his modernist restraint: "He never camouflages the wood with carved decoration which might detract from the intrinsic pattern in the material itself. Instead, he makes the inbred beauty of the material—the grain, texture, and natural color of each wood used—the object's sole ornament."[28]

The critical attention devoted to modern Scandinavian bowls and Prestini's pure bowls and plates had an enormous impact on the growing amateur turning community in America, inspiring a new enthusiasm for bowl turning and opening up sales opportunities. Bowls became the object of choice because of the confluence of aesthetic preferences and fabrication skills: their explicit function and simple lines appealed to modernist ideals, and they were easily shaped with the scraping techniques used by amateurs.

Turned bowls by Finn Juhl and the American Bob Stocksdale were

James Prestini
8 *Bracelet*
ca. 1933–53
Cuban mahogany
W 3 ¹⁵/₁₆ × Diam 3 ¹¹/₁₆
The Museum of Modern Art, New York,
Gift of the Designer, 35.81.sc

Though normally thought of as the first
"studio" turner, Prestini was also an
active maker of production items. The
hyperbolic curves of this bracelet are
typical of his interest in clean, linear
design; but they also resonate with the
heavy cuff bracelets, often made in
colored plastic, that were in vogue in
the 1930s. It is perhaps typical of
Prestini's noncommercial mentality
that he chose a shape that would have
been relatively difficult to turn on
the lathe; the perfect symmetry of the
form attests to his fine tool control.

James Prestini
9 *Cigarette Cup*
ca. 1933–53
Poplar impregnated with dye
H 2 ¼ × Diam 2 ¼
The Museum of Modern Art, New York,
Gift of the Designer, 26.81.sc

This small cup is evidence of Prestini's
adventurous experimentation with
material. The wood is a garden-variety,
unfigured poplar that was impregnated
with green dye during the tree's
growth cycle. Prestini apparently acquired
the wood from the United States
government, which launched the
experimental project as a way of using
relatively low-value timber. Because
of the small dimensions of the available
samples, Prestini adopted the laborious
procedure of joining the piece with
a small dovetail at the midsection.

James Prestini
10 *Salad Set*
1939
Cuban and Honduran mahogany
Tray: Diam 21 7/8, Small bowls:
Diam 6 15/16; Large Bowl: Diam 11 3/8
Stamped on underside of each piece:
PRESTINI
The Metropolitan Museum of Art,
Gift of the Artist, 1975, 1975.135.1–.8

Here Prestini envisioned the normally pedestrian, functional format of a salad set as a sculptural grouping composed of eight interlocking forms. The smaller bowls were designed and precisely turned to fit perfectly around the larger central bowl. The rims of the six outer bowls not only touch each other and the sides of the central bowl, but also line up directly above the outer edge of the platter. Because he privileged form over material, Prestini chose mahogany with a relatively subdued figure as the medium for his exacting craftsmanship. Eventually, he decided that wood was unsuitable for his goals and moved to fabricating his pure geometric forms in the more stable material of metal.

James Prestini
11 *Bowl*
ca. 1933–53
Mexican mahogany
H 5¾ × Diam 16⅛
Stamped on underside: PRESTINI
The Museum of Modern Art, New York,
Gift of the Designer, 1261.68

This bowl is a remarkable demonstration
of Prestini's interest in "pure form."
In effect, he has reimagined the bowl
as a sculptural form and reduced it to
its essence. The piece is perfectly round,
and both the interior and exterior
profiles describe a perfect parabolic
arc that is uninterrupted at the base. It
thus rests on a single point of contact,
freely rocking or spinning with a touch
of the hand. The bowl is also unusual
in that it is relatively large by Prestini's
standards. He was able to achieve this
size by gluing three boards of mahogany
together into a block, and then turning
that block on the lathe. He was careful
when laminating the wood not to
interrupt the flow of the figure, so that
no lines or breaks in the pattern of
the wood detract from the form of the
finished piece.

James Prestini
12 *Bowl*
1950
Sandblasted chestnut
H 1¾ × W 8⅝
Stamped on underside: PRESTINI
Philadelphia Museum of Art,
Gift of James Prestini, 1979.167.8

13 *Platter*
ca. 1933–53
Ebonized ash
H ¾ × Diam 9
Stamped on underside: PRESTINI
The Museum of Modern Art, New York,
Gift of the Designer, 1262.68

Though Prestini worked mostly with
solid hardwoods with quiet figure, he
did occasionally experiment with surface
finishes. His sandblasted and ebonized
pieces, like these two examples, were
the first instances of the use of these
processes in American studio turning.
Tellingly, however, Prestini chose treatments that preserved the uniformity
of the color and texture of the wood
surface and did not break up the purity
of the turned form. On both of these
pieces, the execution of the turning is
flawless, with the interior and exterior
profiles of the thin walls mirroring each
other perfectly. Prestini used scraping
tools, which remove the wood from
the workpiece slowly, in order to attain
this degree of precision.

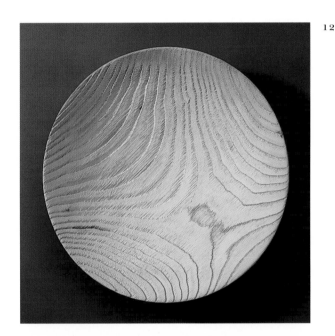

12

13

Fig. 13a. Price list for Arthur Espenet Carpenter, ca. 1953. Courtesy, Art Carpenter.

BOWLS

diameter	2" depth	3" depth	4" depth	5" depth	6" depth
5"	3.00	4.50	6.00	8.50	15.00
6	3.50	6.00	7.50	10.00	17.50
7	4.50	7.50	8.50	12.50	20.00
8	6.00	8.50	10.00	15.00	25.00
9	7.50	10.00	12.50	17.50	30.00
10	8.50	12.50	15.00	20.00	35.00
11	10.00	14.00	17.50	22.50	40.00
12	12.50	16.00	20.00	25.00	50.00
13	15.00	17.50	22.50	27.50	———
14	17.50	20.00	27.50	35.00	———
16	20.00	27.50	37.50	50.00	———
18	25.00	40.00	50.00	65.00	———

TRAYS

diameter	plain	hors d'oeuvre	suzans
8"	4.00		
9	5.00	———	———
10	6.00	7.50	———
11	7.50	8.50	———
12	8.50	10.00	12.50
13	10.00	12.50	15.00
14	12.50	15.00	17.50
16	15.00	17.50	20.00
18	17.50	20.00	22.50
20	20.00	22.50	25.00
22	22.50	25.00	27.50
24	25.00	30.00	32.50
26	30.00	35.00	37.50

ASHTRAYS

6"	4.00
7	5.00
8	6.50
9	8.00

CIGARETTE CUPS

3x3	5.00

Fig. 13b. Detail, price list for Arthur Espenet Carpenter, ca. 1953. Courtesy, Art Carpenter.

Fig. 14. Ebony pepper mill made by John (Jake) May, 1948–54. Collection of Samuel May.

featured in the "Good Design" exhibitions sponsored by MOMA between 1950 and 1954. Stocksdale had honed his self-taught turning skills while in a Conscientious Objectors camp during World War II and then established his own shop in Berkeley, California, in 1946. He concentrated on making bowls whose shapes were inspired by Chinese and Japanese ceramics as well as by Scandinavian bowls, and whose main decorative feature was the color and figure of the wood. Although he liked to turn production ware out of black walnut, he collected a variety of exotic, richly figured woods such as bubinga, harewood, rosewood, and zebrawood to use on special bowls. Unlike Prestini, who demonstrated a preference for quiet figure, Stocksdale sought out richly figured imports (14–17). In a letter to Prestini in 1948, he indicated he had twenty-three varieties of wood in stock, of which only a third were native. Stocksdale found ready markets in exclusive department stores such as Gump's in San Francisco, Fraser's in Berkeley, and Bullock's in Pasadena and became the first turner to earn his living exclusively by making bowls.[29]

Art Carpenter, a Dartmouth College graduate and World War II veteran, saw Prestini's work at the 1947 exhibition at the Museum of Modern Art and was inspired to drive to the West Coast, buy a lathe, and begin turning teak bowls (Fig. 13; 18). As he explained it, "I chose the lathe because it was the simplest tool for making the simplest object I could think of. In the forties there were no bowls from Denmark or Taiwan. Bob Stocksdale, so far as I knew, was the only bowlmaker who attempted more than the uncaring utility of Michigan kitchenware or the lacquered atrocities of redwood and bay sold to tourists on Highway 101." MOMA's 1953 "Good Design" exhibition featured Carpenter's work and provided him with the confidence to expand into furniture. By 1957, when he moved to rural Bolinas, California, Carpenter had stopped his commercial turning and concentrated on furniture.[30]

John (Jake) May of Jackson, New Hampshire, was another pioneer in the use of richly figured imported woods (19–20). May began as a furnituremaker who made meticulous reproductions of colonial furniture, but found the market for his turnings to be more profitable. His bread-and-butter works were doorknobs and a distinctive wasp-waisted pepper mill (Fig. 14), the hourglass shape of which also recalls the candlesticks of Rude Osolnik (21) and many tablewares of the 1950s designed by other prominent designers of the period including Freda Diamond and Walter Dorwin Teague. May's bowls of cocobola, ebony, lignum vitae, satinwood, rosewood, zebrawood, and African padouk were featured in the "Design for Christmas" shows from 1949 through 1953. He made several winter trips to Florida in the early 1950s to look for logs with interesting figure and relied on importers such as Palmer & Parker in Charleston, Massachusetts, and Paul St. Gaudens in Miami. From these sources he procured suitable logs, the density of which also led him to become one of the first modern turners to revive an old technique, turning bowls from green wood. The use of green wood made the actual cutting easier and permitted the turner to use large blocks of wood suitable for salad bowls without having to wait for years while the block lost its moisture and became more stable.[31]

May's prominence as a designer/craftsman during the early 1950s can be documented in several ways. He, along with Jack Lenor Larsen, the leading designer/craftsman in textiles, were on the inaugural faculty of the Haystack Mountain School of Crafts in Liberty, Maine. May taught wood turning and woodworking there from 1952 to 1955. In 1951,

Bob Stocksdale
14 *Plate*
ca. 1953
English harewood
H ⁷⁄₈ × Diam 13 ⁵⁄₈
Burned on underside in script: Harewood/
from/England/-Bob Stocksdale-/-circa 1955
[date added later]
Collection of Kay Sekimachi and
Bob Stocksdale

Bob Stocksdale is attracted by the
inherent qualities of wood and seeks
high-quality samples of exotics from
around the world. For him, the "hunt"
for and eventual acquisition of each
piece of wood are a crucial part of
the craft process. This plate is an early
example of Stocksdale's ability to
capitalize on the features of a special
find, a block of English harewood with
a spectacular streak of color variation
through its center. Stocksdale treats
the broad, flat face of the piece like
a canvas, leaving it unembellished
so that it does not interfere with the
wood's figure. The result is an unusually
painterly composition of a single,
calligraphic brushstroke balanced inside
a perfect circle. This piece was included
in the important early American
Craftsmen's Educational Council exhibition, "Designer-Craftsmen, U.S.A.,
1953."

Bob Stocksdale
15 *Bowl*
1958
California black walnut
H 5 ³⁄₈ × Diam 6 ¹¹⁄₁₆
Burned on underside in script:
Black Walnut/from/California/-Bob
Stocksdale-/1958
Collection of Kay Sekimachi and
Bob Stocksdale

The generally Asian flavor of Stocksdale's
work is evident in this early piece.
In particular, the interplay between the
relatively angular foot and the curva-
ceous belly of the form is reminiscent
of Eastern ceramic and lacquer rice
bowls; Stocksdale has wryly noted that
he was amazed to discover that Chinese
potters had been imitating him for
thousands of years. Though the wood
in this case is a local California walnut
rather than an exotic species like those
he often uses, Stocksdale has taken
care to select a sample with a dramatic
figure. The bowl was exhibited at the
World's Fair in Brussels in 1958.

Bob Stocksdale
16 *Fluted Birdmouth Bowl*
ca. 1965
Macassar ebony
H 2 ¾ × W 6 ³/₁₆ x D 5 ¹¹/₁₆
Incised on underside: Macassar Ebony/
from/East Indies/Bob Stocksdale
Collection of Forrest L. Merrill

One of Stocksdale's signature pieces is
the "birdmouth" bowl, in which two
sides of the rim sag slightly. Although
Stocksdale may have been inspired by
the similar forms of Scandinavian
designer Finn Juhl's bowls (see fig. 10),
the shape is also derived directly from
the swell in the exterior profile of the
tree. This early rendition of the form is
more angular and less exaggerated
than later "birdmouths" by Stocksdale,
which are nearly hemispherical. The
bowl is also distinguished by an unusual
band of fluting, which was executed by
touching it against a bandsaw at small
increments while rotating it by hand.

Bob Stocksdale
17 *Bowl*
ca. 1970s
Boxwood
H 3 ¹/₁₆ × Diam 6 ³/₈
Incised on underside: Boxwood/from/
Malaysia/Bob Stocksdale
Collection of Forrest L. Merrill

Boxwood is one of Stocksdale's preferred materials because it cuts
cleanly and shines with a dim luster.
The precision afforded by the wood is
demonstrated in this delicate bowl,
which features a tall cylindrical foot
and extremely thin walls. Like many
of Stocksdale's forms, the general layout of the composition is inspired
by Chinese porcelains. The ceramic
precedent is somewhat distant, however,
as the shape has been lightened considerably and curved inwards. The
delicacy of the turning harmonizes with
the subdued color and figure of the
material, particularly at the rim of the
bowl, which tapers off into thin air.

Arthur Espenet Carpenter
18 *Bowl*
1962
Teak
H 6 × Diam 11 ¾
Incised on bottom: Re 96/Drew/Espenet
[burned]/5800/Siamese Teak/1962
Collection of the Artist

This bowl was made near the apex of
Carpenter's decade-long wood turning
career, which he describes as a pro-
gression from "thick crudities to thin
pleasing shapes." His work was inspired
by bowls by James Prestini, which
Carpenter had seen at the Museum of
Modern Art; and appropriately, his
work was in turn accepted as good
design by the museum, where his pieces
were shown in 1953. Unlike Prestini,
though, Carpenter did not think of his
work as pure sculpture. The condition
of this bowl, with its interior scratches
and stove-top burn marks on the base,
attests to the fact that he meant his
pieces to be used. Indeed, he has been
using this bowl in his own kitchen
since it was made.

John (Jake) May
19 *Shallow Bowl*
ca. 1954
Unidentified tropical hardwood, perhaps of
the rosewood family
H 1 ¾ × Diam 9 ½
Incised on underside in script: JOH[N] MAY
Collection of Jane and Arthur Mason

In his day, John (Jake) May was as
prominent a figure in turning as his contemporaries James Prestini and Bob
Stocksdale, with whom his simple forms
in exotic woods have much in common.
This shallow bowl, typical of most of
his 1950s production, was originally
owned by weaver and textile designer
Jack Lenor Larsen. It is a good example
of May's technique of turning the wood
while it is still green, so that the form
warps slightly and the grain rises from
the surface during the drying process
(compare with 5).

John (Jake) May
20 *Footed Bowl*
1950–53
Ebony
H 3 ¼ × Diam 7 ½
Stamped on underside in circular formation:
JOHN MAY & BROS. JACKSON, N.H.;
incised within circle: III–XXXVIIII
Collection of Samuel May

Though many of May's bowls were in
the organic idiom of Scandinavian
modern design, he also executed footed bowls in a colonial revival style. His
pieces in this vein are unusual in that
they combine this historicism with
a delicate finesse usually reserved for
more up-to-date forms. The strong
transition from foot to bowl and the
gradual thinning of the rim on this
piece are the equal of any contemporary work by Bob Stocksdale. This is
quite clear when the piece is compared
with a superficially similar, but much
heavier design by May's contemporary
Paul Eshelman (7).

Rude Osolnik
21 *Candlestick Set*
ca. 1952
Walnut, brown felt
H 17 ¼ × Diam 3 ¼; H 15 ¼ × Diam 3;
H 12 ¼ × Diam 3
Inscribed on each, on the felt in black ink:
(a cipher of a pair of interlocking Os)
Mobile Museum of Art, Museum Purchase
with Funds from John B. Waterman by
exchange, P1998.04.01–.02–.03

Osolnik claims to have made enough
turnings during his long career to cover
the entire surface of a football field. If
so, much of the turf would be occupied
by candlesticks like these, which have
long been his signature sales item.
Their gentle curves make an interesting
comparison to the rigid geometry of
James Prestini's bracelets (8). Unlike
Prestini's production items, Osolnik's
were ideal as a commercial ware. They
could be sold singly, or in sets of three,
five, or more; and though most were
made of walnut, they were also available
in a variety of woods, including expensive tropical hardwoods.

Fig. 15. Bowls of walnut and mahogany made by Lemurian Crafts, ca. 1950, from *Current Design* 1, no. 1 (Spring 1950): 1.

Fig. 16. Teakwood bowl by Paul Killinger of Stowe, Massachusetts, ca. 1960, from *Craft Horizons* 20, no. 4 (July/August 1960): 19.

Fig. 17. Ebonized bowl with silver foot turned by Helen Warren and sold by Towle Silversmiths, ca. 1950. Yale University Art Gallery.

Edgar Kaufmann, Jr., helped organize a show of American design and craft that opened in Stuttgart, Germany. Included among the foremost examples of American work were furniture by Charles Eames, George Nelson, Edward Wormley, Paul McCobb, and Russel Wright; ceramics by Eva Zeisel, Gertrud and Otto Natzler, and Mary and Edwin Scheier; glass by Maurice Heaton; and turned works by Prestini, Stocksdale, and May.[32]

While Prestini, Stocksdale, and May were considered the leading design turners, others also took advantage of the new interest in wooden salad bowls and platters. The work approved by the Institute of Contemporary Art for its Christmas shows included not only the leading designers/craftsmen but also work by production turners such as Beaumont in Coos Bay and Lemurian Crafts of Ramona, California (Fig. 15). Such firms were producing great quantities of bowls and seeking broad national markets. Stores specializing in exclusive housewares, such as Gump's in San Francisco and George Jensen in New York, also offered designed bowls by turners such as Stocksdale and Paul Killinger (Fig. 16). These same stores and jewelers also sold another type of bowl: the silver-footed fruit/salad/dessert bowl. For example, Towle Silversmiths of Newburyport, Massachusetts, contracted with Helen Warren to turn mahogany bowls, which were then ebonized to minimize figure and lacquered (Fig. 17).[33]

Another pioneer woman turner was the furnituremaker Joyce Anderson of Morristown, New Jersey. Anderson and her husband Edgar became designers/craftsmen as a lifestyle choice in 1948; they sought to be self-employed and "totally responsible" for their work. She gradually learned turning by experimenting, first making legs and furniture parts, then expanding to platters, bowls, and stools that consisted of turned platters with turned legs (22). Although she did not meet Bob Stocksdale until an American Craft conference towards the end of the 1950s, Anderson shared a similar interest in a wood's color and figure. While she experimented with laminations and inlaid brass in the mid-1950s, she preferred to make simple forms from rare or special woods. In the New Jersey area she found markets similar to her fellow design turners: the Christmas design show at the Newark Museum and New Jersey Designer-Craftsmen Shows.[34]

The legacy of the late 1940s and early 1950s affected others in fields related to design. Engineers such as Jerry Glaser and Melvin Lindquist, who had been introduced to spindle and faceplate turning in industrial arts classes during the late 1920s and early 1930s, recognized the design and engineering challenges of turning in the 1950s. Glaser, who had seen Stocksdale's work as well as Scandinavian modern design at Frank Brothers in Long Beach, California, combined shapes from Finn Juhl with gouged exterior surfaces, joined the Southern California Designer Craftsmen group (where he and furnituremaker Sam Maloof were among the few who worked in wood), and then developed a more effective bowl gouge out of high-speed steel (23). Like his friend Stocksdale, Glaser also collected many different types of exotic woods that allowed him to explore figure and color. Lindquist popularized the use of spalted wood to highlight natural deformities of figure and color, pursued the vase form as an organic rather than classical shape, and developed tools for blind boring, or the hollowing of vessels through narrow neck openings (24).[35]

Thomas Nicosia, an engineer and cabinetmaker who designed and fabricated aircraft interiors and aeronautic equipment, also began to

Joyce Anderson
22 Stool
1969
Birch, walnut
H 29 ¼, Diam (seat) 13 ³/₁₆, W 20 ½
Incised on underside of seat: 148–07–1943
Collection of Gloria Roby

Joyce Anderson began collaborating with her husband Edgar on furniture projects in the 1950s, learning from him how to turn legs and spindles. Joyce did the turning for the furniture they designed together. She found the process of lathe turning highly satisfactory for making simple forms from figured woods, often harvested on their own property. This stool, a classic example of the Andersons' production line, which they began to develop in the 1950s, shows the influence of Scandinavian design and Shaker furniture. The construction of the piece is typical of the period, with simple tenoned joints and gentle contours on the seat, legs, and rungs. The meeting points of the legs and seat are finely executed, with wedges that fix the tenons in place and sloped shoulders on the upper legs underneath the seat.

Jerry Glaser
23 Bowl
1963
Teak
H 6 × Diam 11 ½
Inscribed on underside: TEAK/FROM/
THAILAND/GLASER/11–12–63
Collection of the Artist

Along with his close friends Bob
Stocksdale and furnituremaker Sam
Maloof, Jerry Glaser was influenced by
the directness and simplicity of mid-
century "Good Design," as it was
defined by the Museum of Modern Art
in New York. Inspired by Swedish turnings he had seen in the 1950s, Glaser
made several versions of this bowl in
walnut or teak. This particular example
was included in the exhibition "California Design Nine," held in 1965 at
the Pasadena Art Museum (see also
44). The rim was cut to shape with a
saw, the exterior textured with a gouge,
and the three feet hand-carved. Later
in his career, Glaser made a "natural
variation" of this piece in which the
curve of the rim was developed from
the exterior profile of the round log,
similar to Stocksdale's "birdmouth"
bowls (16). Glaser always tried for simple shapes, taking as his motto Antoine
de Saint-Exupéry's advice: "Perfection
is finally attained not when there is no
longer anything to add, but when there
is no longer anything to take away."

Melvin Lindquist
24 Bud Vase
1974
Spalted rock maple
H 5 ⅛ × Diam 2 ¾
Incised on underside: L 4–74/Rock Maple
Lindquist Studios Archive Collection

Although sold as production pieces,
each of Lindquist's bud vases has a
unique character because of the wood
from which it is made. In this case, the
piece has a spectacular pattern of spalting that overlays the grain of the maple,
like an ink drawing on paper. Lindquist
was especially fond of this bud vase
because the spalting pattern suggested
a flower blossom, so he never sold it
at a craft fair. Of thousands of such
production items, it is one of the few
that remain in the artist's collection.

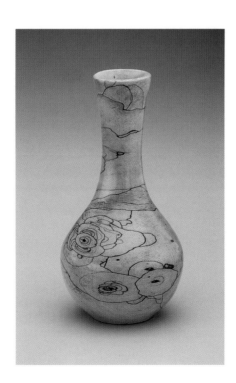

turn vessels in the late 1940s. While he derived his forms from classical prototypes, he developed a particular expertise in polychrome turning. Rather than simply gluing up different types of wood and turning a laminated vase, he used a metal lathe to turn small parts that he assembled with tongue-and-groove and rabbet joints into a rough shape. He then turned this construction and finished it with a high-gloss lacquer (25). Another hobbyist who explored an aesthetic of precision was New York City's Frank Knox, a former management consultant who began the gentlemanly pursuit of ornamental turning on a Holtzapffel lathe in the early 1960s. The lathe allowed Knox to turn forms with more than one axis of revolution and to decorate precisely by moving a rotating cutting tool exactly and predictably around the work. Knox did not merely preserve the traditional overall cut decoration of ornamental turning, but updated it by using boldly figured tropical woods embraced by the modern turners of the 1950s (26).[36]

The fascination with bowls and faceplate turning carried over into the educational system and the popular base of turning. Industrial arts teachers rediscovered the applications of the lathe and began to recognize the pedagogical possibilities of bowl turning: the students could work the wood while it was green, develop design based on figure, and discover the relationship between speed and tool (Fig. 18). From start to finish, turning came to be seen as the woodworking skill that gave the students the closest contact with wood structure, properties, and appearance. Whereas previous articles in the hobbyist publications focused primarily on spindle turning for furniture legs, articles in the 1950s began to focus upon bowls. A 1950 article advised do-it-yourselfers to buy turning blocks from craftsmen's supply houses or to find material in their own backyards. In 1954, the third edition of William Klenke's *The Art of Woodturning* featured several new designs for salad and fruit bowls. Bob Stocksdale became the "poster turner" for *Popular Science* and *Craft Horizons* in 1956; both magazines published step-by-step photographs of him turning a bowl, making the process seem so simple (Fig. 19).[37]

Creative Wood Turning

Prestini, through his acceptance and promotion by the Museum of Modern Art, attracted the interest of the design community and greatly increased the visibility of turned wood. When he stopped turning in 1953 and began to carve bowls and make plywood sculptural forms, however, turned bowls became less visible in the design world. The last Museum of Modern Art "Good Design" exhibition occurred in 1954, and the "Design for Christmas" exhibitions in Boston began to focus on European household wares in 1954. Without Prestini promoting turning as a design exercise, lathe-made objects became marginalized within the field of design.

Instead the interest in turning migrated over to the craft world, which was becoming increasingly visible and organized during the 1950s. The American Craftsmen's Educational Council came to the fore, arguing for the role of small shop craftsmen in producing functional domestic objects with skill, feeling, and intelligence. The Council collaborated with the Brooklyn Museum in 1953 to mount the pioneering and influential "Designer-Craftsmen, U.S.A., 1953," an exhibition that traveled under the auspices of the American Federation of Arts to several other museums including the Art Institute of Chicago, the Virginia Museum of Fine Arts, and the San Francisco Museum of Art. In the wood section, nine of the

Fig. 18. Industrial arts student work made between 1918 and 1954 at Olathe High School in Olathe, Kansas, from *Industrial Arts and Vocational Education* 43, no. 8 (October 1954): 284.

Fig. 19. Photographic essay illustrating Bob
Stocksdale's bowl turning technique, from
Craft Horizons 16, no. 6 (December 1956): 38.

Thomas Nicosia
25 *Standing Cup*
ca. 1960
Purpleheart (Mexico), rosewood, tulipwood,
cocobolo (Brazil), satinwood (Ceylon), ebony,
mahogany, bubinga, poplar, limba (Africa),
felt
H 11 ¹/₈ × W 7 ⁵/₈
Stamped on underside: NICOSIA PHILA.
Collection of Samuel M. Freeman II

Thomas Nicosia was an amateur turner
who independently developed a complicated system of constructing vessels
from many pieces of contrasting woods.
Unlike later turners who used lamination, Nicosia joined the fragments of
his works together not only with glue,
but also with internal tongue-and-
groove and rabbet joints. Despite this
careful craftsmanship, he was not
concerned with the color and natural
texture of the woods he was using, as
other early postwar turners were; most
of his pieces are made up of small,
alternating bands of color. Furthermore,
Nicosia usually covered his wood with a
thick layer of high-gloss lacquer polish
that emphasizes his graphic, rather
than sensual, approach to the material.
The forms he made are as idiosyncratic
as his technique was laborious. Perhaps
influenced by vessels he saw as a
child in Sicily, he created extravagantly
baroque interpretations of classical
Greek and Roman trophy forms, as in
this standing cup.

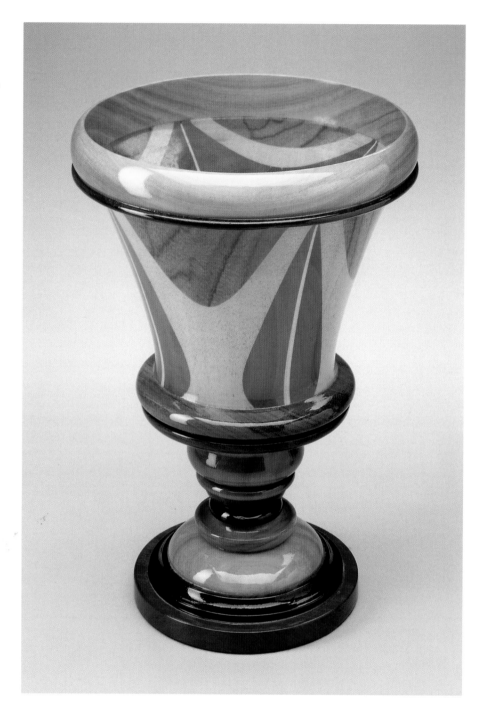

Frank Knox
26 *Compote*
1976
California Clara walnut, ebony; unidentified
wood on incienso
H 9 ½ × Diam 7 ⅜
Incised on underside: Bowl & Stem-/Clara
Walnut, California./Base, an unidentified
wood on/Incienso. Decorated and fluted/on
the Holtzapffel/Ornamental/lathe made in
London in 1853./Crafted by Frank M. Knox
[script]/Item No. 100, May 1976
Wood Turning Center, Anonymous Loan,
1995.01.01.119L

Though he was a hobbyist, Frank Knox
initiated the contemporary practice
of American ornamental turning. His
goal was to explore the full potential of
the ornamental lathe, using its full
complement of cutters. But he was also
interested in well-designed objects as
ends in themselves. Unlike most historical practitioners of ornamental turning,
he tried to balance the complex surface
patterns made on the lathe with the
beauty of the unadorned wood. This
compote is constructed of three separate
sections: the base and bowl, turned
on a faceplate; and the stem, which was
spindle turned. Ebony rings hide the
joints between each component.
The piece also features three distinct
patterns, each of which is executed with
the assistance of an indexing system
(which allows the turner to rotate the
piece in regular increments between
each cut). A band of waves, made with
an angled, disk-shaped cutter, runs
around the exterior of the bowl. The
stem and base have two different
patterns of diagonal flutes, made by
moving a cutter laterally across the
surface while rotating the workpiece.
These operations were accomplished
using Knox's 1853 Holtzapffel
ornamental lathe.

twenty-four woodworkers turned bowls. In the catalogue, the designer Edward Wormley explained the large proportion of turners while describing the niche of the craftsman: craftsmen working in small shops, in contrast with those in industry, could view and exploit the beauty of a particular piece of wood. Unhindered by the time constraints and market expectations of the factory, the woodworker could take the time to find a piece of wood's distinctive figure, base a design on that unique marking, and draw on consummate skill to make it: "With his experience and skill he knows that his shaping of the elements of design must take advantage of the wood figure."[38] Turners, more than furnituremakers, had the opportunity to use and showcase different woods, an advantage that explains the great number of turners (twelve of the fourteen woodworkers) in the inaugural 1956 exhibition at the Museum of Contemporary Crafts.[39]

Over the course of the 1950s, wood turning, like other crafts such as ceramics and fiber, began to push in a new, "freewheeling" direction and develop a more individualistic approach. Rejecting the focus on form and the modernist notions of utility, some turners began to highlight the character of imperfect materials and unregulated workmanship to distinguish the individual personality of their work from the consistent uniformity of industrial design. Both turners who had learned turning as part of a college program as well as those who learned on their own began to explore the various uses of the lathe as a form of personal creativity. It was at this time that these turners transformed the lathe from an industrial or engineering tool used for production to an artistic tool used for individual expression. The new directions in turning can be seen in the exploration of different materials and forms as well as the interest in manipulating objects off the lathe, after they were "finished."[40]

Whereas the design turning of the 1940s and 1950s emphasized perfectly round shapes of plain-figured woods (for example, the work of Prestini and Juhl) or richly figured exotics (for example, Stocksdale and May), the new creative turners expanded the types of woods they used and the manner in which they used them. The dominant attitude of the design turners was subservience to the wood and absolute pursuit of clear wood. Stocksdale remarked that his forms develop on the lathe, "for many times I have to change my initial design to eliminate flaws in the piece of wood."[41]

Rude Osolnik, who majored in industrial arts at Bradley University, where turning had been a major part of the woodworking curriculum since the 1920s, was one of the leaders in using "flawed" woods, partly out of frugality and partly out of interest in exploring the inherent design qualities of the medium (27–28, 30). He brought his experience as a production turner, where every motion had to be efficient and every finished product priced appropriately, to the field of individual turning. He was always aware of aligning costs of material and labor with the interests and demands of the market. In the 1940s, Osolnik found a source of cheap wood—the knotty and gnarly spurs (the enlarged areas of a tree just above its roots) considered scrap by the local veneer mills. To facilitate his cutting, he turned these spurs green and discovered that he liked the asymmetrical shape and uneven rim that resulted as the wood lost its moisture. In exploring stumps, roots, spurs, and burls, Osolnik developed his own vocabulary of free-form rims (sometimes even sawing the rim into an irregular profile) and natural-edge rims in which the bark and cambium layers were preserved along some part of the bowl's rim. Rather than searching only for flawless wood and seeking an absolutely

Rude Osolnik
27 *Salad Set*
ca. 1950
Rosewood
Large bowl: H 4 ¼ × Diam 12;
Small bowls: H 2 ⅓ × Diam 7
Inscribed on underside of each piece:
Osolnik Originals/Rosewood
The Speed Art Museum, Louisville, Kentucky,
1999.4.1–6

This early salad set by Rude Osolnik makes an instructive comparison with a set of bowls made by James Prestini (see 10). Prestini meant his set as a demonstration of precision turning, in which each of the smaller bowls is identical in size and profile. By contrast, Osolnik's bowls are unique because of their eccentric rims, which follow the curved edges of the salvaged tree cross sections from which the pieces were turned. Osolnik often turned bowls of this kind as individual pieces; it was unusual for him to group several of them together in a set.

Rude Osolnik
28 *Spur bowl*
ca. 1950
Walnut
Inscribed on underside: Osolnik Originals
H 3 × Diam 18
Southern Highland Craft Guild Permanent
Collection, Gift of Virginia King, 1997.22.1

Carl Huskey
29 *Fruit*
ca. 1950
Walnut, cherry, maple
H 1 ½ × Diam 1 ½ to H 4 ½ × Diam 4 ½
Southern Highland Craft Guild Permanent
Collection, Gift of Virginia King, 1997.22.2–8

Virginia King purchased this bowl and turned wooden fruit separately from Rude Osolnik and Carl Huskey at the same Southern Highland Craft Guild craft show in the 1950s. The bowl and fruit were displayed together in her home until their gift to the Guild. The fruit was one of many production wares made in a variety of woods by the Huskey family business, which sold items to the Great Smoky Mountains National Park tourist trade. Carl Huskey's son Ray still makes turned fruit today. The bowl is typical of Rude Osolnik's early work, which was often made out of waste scraps from local veneer mills, an inexpensive source of figured wood. Osolnik preserved the profile of the log in the shape of the rim.

Rude Osolnik
30 *Bud Vase*
ca. 1965
Redwood burl twig
H 6 ⅛ × Diam 10 ¾
Mayo Clinic Art Collection

In this organic bud vase (or weed pot), Osolnik capitalized on the cracks, bark inclusions, and varied color of a piece of found wood. The heavy, broad shape of the piece offers a top view down into the fissures in the material, conveying a sense of depth and massiveness. Like his contemporary Melvin Lindquist, Osolnik combined this sensitivity to the wood with a straightforward, albeit minimal, functionality: a narrow hole drilled into the interior was meant to hold a single stem.

Rude Osolnik
31 *Bowl*
1975
Laminated Baltic birch plywood
H 7 × Diam 10 ¹⁵/₁₆
Inscribed on underside in ink: OSOLNIK ORIGINALS/LAMINATED WOOD; inscribed on bottom edge in black: 121
Renwick Gallery of the Smithsonian American Art Museum, 1975.175

In 1975, continuing decades of wide-ranging experimentation, Osolnik found a new material in birch plywood. To make a bowl like this one, he first glued a stack of plywood planks and walnut veneers into a block, often using scrap woods from his shop. He then mounted the block on the lathe and turned it to shape, creating a symphony of intersecting curvilinear patterns. This particular bowl was made for the Renwick Gallery's 1975 "Craft Multiples" exhibition, which featured functional objects that could be dupli-cated in production runs. Ironically, this exercise began a series of one-of-a-kind plywood bowls that are among Osolnik's best known works.

smooth and consistent surface, Osolnik also embraced natural defects—
bark inclusions, voids, and checks on the bodies of his bowls—as a way
to highlight his craftsmanship. In the mid 1970s, he even laminated Baltic
birch plywood to form an artificially grained wood that he turned into
refined shapes (31).[42]

Another turner who saw the aesthetic possibilities of what had
earlier been viewed as inferior wood was Melvin Lindquist, who began to
turn spalted maple (wood streaked and discolored by carbonaceous
deposits introduced by fungi) in the late 1950s. The varying hardness of
the material (the black zone lines in the spalting were hard, while much
of the lighter wood was soft) tended to result in chipped and pitted surfaces.
To accentuate the full-grain configuration with a smooth surface, Lindquist
developed carbide-tipped tools for some of the harder examples and
"abrasive turning" with a flap wheel or grinder applied to a rotating blank
in the lathe for the softer blocks. Like Osolnik, Lindquist also explored
the irregularities of distressed woods with bark inclusions or voids, burls,
and natural edges and was one of the first turners to use a natural edge
around the entire circumference of a lip (32–35). Manzanita root, a
gnarly shrub with no commercial lumber use, became another favorite
wood on the West Coast. Prized for its interlocking grains and rough surface,
manzanita became the wood of choice for self-taught California turners
such as William Hunter and Hap Sakwa in the 1960s and early 1970s
(36).[43]

The interest in irregularity and natural defects in the materials
also led to the development of new forms. Eschewing the regularity and
architectonic elements of a classical vase, Osolnik and Lindquist pioneered
the organic vase, a bulbous shape characterized by thick walls, small
openings, and celebration of irregularities such as checks, knots, and bark.
Lindquist even sanded the edges of checks to accentuate the fissured
appearance of his vases. Instead of focusing upon predictable, explicitly
utilitarian bowls and platters, turners began to produce weed pots, semi-
functional vessels with thin necks, in which the bodies featured contrasting
heartwood/sapwood or smooth surface/distressed wood.

Part of the move from open bowls toward thin-necked, closed
vessels can also be attributed to the influence of potters like Toshiko
Takaezu. The growth of studio craft programs in the 1950s and the net-
works encouraged by the American Craftsmen's Council had contributed
to cross-fertilization of ideas among different media over the course of
the decade. The new ceramic approach to turning can be seen most clearly
in the work of Mark Lindquist, Mel's son, who came out of a studio art
background and experience as a potter. Profoundly influenced by Japanese
aesthetic theories of the period and Japanese Tamba pottery, Lindquist
deliberately pursued impure forms and used rough workmanship, often
leaving visible gouge marks. He even carved rims and other parts already
turned as a way of asserting himself in opposition to the dominant design
trends (37).[44]

Another turner who pioneered new vessel forms in spalted wood
was Ed Moulthrop, an architect who pursued turning as a serious sideline
and then as a full-time career. Moulthrop harvested local spalted, diseased,
and lightning-struck woods, which he then turned into large spherical
vessels that are distinguished not only by scale but also by a plastic-like
finish achieved through immersion of the rough turning in polyethylene
glycol and a final surface of rubbed epoxy. To accentuate the "subtle or
exotic range of colors and the etching-like patterns of growth rings," he

Melvin Lindquist

32 Fluted Vase

1965

Spalted maple

H 10 ¾ × Diam 5

Burned on underside: 87 [?]–65

Lindquist Studios Archive Collection

Melvin Lindquist first ran across spalted wood near his house in Schenectady, New York, in the 1950s. Traditionally, spalted wood has been thought of as a waste material; Lindquist recalls that woodworkers in the Northeast nicknamed it "pig wood." It is difficult to turn the material to a smooth finish because the fungus that creates the black spalting lines also weakens the structural integrity of the wood. By abrading the wood with a disc sander, Lindquist was able to turn the wood to shape without creating a rough, pecked surface. He could also then exploit the fungus lines as a decorative, calligraphic pattern running across the regular grain of the wood. In this vase, Lindquist bored out the center using a long scraper of his own manufacture, and then fluted the neck with carving tools.

Melvin Lindquist

33 Pot

1976

Sugar maple burl

H 7 ½ × Diam 7 ⅝

The Metropolitan Museum of Art,

Gift of the Artist, 1978, 1978.180

Unlike the slightly later hollow vessels of David Ellsworth (see 53), this piece is not a technical tour-de-force; it has a wide mouth and is uniformly thick. But one should not assume that the vessel is unsophisticated; Lindquist's finesse lay not in turning thin walls, but rather in capturing the qualities of his raw material. He has left the shape a simple ovoid to complement the extravagant effect of the maple's burl pattern and a bark inclusion, which cascades down the side. This piece was acquired by the Metropolitan Museum of Art in 1978, just after it had been shown in the Renwick Gallery's exhibition "The Art of the Turned Bowl."

Melvin Lindquist

34 *Bowl*

1976

Wild cherry burl

H 5 ¾ × Diam 11 ½

Inscribed on underside:

L [script] 3–76 WILD CHERRY BOWL

Schenectady Museum,

Gift of Mark and Melvin Lindquist, 77.84

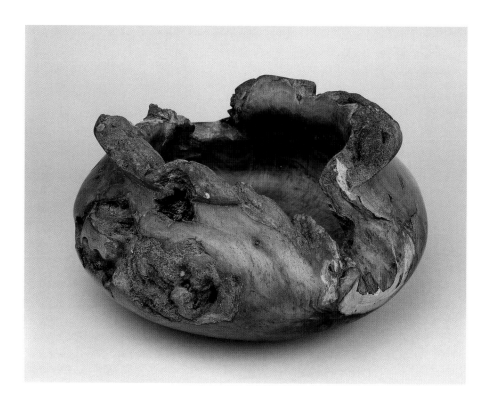

Lindquist has written that he approaches every piece of wood with enthusiasm and respect, "as if it will make the best object I've ever made." He invariably leaves something of the raw, untransformed condition of his material. In this case, Lindquist exploited the bark edge of the log and the serpentine pattern of the cherry burl. He was also daring in allowing the finished vessel form to be interrupted by the natural gaps in the wood, which are highlighted by outlines of light-colored sapwood. The profile of the bowl was inspired by Hopi pottery, to which Lindquist was introduced by his son Mark. The shape—and variations upon it—would become one of his signatures in the early 1980s.

Melvin Lindquist

35 *Root Bowl*

1979

Manzanita burl

H 7 ⅛ × W 13 ¼ × D 8 ¾

Incised on underside: Mel Lindquist/

Manzanita/Burl/10–79

Lindquist Studios Archive Collection

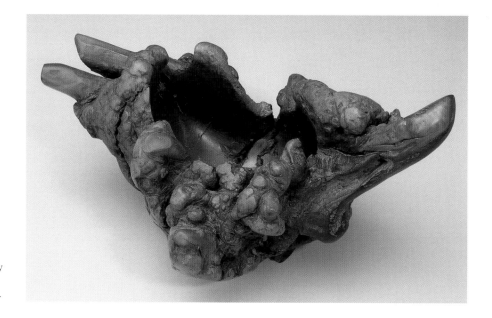

Lindquist's preservation of the shape of the natural wood he was turning reached its zenith in the late 1970s in a series of "root bowls." This spectacular example alludes to the form of a traditional bowl, but its turned cavity is overwhelmed by the dynamic surrounding root forms. In this sense, the piece epitomizes Lindquist's philosophy of restraint in approaching wood. The turning and finishing of the interior do, however, serve the purpose of revealing the deep color and exciting figure that the manzanita burl exhibits at the intersection of its roots.

William Hunter
36 Vase
1971
Manzanita burl
H 10 ⅜ × Diam 6 ½
Incised on underside: HUNTER/1971
Yale University Art Gallery,
Gift of the artist in memory of his parents
Charldon and Bonnie Hunter, 2000.48.1

William Hunter began his career making a multitude of production items, including letter openers, bud vases, and smoking pipes. This vase, one of his first significant one-of-a-kind pieces, represented an increase in his ambitions. After the piece was taken off the lathe, the broad facets that run down the vessel sides were fashioned with a power disc sander, a tool that Hunter has continued to use to shape and finish his forms (see 101, 102). To a degree unusual at the time of this piece's creation, Hunter was interested in highlighting the natural irregularities of the raw material. The vase is topped with an outcropping of natural burl that is riddled with cracks and crevices, and the vessel side is punctuated with deep, bark-lined cavities. The rest of the surface is highly polished, creating a vivid contrast of natural and worked surfaces.

Mark Lindquist
37 Meditating Vessel
1972
White birch root burl
H 3 ⅞ × W 7 × D 6
Inscribed on underside: (a cross) Mark Lindquist/White Birch/Root Burl 1972
Lindquist Studios Archive Collection

In the early 1970s, Mark Lindquist began to use the lathe to create one-of-a-kind objects in which the form captured the qualities of a specific piece of wood. In this case, he showed his appreciation for the natural beauty of a hemispherical piece of birch burl by deciding not to transform it. Apart from the base, the entire exterior of the bowl is covered with the intact bark of the tree. This rough surface is linked to the turned, polished interior by a small aperture in the side. Lindquist had only recently made the transition from pottery to wood turning when he made this bowl, and the shape of the piece, its irregularity, its thick walls, and its contrasting textures are all reminiscent of Japanese tea ceremony ceramics. The title *Meditating Vessel* further points to the Asian flavor of Lindquist's work at this time.

turned with the pith on the axis of rotation. For these hyperbolic vessels, which have diameters as great as forty inches and heights up to four feet, Moulthrop developed a special large lathe and turning tools (38).[45]

Other graduates of craft and industrial arts programs also pushed the parameters of the field. C. R. (Skip) Johnson, a 1960 MFA graduate of the School for American Craftsmen at the Rochester Institute of Technology, found the furniture emphasis of that program stifling. His teacher Tage Frid had demonstrated the use of the lathe, but did not incorporate it into the class assignments. Johnson, responding to the toys of Kay Bojesen, did his entire thesis show on turned figures and animals. His whimsical "Mountain Men" were part of that show, and Johnson's subsequent work often explored humor and narrative through objects comprised of lathe-turned parts (39–42). Frank Cummings, a graduate of and teacher at California State University at Long Beach, made a wide variety of vases, mirrors, and small objects that incorporated turned wooden elements with many other materials including feathers, plastics, and ivory. He sought to synthesize other woodworking traditions such as the Shaker belief that good craftsmanship was a devotional pursuit and the African tradition that bestowed ceremonial meaning on everyday objects (43).[46]

In addition to materials and forms, techniques were a third frontier that turners pushed at this time. Robert Trout, another Long Beach graduate, viewed the lathe not as a precious tool to revere, but rather simply as another machine tool to use efficiently. He made objects on a lathe, then embellished their surfaces off of the lathe, carving decorative patterns into the vessel or cutting facets into the body (44). His work stood out in the California Design exhibitions of the 1960s and in Dona Meilach's pathbreaking book, *Contemporary Art with Wood*. Published in 1968, Meilach's book linked developments in wood sculpture of the 1950s with furniture and turning of the 1960s, showcasing some of Trout's unusual bowls.[47] Meilach also illustrated multi-axis turning and argued that the lathe was useful for more than spindles, legs, and bowls. To demonstrate this point, she included photographs of off-center turned exercises executed at the Institute of Design in Chicago, where Ray Pearson had succeeded Prestini (Fig. 20). The resulting forms, described by Meilach as "odd and graceful," suggested the vast potential that turners only began to tap several decades later.[48]

Another pioneer in the manipulation of turned objects off the lathe was Stephen Hogbin, a furniture designer trained in England at Rycotewood College and the Royal College of Art. After teaching for three years at Sheridan College of Design in Ontario, Hogbin struck out as an independent craftsman in 1971 and chose turning since it seemed to be a "low risk means to set up with minimal equipment and try ideas in rapid succession."[49] He quickly developed a specific approach: after turning a form he would cut it into segments, then turn them around, inside out, or upside down to explore the interrelationships and form new objects (45). His "fragmentals" were a form of deconstruction far ahead of their time and inspired a number of turners to try their hand at the "Hogbin cut."[50]

After focusing initially on smaller objects, Hogbin turned his attention to large-scale turnings, either long totemic posts or laminated fragmentals that were cut up into furniture forms (46). In 1972, with the help of his father-in-law Bud Thomas, Hogbin made his own lathe from a truck axle for this body of work. His work resonated with some

Fig. 20. Examples of student multi-axis turning exercises made in Ray Pearson's classes at the Institute of Design of Illinois Institute of Technology, from Dona Meilach, *Contemporary Art with Wood: Creative Techniques and Appreciation* (New York: Crown, 1968), 49.

Ed Moulthrop
38 *Super-Ellipsoid*
1978
Tulipwood
H 13 × Diam 25
High Museum of Art, Atlanta, Georgia,
Gift of the Junior Committee of the
Members Guild, 1978.1000.20

This is a typical example of Ed Moulthrop's signature "spheroid" vessels, which he began making in the early 1970s. By the latter part of the decade, he had increased the size of the pieces to unprecedented proportions. This necessitated the development of a unique lathe and long-handled tools designed and made from salvaged parts by Moulthrop himself. He also invented a unique method of strengthening the wood to prevent splitting and warping. After turning the rough shape of his pieces, Moulthrop cures them for six to nine weeks in vats of the chemical polyethylene glycol (PEG), which replaces the natural moisture in the cells and stabilizes the material, fixing the color of the wood. He then finishes the pieces on the lathe and covers them with a thick layer of plastic resin that further protects the surface. This process allows Moulthrop to create huge pieces such as this one out of local woods like tulip, which is spectacularly colored and figured but relatively unstable in its unprepared state.

C. R. (Skip) Johnson
39 *Mountain Man*
ca. 1965
Mahogany, leather
H 9 ¾ × W 5 ⅝ × D 2 ½
Collection of the Artist

40 *Mountain Woman*
ca. 1965
Mahogany
H 8 ⅛ × W 4 ½ × D 2 ¼
Collection of the Artist

41 *Pig*
ca. 1965
Mahogany, leather, brass
H 1 ½ × W 1 ½ × D 3 ⅞
Incised on underside: Cjon
Collection of the Artist

With the exception of the leather hat brim on one figure, Johnson's ingeniously designed figures are made entirely of turned elements. They were made while the artist was a resident of North Carolina, and were originally designed as a thesis project for his woodworking class with Tage Frid at the School for American Craftsmen at the Rochester Institute of Technology. Though the toys were intended to be a souvenir of Appalachia, their basic construction is indebted to similar designs by the Danish designer Kay Bojeson. After designing these toys, Johnson thought better of involving himself in day-to-day mass production. He had the pieces made by the Huskey family of turners (see 1, 29), and sold through the Southern Highland Handicraft Guild. Johnson received a small commission for each one sold, which allowed him to concentrate on one-of-a-kind studio pieces (see 42).

C. R. (Skip) Johnson
42 The Itinerant Turner's Toolbox
1981
Mahogany, basswood, walnut, padauk,
honey locust
H 42 ⅜ × W 26 1/16 × D 9 ¾
Wood Turning Center,
Gift of the Artist, 1995.01.01.103G

Here Johnson, a furnituremaker by
training, reflects humorously on the
history of the turning craft. This toolbox
is a creative interpretation of the gear
of an itinerant turner of the early
1800s, who made his living with nothing
but a horse and wagon, his tools, and
a lathe. All of the objects in the box are
fashioned in wood, including gouges,
scrapers, chucks, calipers, spare lathe
parts, and even slip stones for sharpening tool edges. Knowing that, like the
lathe, the craftsman gets hot while
working, Johnson also provided an easy
method for turners to refresh themselves
without having to stop turning. The
tool box is meant to hang conveniently
above the lathe, and a tube extends
from the beer keg in the top of the box
to a nipple projecting from the front.
Within the fiction of the piece, the
flow of fluid is activated by pressing
one's cheek against a round lever nearby.
The box was made for the 1981
"Turned Object Show."

Frank E. Cummings III
43 *Vessel*
ca. 1960
East Indian rosewood, buffalo fur, goat hair,
horse hair
H 11 ³⁄₈ × Diam 7 ¹⁄₂
Collection of Harland and Elizabeth Goldwater

The free design approach that Frank
Cummings took in creating this piece
was typical of his wide-ranging work of
the 1960s, which embraced furniture,
jewelry, and clock-making in a variety of
materials. Cummings was one of the
first contemporary turners to use the
lathe as a roughing tool, creating a
basic form that could then be extensively carved. He was also one of the
first to take a mixed-media approach to
decorating turned objects. Only the
bottom third of this vessel retains its
smooth, turned surface. The other
areas are hand-carved and decorated
with applied animal hair, evoking the
ceremonial objects Cummings had seen
on a trip to Africa just before making
this piece. The densely worked surface,
reminiscent of the hide of a rhino or
elephant, further establishes an organic,
ritualistic feel. The wave pattern running
around the top of the vessel is an early
example of Cummings's lacework
motif, which would become increasingly
complex and refined over the course
of his career.

Robert Trout
44 *Bowl*
1964
Teak
H 4 ¾ × Diam 9 ¾
Incised on underside: Trout '64/Teak
Collection of the Artist

Robert Trout was a broadly skilled craftsman who worked in clay and metal as well as wood; he thought of the lathe as one machine tool in the shop, rather than as the exclusive focus of his practice. This attitude may have contributed to his interest in embellishing the surfaces of his turnings with hand-carved pattern. Though a number of California turners in the 1960s tried their hand at surface texturing (see 16, 23, 43), Trout's sensibility was unusual for its overtly ornamental character. The oval forms encircling the exterior walls of this bowl remind one of the graphic design styles of the 1960s. The choice of teak and the simple form of the piece, however, hearken back to the Scandinavian-influenced turnings of the previous decade. Trout's work was shown alongside Stocksdale's and Jerry Glaser's in the "California Design" shows at the Pasadena Art Museum.

Stephen Hogbin
45 *Rocking Bowl*
1979
Mahogany
H 3 ¾ × W 7 ⅞ × Diam 6 ⁹⁄₁₆
Incised on exterior near rim: SH
Arizona State University Art Museum,
Gift of Edward Jacobson, 90.18

Stephen Hogbin's early experiments on the lathe included off-center turnings, lamination, and cut and reassembled bowls and plates, which he called "fragmentals." From his background in industrial design, Hogbin knew that patternmakers often used these processes in designing forms for manufacture, but he saw them as creative ends in themselves. He often worked scientifically, making a series of objects using the same technique with small variations. This "fragmental" bowl is typical of this period of intense innovation. It is a bowl with a flared lip cut in half and rejoined by gluing the rims of the halves together. The result is an organic ridge that runs from edge to edge underneath the form, creating a "rocking" bowl. The piece was in the 1985 landmark exhibition and publication of Edward Jacobson's collection, "The Art of Turned-Wood Bowls."

Fig. 21. "Triple Cocktail Table" made by Tom Lacagnina of Alfred, New York, ca. 1970–74, from Dona Meilach, *Creating Modern Furniture* (New York: Crown, 1975), 233.

furnituremakers who had been influenced by Wendell Castle's innovative stack-laminated and carved work of the 1960s. Tom Lacagnina used stack-laminated construction, but instead of simply shaping the final form with chainsaws, grinders, and gouges, he turned certain elements. In blending Castle's lamination construction techniques with Lindquist's interest in checked wood and solid mass, Lacagnina offered a distinctive perspective on freewheeling turning (Fig. 21). Curiously, it was never followed by others, perhaps because he inhabited a tenuous middle ground between furniture and vessel turning.[51]

Like many of the new turners of the 1960s and 1970s, Hogbin relied on a small line of production ware to develop skills and to earn a living through sales. For lathe operators working in commercial shops, production turning—in which speed, repetition, and accuracy were most highly prized—was an end unto itself; but for the new breed of craftsmen who emerged in the post-World War II era, making and selling production items was a means towards another, more personal end. Batch work provided financial stability due to the scales of efficiency and also increased the turner's skills. Once these new turners built a financial and technical base with a line of common wares, they often abandoned it in favor of expensive one-of-a-kind work. For example, in order to develop the necessary skills and to explore the textural relationship between turning and carving with gouges, Hogbin made salad servers from split turnings— the historical basis of his individualistic fragmentals (47). David Ellsworth and Al Stirt both began with production work to build their technical levels and to support their chosen field. The former sold many sets of salt-and-pepper shakers in craft shows, and the latter focused on bowls for craft stores and shows (48–49 and 50). Jack Straka, a former electrical engineer, changed careers in his forties and moved to the warmer climate of Hawaii, where he learned turning from a production turner. He brought a production mentality to his own work, which specializes in bowls of Hawaiian woods with shapes and conventions derived from such traditional carved Hawaiian forms as the calabash (51).[52]

While the design shows of the early 1950s had brought turning to the attention of a larger public through articles and illustrations in magazines, the period from about 1955 to 1975 witnessed a broadening of exposure to the actual turned objects. These were years of significant expansion in the number of regional craft shows and sales, some organized by the American Craftsmen's Council and some by regional or state organizations. The ACC exhibitions of the early 1960s always included turners, and America House, established in 1949 as the official store of the ACC, became the premier sales gallery for turned objects in New York. Prestigious exhibitions such as the "Finger Lakes Exhibition" in Rochester or "California Design" in Pasadena also continued to show turned objects. Popular venues for the sale of turnings were regional craft shows such as the Southern Highland Craft Guild's craft show, which debuted in 1952, and the Northeast Craft Fair, established in 1966 in Stowe, Vermont, and subsequently relocated to Rhinebeck, New York, from 1973 to 1984. At all of these craft fairs, turners sold their goods, enjoyed the opportunity to socialize and escape the isolation of their shop, and often demonstrated turning. Osolnik always drew a crowd at the former, while the Lindquists were main attractions at the latter. The mesmerizing effect of demonstrations made the products very seductive, increased sales, and attracted other amateurs to turning.[53]

The broader exposure of turning as a craft and as a form of

Stephen Hogbin
46 Chair
1974
Cedar
H 32 × W 28 ½ × D 38 ½
Collection of the Artist

Stephen Hogbin initially saw the lathe as a low risk and inexpensive means of rapidly executing design ideas. In retrospect, it is clear that he was also attracted to the clarity and flexibility provided by the tool. Influenced by early popularizations of the philosophy of deconstruction, such as John Berger's book *Ways of Seeing*, Hogbin privileged the conceptual possibilities of the turning process over the dictates of function or beauty. In 1972, with the help of his father-in-law Bud Thomas, he built a new lathe from a truck axle mounted on a steel frame to handle large masses of wood. This massive chair was made from a single laminated disk seven feet in diameter and one foot thick. Hogbin turned concentric grooves into the disk, and then cut and reassembled it, yielding two of these chairs, a table, and two shelves.

Stephen Hogbin
47 *Spoons*
ca. 1978
Birch
L 11 ½ × W 3; L 11 ⅝ × W 3
Incised on one handle: SH [conjoined]
Wood Turning Center,
Gift of Alan LeCoff, 1995.01.01.083a.b.c

These serving spoons brought Hogbin's
innovative "fragmental" turning to
the affordable level of production ware.
The basic shape is fashioned from a
single split spindle turning, but Hogbin
has made the spoons more appealing
by hand-carving the handle and the
inside of the bowl. The ribs that run
around the back of the spoons have
both a decorative and a functional
role, as they can be used to hold an
elastic band in place so the pair can
be shipped or stored as a unit.

David Ellsworth
48 *Salt & Pepper Shakers*
ca. 1976
Brazilian rosewood, padauk, walnut
H 2 ½ × Diam 2 ¾ (each)
Wood Turning Center,
Gift of Jesse LeCoff, 2000.08.23.01

49 *Sugar Container*
ca. 1976
Brazilian rosewood, padauk, walnut
H 1 ¾ × Diam 5
Burned on underside: (barred circle cipher)
Wood Turning Center,
Gift of Jesse LeCoff, 2000.08.23.01

Ellsworth produced these functional
shaker sets in quantity from 1974 to
1977 in order to support himself
financially. The design features exotic
rosewood and padauk laminated to
walnut. Each shaker has a dovetail slide
or plug in the base so that it can be
refilled. Once Ellsworth's hollow vessels
(53, 55) began to garner recognition,
he abandoned production work entirely.

Alan Stirt
50 *Fluted Bowl*
1979
Black cherry
H 4 ½ × Diam 10 ¼
Incised on underside: Al Stirt '79/
BLACK CHERRY/FROM VERMONT
The Society for Contemporary Crafts,
Pittsburgh, Pennsylvania

Alan Stirt is among the few professional studio turners whose one-of-a-kind work developed directly out of an earlier body of production wares; in fact, it is difficult to draw a line between the two. This early cherry bowl, by virtue of its small size, could be produced in relatively large quantities. Despite its modest proportions, however, it has much of the appeal of the artist's later monumental fluted bowls (72).

Jack Straka
51 *Bowl*
ca. 1979
Koa
H 6 × Diam 10 ¾
Incised on underside: Straka/Koa Wood
Wood Turning Center, Anonymous Loan,
1995.01.01.241L

Jack Straka, a turner living in Hawaii, was influenced by the local tradition of "calabash" bowls. Though gourds are used for vessel-making in Africa and throughout much of the Pacific, the Hawaiian calabash tradition is unusual for its use of patches to fill natural cracks in the walls. When wood turners such as Straka emulated the gourd-shaped bowls in wood, they replaced the patches with wooden dovetail keys that resemble those used by American furnituremaker George Nakashima (suggesting, perhaps, a Pacific origin for this motif in Nakashima's work). Straka also captures something of the natural softness and sturdiness of the calabash by turning his bowls from koa, a local Hawaiian wood with rich color and quiet figure.

individual expression can also be seen in the hobbyist literature of the period. Rather than emphasize utility, traditional designs, and satisfaction with exacting tool processes, the articles of the late 1960s and early 1970s remarked that although the lathe had almost been forgotten as a power tool "the word is getting around about the creativity and sheer pleasure— akin to sculpturing—that the lathe makes possible."[54] There was a sudden surge in sales of lathes, a concern with sufficient swing (the height from the ways to the mandrel) that would allow large vessel and bowl turning, and even the emergence of shops specializing in lathes and turning tools.[55]

The broadening base of creative wood turning and the emerging market for wood turning equipment and objects can also be seen in the publication of *Fine Woodworking* magazine, which debuted in 1975, and Dale Nish's book *Creative Woodturning*, also in 1975. *Fine Woodworking* published articles by Mark Lindquist, David Ellsworth, and others that disseminated new techniques, illustrated current work, and commissioned reviews of symposia. Nish, a professor of industrial arts at Brigham Young University, covered a wide variety of techniques in his well-illustrated volume. In one source, a turner could see the most comprehensive treatment of techniques and final products. Yet there were no measured drawings, suggesting that readers understand the possibilities and experiment on their own.

Conclusion

The socialization at craft shows and the appearance of new publications began to link together a group of craftsmen who previously had toiled largely on their own. Turners may have had some associations with local craftsmen in a variety of media, but it was only in 1976, with the advent of the George School Symposia, that turners began to communicate with each other. Professional turners, academic woodworkers, shop teachers, and hobbyists all began to interact and take the initiative to shape the field themselves. Their sharing of techniques and approaches quickened the impulse to experiment and fostered a dramatic growth in the number of turners, the types of tools, and the variety of work. This flourishing did not spring up unexpectedly or by chance, but rather grew from a long and complex foundation of industrial arts training, hobbyist involvement, modern design philosophy, and craft concerns about processes.

Notes

For their help in research for this essay, I would like to acknowledge the following: Suzanne Baizerman of the Oakland Museum, various members of the Brubaker family, Patty Dean of the Minnesota Historical Society, Nora Donnelly of the Institute of Contemporary Art in Boston, Hugh McKay, various members of the May family, Mark Salwasser, Tricia Schreck, Bruce Smith, Duncan Smith, and Alana VanDerwerker. Patricia Kane, Glenn Adamson, Charles Hummel, and John Kelsey also provided important feedback on an earlier version of the essay. W. Scott Braznell generously shared references to turners and turned bowls from his extensive files on 1940s and 1950s design.

1 For typical interpretations see John Kelsey, "The Turned Bowl: The End of Infancy for a Craft Reborn," *Fine Woodworking* 32 (January/February 1982): 54–60; Edward Jacobson, *The Art of Turned-Wood Bowls* (New York: E. P. Dutton, 1985); Mark Lindquist, *Sculpting Wood: Contemporary Tools & Techniques* (Worcester, Mass.: Davis Publications, 1986), 210–16.

2 The Russian system of abstract exercises was popularized by the display of the Imperial Russian Technical School at the 1876 Centennial Exposition in Philadelphia. The Sloyd system of physical training in wood work, pioneered by Dr. Otto Salomon of Sweden, debuted in America at the 1885 Cotton Centennial Exhibition in New Orleans.

3 For a discussion of the manual training movement and its effect upon woodworking, see Ray Stombaugh, *A Survey of the Movements Culminating in Industrial Arts Education in Secondary Schools* (New York: Teacher's College, Columbia University, 1936); Charles Richards, "The Relation of Manual Training to Industrial Education," *Manual Training Magazine* 9, no. 1 (October 1907): 2–9; and Paul Klein, "Fifty Years of Woodworking in the American Schools," *Industrial-Arts Magazine* 16, no. 1 (January 1927): 1–5, and no. 2 (February 1927): 48–51.

4 Calvin Woodward, *The Manual Training School* (Boston: D. C. Heath, 1887); Michael Golden, *A Laboratory Course in Wood-Turning* (New York: Harper & Brothers Publishers, 1897); Charles Bennett, "An Experiment in Wood-Turning," *Manual Training Magazine* 2, no. 3 (April 1901): 155–62; and Fred Crawshaw, *Problems in Wood Turning* (Peoria, Ill.: Manual Arts Press, 1909). It is noteworthy that Crawshaw believed spindle work to be more valuable for it taught skill in tool work, called for analysis of relationship between action and result (best seen in the various uses of the skew chisel), instilled the comprehension of mathematical principles, and introduced the student to pleasing design. In contrast, faceplate turning only contributed to a better understanding of form and the application of technical principles.

5 Charles Bennett, "The Manual Arts: To What Extent Shall They be Influenced by the Recent Movement Toward Industrial Education?" *Manual Training Magazine* 8, no. 4 (July 1907): 189–95; "Introductory," *Industrial-Arts Magazine* 1, no. 1 (January 1914): 1–2; Frederick Bonser, "The Significance of a Name," *Industrial-Arts Magazine* 1, no. 3 (March 1914): 112; F. D. Crawshaw, "The Present Day Opportunity in Manual and Industrial Arts," *Industrial-Arts Magazine* 1, no. 3 (March 1914): 79–83; A. B. Mays, "The Determining Factors in the Evolution of the Industrial Arts in America," *Industrial-Arts Magazine* 13, no. 3 (March 1924): 85–90.

6 J. E. Painter points out the need for proper lathe equipment in "A Problem in Wood-Turning Equipment," *Manual Training Magazine* 10, no. 5 (June 1909): 425–29. Descriptive advertisements for school lathes can be found in *Industrial-Arts Magazine* 4, no. 3 (September 1915): xiii; 8, no. 1 (January 1919): x; 9, no. 1 (January 1920): v; 9, no. 5 (May 1920): iii; 9, no. 11 (November 1920): v; 9, no. 12 (December 1920): iii; 11, no. 6 (June 1922): ix; 18, no. 7 (July 1929): 23A; 19, no. 1 (January 1930): inside of back cover; and 19, no. 4 (April 1930): inside of back cover. Metal screw-cutting lathes also appeared in advertisements. Such machines continued to be popular in the industrial arts magazines into the 1940s and 1950s because metal shops and automobile shops remained integral to the curriculum.

7 Archie Milton and Otto Wohlers, *A Course in Wood Turning for High Schools* (Milwaukee, Wis.: The Bruce Publishing Company, 1919); and William Klenke, *Art and Education in Wood Turning* (Peoria, Ill.: Manual Arts Press, 1921). For articles on the popular projects, see the following in *Industrial-Arts Magazine*: G. C. Polson, "Wood Turning Projects," 4, no. 2 (August 1915): 72–75; DeWitt Hunt, "Adding Interest to Practical Problems in Shopwork," 9, no. 9 (September 1920): 341–43; A. M. Hahn, "A Better Way to Turn Built-up Projects," 13, no. 4 (April 1924): 150–51; J. R. Vertrees, "An Artistic Candlestick," 14, no. 9 (September 1925): 356; E. Crawford Houston, "Table Lamp," 19, no. 4 (April 1930): 156; and Paul Wenger, "Vase Lamp," *Industrial Arts and Vocational Education* 19, no. 10 (October 1930): 403; and F. E. Hardin, "Lamps," ibid. 20, no. 9 (September 1931): 333–35. Examples of the interest in inlay are found in *Industrial-Arts Magazine*: Joseph Park, "Inlay Applied to Turned Wood for Decorative Effects," 8, no. 6 (June 1919): 21–13; Paul Wenger, "A Turned Jewel Case," 18, no. 1 (January 1929): 20; Paul Wenger, "Cake Salver," 18, no. 7 (July 1929): 277; and Paul Wenger, "A Mint Tray," 18, no. 11 (November 1929): 443. On polychrome laminations, see W. I. Tawes, "An Interesting Table Lamp," *Industrial Arts and Vocational Education* 21, no. 1 (January 1932): 23; H. H. Grauman, "Table Lamp," ibid. 21, no. 2 (February 1932): 67; and Wayne Judy, "Fruit Bowls That Are Different," ibid. 21, no. 7 (July 1932): 228–29.

8   Prestini took manual training classes while growing up in Westerly, Rhode Island (he took woodworking and turning with a Scottish teacher and machine shop with another teacher), and Osolnik was greatly influenced by John Rohner, his industrial arts teacher in Johnson City, Illinois. Both turners responded to the emphasis on tool control and the new emphasis on design. See John Cooper, "Woodturner," *The Westerly Sun* (May 22, 1988); Suzette Zurcher, "Prestini, A Contemporary Craftsman," *Craft Horizons* 8, no. 23 (November 1948): 25–26; and Jane Kessler and Dick Burrows, *Rude Osolnik: A Life Turning Wood* (Louisville, Ky.: Crescent Hill Books, 1997), 33–34.

9   On Mattil and Huskey, see James Jordan III et al., *Southern Arts and Crafts 1890–1940* (Charlotte, N.C.: Mint Museum of Art, 1996).

10   In June of 1930, *Industrial-Arts Magazine* changed its name to *Industrial Arts and Vocational Education* in response to the changing attitudes towards the older manual training. For specific comments on the change of this time, see Walter Collins, "Industrial-Arts vs. Smith-Hughes Education," *Industrial-Arts Magazine* 17, no. 2 (February 1928): 44–45; Omar Day, "Why Industrial Arts in America," *Industrial Arts and Vocational Education* 19, no. 11 (November 1930): 413–17; and Arthur Mays, "Industrial Arts in the New Curriculum," ibid. 26, no. 2 (February 1937): 35–36. In the 1930s, the Bruce Publishing Company produced a special issue of *Industrial Arts and Vocational Education* each March that was subtitled the "School Shop Annual." The table of contents clearly reveals the managerial role of the teachers in vocational education.

11   On the rise of do-it-yourself home shops and value placed on productive leisure, see Steven Gelber, "Do-It-Yourself: Constructing, Repairing, and Maintaining Domestic Masculinity," *American Quarterly* 49, no. 1 (March 1997): esp. 81–90. A typical period approach was *Woodworker's Turning and Joining Manual* (New York: Popular Science Publishing Company, 1934). Many of the earliest hobbyists had probably been introduced to turning in shop classes.

12   Gelber, 88. On Whipple, see Harriet Morrison, "Creative Design in Wood Inlay," *Craft Horizons* 10, no. 2 (Summer 1950): 21–23; and on Read, see *St. Paul Pioneer Press*, October 19, 1959: 8.

13   Sam Brown, ed., *Getting the Most Out of Your Lathe* (Milwaukee, Wis.: Delta Manufacturing Co., 1935), 5. Another lathe manual was *A Comprehensive Handbook on Uses and Applications of the Lathe* (Plainfield, N.J.: Walker-Turner Company, 1934). Also helpful are the advertisements in School Shop Annual of *Industrial Arts and Vocational Education* 26, no. 3 (March 1937), as well as Harold Barker, "A Pictorial History of the American Wood Lathe (1800–1960)" (1986 manuscript; copy on file at the Wood Turning Center, Philadelphia).

14   Ernest Brace, "Planning a Woodworking Shop," *Craft Horizons* 5, no. 12 (February 1946): 26.

15   William Klenke, *The Art of Wood Turning* (Peoria, Ill.: Manual Arts Press, 1937), 11.

16   W. Clyde Lammey, "How to Grind and Hone Your Wood Turning Tools," *Popular Science* 118, no. 5 (May 1931): 94–95; and "Tips on How to Develop Your Skill in Wood Turning," *Popular Science* 118, no. 6 (June 1931): 128–31. In *Popular Mechanics*, see "How to Use Wood-Turning Tools," 63, no. 1 (January 1935): 147–49; "Spindle Turning," 68, no. 6 (December 1937): 948–53; "Faceplate and Chuck Turning," 69, no. 1 (January 1938): 151–55; "Special Spindles," 69, no. 2 (February 1938): 307–10; and "Production Turning," 69, no. 3 (March 1938): 467–70. In 1942, Edwin M. Love wrote a three-part series for *Popular Science:* "A Royal Hobby," 140, no. 2 (February 1942): 152–56; "Making Furniture Legs on the Lathe," 140, no. 3 (March 1942): 176–79; and "Faceplate Turning for Creative Craftwork," 140, no. 4 (April 1942): 164–67.

17   *Popular Mechanics* 69, no. 1 (January 1938): 151.

18   *Woodworker's Turning and Joining Manual*, 116.

19   Perry Trout, "Homemade Lathe for Woodworking," *Popular Mechanics* 58, no. 1 (July 1932): 157–58; and in the same magazine, Albert Larson, "Homemade Wood Lathe Mounted on Floor Stand," 68, no. 4 (October 1937): 621–23; and Jack Mellinger, "Modernize that Old Lathe," 88, no. 1 (July 1947): 202–4. Leonard Wiley, "How to Select and Season Wood for Turning," *Popular Science* 141, no. 1 (July 1942): HW72–73.

20   On Dubuke and Rossiter, see Alan Eaton, *Handicrafts of New England* (New York: Harper & Brothers, 1949), 41–43. Both Dubuke and Rossiter were among the featured turners in the 1943 New England Craft exhibition and the 1944 Contemporary American Craft exhibition (where the only other turner was James Prestini); see *Contemporary New England Handicrafts* (Worcester: Worcester Art Museum, 1943); and *Contemporary American Crafts* (Baltimore: Baltimore Museum of Art, 1944).

21   Information on the myrtlewood turners was drawn from interviews with Hugh McKay of Gold Beach, Oregon, whose grandparents took over Orin Hess's myrtlewood shop in that town in 1967 (June 27, 1999); and Edsil Hodge of Coos Bay, who was the shop foreman for Beaumont, which became House of Myrtlewood and is now known as the Oregon Connection (July 7, 1999). Hodge estimates that he made a salad bowl every ten to fifteen minutes. For a modern account of the business, see Joan Chatfield-Taylor, "Silky Myrtlewood of Oregon's Coast," *New York*

Times, March 15, 1987, Travel Section. On the Grass company, see John Bowie, "The John Grass Wood Turning Company," in *A Sampling of Papers from the 1993 World Turning Conference* (Philadelphia: Wood Turning Center, 1997), 27–32.

22 The 1934 publication *Woodworker's Turning and Joining Manual* referred to "the last of the professional turners" (116). The sense of turning as a dying craft practiced only by older artisans has been articulated by the designer/furnituremakers Art Carpenter of California and Charles Webb of Massachusetts. See Arthur Espenet Carpenter, "Memoirs of an Opinionated Woodie," in *Furniture Studio One*, ed. John Kelsey and Rick Mastelli (Free Union, Va.: The Furniture Society, 1999), 45; and Edward S. Cooke, Jr., "Turning and Contemporary Studio Furniture: An Uneasy Relationship," *Papers from the 1997 World Turning Conference* (Philadelphia: Wood Turning Center, 2000), 14–21. See also Marshall Ensor, "Bringing the Wood Lathe to the Front," *Industrial Arts and Vocational Education* 43, no. 8 (October 1954): 282–85; and Arthur Gardner, "Beginner Wood-Turning Projects," *Industrial Arts and Vocational Education* 32, no. 10 (October 1943): 320.

23 Albert LeCoff and Tina Van Dyke, *Pennsylvania Lathe-Turned Objects: Trends, Transitions, Traditions 1700–1990* (Philadelphia: Woodmere Art Museum, 1990); and Jake Brubaker file, Wood Turning Center Archives.

24 On the value of amateurs, see Wayne Booth, *For the Love of It: Amateuring and Its Rivals* (Chicago: University of Chicago Press, 1999). On the individual makers, see "Artist With a Lathe," *Popular Mechanics* 108, no. 6 (December 1957): 109–11; Susan Stebbins, "Harry Nohr and His Heritage Bowls," *Wisconsin Trails Magazine* 7, no. 4 (Winter 1966): 20–22; "Harry Nohr, Maker of Bowls," in Bertha Whyte, *Craftsmen of Wisconsin* (Racine, Wis.: Western Publishing Co., 1971), 44–51; and Allen Androkites, *Measured Drawings of Selected Pieces of Woodwork by Paul W. Eshelman, Craftsman and Educator* (Millersville, Penn.: by the author, 1980).

25 Arthur Pulos, *The American Design Adventure, 1940–1975* (Cambridge, Mass.: MIT Press, 1988), 79–83; Esbjørn Hiort, *Finn Juhl: Furniture — Architecture — Applied Art* (Copenhagen: Danish Architectural Press, 1990); Arne Karlsen, *Contemporary Danish Design* (Copenhagen: The Danish Society of Arts and Crafts and Industrial Design, 1960); Edgar Kaufmann, Jr., "Kay Bojesen: Tableware to Toys," *Interiors* 112, no. 7 (February 1953): 64–67; and Mary Lyon, "A Master Plays Wide Field," *Craft Horizons* 13, no. 4 (July/August 1953): 26–31. A good introduction to the

period view of turning not as a craft but as design art is Gerald James, *Woodturning: Design and Practice* (London: John Murray, 1958). James warned against the monotonous tyranny of symmetry and emphasized the importance of abstraction, restrained decoration, and inherent color and figure of the wood. A later publication that also promotes good restrained design with consistent clear wood and little decoration is Eldon Rebhorn, *Woodturning* (Bloomington, Ind.: McKnight & McKnight, 1970).

26 Kendall Bassett and Arthur Thurman, *How to Make Objects of Wood* (New York: The Museum of Modern Art, 1951), 66.

27 Zurcher, "Prestini, A Contemporary Craftsman"; and Edgar Kaufmann, Jr., *Prestini's Art in Wood* (New York: Pantheon Books, 1950). As a designer for the team from the Armour Research Foundation, Prestini also received a first-place award from MOMA for his entry in the Low-cost Furniture Design Competition of 1948. A useful compilation of articles relating to Prestini is *James Prestini, 1938–1988* (Petaluma, Calif.: Creators Equity Foundation, 1990).

28 Elodie Courter, "Wood as Fine as Porcelain," *House Beautiful* 89, no. 12 (December 1947): 133. See also *Design for Christmas* (Boston: Institute of Contemporary Art, 1949); *Design for Christmas* (Boston: Institute of Contemporary Art, 1950); and Elodie Courter, "Wood Shapes by James Prestini," *Arts & Architecture* 65 (August 1948): 27–29. Another influential guide to American design of the 1950s also features Prestini: Don Wallance, *Shaping America's Products* (New York: Reinhold, 1956), 152–53.

29 Bob Stocksdale to James Prestini (March 9, 1948) as published in *James Prestini, 1938–1988;* Bob Stocksdale, "Exotic Woods: Observations of a Master Turner," *Fine Woodworking* 1, no. 4 (Fall 1976): 28–32; Kelsey, "The Turned Bowl," 56; Michael Stone, *Contemporary American Woodworkers* (Salt Lake City: Peregrine Smith, 1986), 34–47; Robert Bruce Duncan, "Bob Stocksdale: Still on a Roll at 75," *Woodwork* 1 (Spring 1989): 16–21; and Harriet Nathan, ed., *Bob Stocksdale: Pioneer Wood-Lathe Artist, and Master Creator of Bowls From Fine and Rare Woods* (Berkeley, Calif.: Regional Oral History Office at Bancroft Library, University of California, 1998).

30 Stone, *Contemporary American Woodworkers*, 95. See also Carpenter, "Memoirs of an Opinionated Woodie," in *Furniture Studio One*, 43–49.

31 May stopped turning for much of the 1960s and 1970s, so his reputation has not endured or been researched. Interviews with John May, Jr., and Nat May (June 1999), Sam May (July 1999), Keith May (August 1999), and Duncan Smith and Joel Pratt (August 1999) have helped shed light on Jake May's career. For published sources on May, see

Richard May, "Bowls From Green Woods," *Craft Horizons* 9, no. 2 (Summer 1949): 20–21; Eaton, *Handicrafts of New England*, 42; "A Hobby Becomes a Paying Business," *Living for Young Homemakers* 5 (April 1952): 90–91; and "How to Be Shibui With American Things," *House Beautiful* 102, no. 9 (September 1960): 148–49. The latter used three examples—May, Lenore Tawney, and Peter Voulkos—to illustrate "shibui," the highest form of inner beauty characterized by refinement and restraint. The prevalence of the hourglass shape as the shape of the 1950s is documented in Lesley Jackson, *The New Look: Design in the Fifties* (New York: Thames and Hudson, 1991).

32 Information on May's teaching at Haystack drawn from a letter from Alana VanDerwerker to the author, April 18, 1999. On the German exhibition, see *Industrie und Handwerk schaffen: neues Hausgerät in USA* (Stuttgart: n.p., 1951).

33 "Design for Christmas" catalogues from 1949 to 1954 include the following turners: Prestini; May; Carpenter; Beaumonts; Lemurian Crafts; Paul Killinger of Arlington, Massachusetts; Fred Brown of Concord, New Hampshire; John Lance of Shelburne, Vermont; and Stanley Johnson. Future research should document more fully the turned work of the 1950s. Reynolds G. Dennis was the head of Lemurian Crafts, according to the catalogue for the inaugural show of the Museum of Contemporary Crafts, *Craftsmanship in a Changing World* (New York: Museum of Contemporary Crafts, 1956). On Jensen and Killinger, see Merryll Saylan, "Paul Killinger," *American Woodturner* 2, no. 3 (September 1987): 18. In "Prestini, A Contemporary Craftsman," Zurcher describes the range of bowls, from "the thick, unpretentious chopping type of bowl of the housewares department" to "the expensive silver-based one of the luxury shop" (25).

34 Michael Stone, "Partners in Craftsmanship," *American Craft* 43, no. 3 (June/July 1983): 6–10; Betty Pepis, "Architect-and-Wife Team Creates Furniture to Fit," *New York Times*, May 5, 1956; and Anderson questionnaire, 1998, Wood Turning Center Archives.

35 Interview with the author, December 29, 1998; Glaser questionnaire, 1998, Wood Turning Center Archives; Mark Lindquist, *Sculpting Wood*, 153–56, 197, 231–34; and Jacobson, *The Art of Turned-Wood Bowls*, 12, 45–46.

36 Glenn Adamson, "Thomas Nicosia (1899–1998): Hobbyist as Revolutionary," *Turning Points* 11, no. 2 (Summer 1998): 4–6; and John Kelsey, "Ornamental Turning," *Fine Woodworking* 1, no. 4 (Fall 1976): 46–49.

37 Ensor, "Bringing the Wood Lathe to the Front," 282–85; Edwin Love, "Turning Disks and Bowls on the Lathe," *Popular Science* 156, no. 1 (January 1950): 236–39; Manuel Madera, "How to Use a Wood-turning Lathe," *Better Homes and Gardens* 28, no. 9 (May 1950): 234–39; William Klenke, *The Art of Woodturning* (Peoria, Ill.: Charles Bennett, 1954); Darrell Huff, "Bowls Are His Business," *Popular Science* 169, no. 2 (August 1956): 165–68; and "Bob Stocksdale Turns a Bowl," *Craft Horizons* 16, no. 6 (December 1956): 38–39. Love even recommended that leaving bark on the finished bowl was "an attractive effect."

38 *Designer-Craftsmen, U.S.A., 1953* (New York: American Craftsmen's Educational Council and the Brooklyn Museum of Art, 1953). On the growth of the American Craftsmen's Council, see *American Craft* 53, no. 4 (August/September 1993).

39 *Craftsmanship in a Changing World* (New York: Museum of Contemporary Crafts, 1956). The list of participants—Art Carpenter, Paul Eshelman, Paul Killinger, Anthony LeRocco, Jake May, Cecil Reed, John Stevens, Bob Stocksdale, Norwood Teague, Richard Wakamoto, and Paul Smith—indicates that the Craftsmen's Council had taken over for the earlier Christmas design shows in the promotion of turning.

40 Rose Slivka coined the term "freewheeling" in the early 1960s to describe how Peter Voulkos, Lenore Tawney, and other cutting-edge craftspeople were challenging past traditions, taking risks to push beyond function, exploring meaning, and breaking new ground; see Rose Slivka, "The New Ceramic Presence," *Craft Horizons* 21, no. 4 (July/August 1961): 30–37; and Slivka, "The New Tapestry," ibid. 23, no. 2 (March/April 1963): 10–19. On the impact within the furniture field, see Edward Cooke, Jr., *New American Furniture: The Second Generation of Studio Furnituremakers* (Boston: Museum of Fine Arts,1989), esp. 15–18. Germane to the discussion of craftsmanship as a cultural term rather than a technical term is David Pye, *The Nature and Art of Workmanship* (London: Cambridge University Press, 1968).

41 Jacobson, *The Art of Turned-Wood Bowls*, 74.

42 Kessler and Burrows, *Rude Osolnik: A Life Turning Wood;* see also *Rude Osolnik: A Retrospective* (Asheville, N.C.: Southern Highland Handicraft Guild, 1989); and *Rude Osolnik: Early Work* (Atlanta, Ga.: Connell Gallery, 1999).

43   Mark Lindquist, *Sculpting Wood*, 24–28, 230–87; Jacobson, *The Art of Turned-Wood Bowls*, 45–46; Mark Lindquist, "Spalted Wood," *Fine Woodworking* 2, no. 1 (Summer 1977): 50–53; and Lindquist, "Turning Spalted Wood," *Fine Woodworking* 11 (Summer 1978): 54–59.

44   On Mark Lindquist, see Mark Lindquist, *Sculpting Wood*, 24; Jacobson, *The Art of Turned-Wood Bowls*, 42–44; and Lindquist questionnaire, 1998, Wood Turning Center Archives. Influential books on Japanese and Asian ceramics were Okakura Kakuzo, *The Book of Tea* (Rutland, Vt.: Charles E. Tuttle, 1956) and Soetsu Yanagi, *The Unknown Craftsman: A Japanese Insight into Beauty* (New York: Kodansha International, 1972).

45   Information on Moulthrop can be found in Jacobson, *The Art of Turned-Wood Bowls*, 53–56; John Kelsey, "The Turned Bowl," 58; Albert LeCoff, *Lathe-Turned Objects* (Philadelphia: Wood Turning Center, 1988), 145; and Dale Nish, "Turning Giant Bowls," *Fine Woodworking* 41 (July/August 1983): 48–53.

46   Johnson has been prolific as a teacher and maker; see Johnson questionnaire, 1998, Wood Turning Center Archives. Cummings began at Long Beach in 1960 and graduated in 1968; see Cummings file, Wood Turning Center Archives.

47   Trout's work appeared in several publications in the 1960s and 1970s; see Dona Meilach, *Contemporary Art With Wood: Creative Techniques and Appreciation* (New York: Crown, 1968), 164, 171–74; *California Design Eight* (Pasadena: Pasadena Art Museum, 1962), 171; *California Design Nine* (Pasadena: Pasadena Art Museum, 1965), 112; *California Design Eleven* (Pasadena: Pasadena Art Museum, 1971), 47; and Dale Nish, *Creative Woodturning* (Provo: Brigham Young University Press, 1975), 222–23, 241–44. On biographical information, interview with the author, December 30, 1998; and Trout questionnaire, 1998, Wood Turning Center Archives.

48   Meilach, *Contemporary Art With Wood*, 48.

49   Hogbin questionnaire, 1998, Wood Turning Center Archives.

50   On Hogbin, see Donald McKinley, "The Wood-Turned Forms of Stephen Hogbin," *Craft Horizons* 34, no. 2 (April 1974): 28–32, 64; Dona Meilach, *Creating Modern Furniture: Trends, Techniques, Appreciation* (New York: Crown, 1975), 168–69; Stephen Hogbin, *Wood Turning: The Purpose of the Object* (Sydney: John Ferguson Pty. Ltd. and Crafts Council of Australia, 1980); and Hogbin questionnaire. Hogbin's *Wood Turning: The Purpose of the Object* may have been the most influential publication of this period and has continued to inspire turners to this day.

51   On Lacagnina, who earned his BFA in 1970 and his MFA in 1974 from RIT, see Meilach, *Creating Modern Furniture*, 158, 165, 212, 232–33; and *New Handmade Furniture* (New York: American Craft Museum, 1979). On the relationship between turning and studio furniture, see Cooke, "Turning and Contemporary Studio Furniture: An Uneasy Relationship," in *Papers from the 1997 World Turning Conference.*

52   On Ellsworth, Stirt, and Straka, see Dale Nish, *Master Woodturners* (Provo: Artisan Press, 1975), 2, 145, 165; see also Ellsworth questionnaire, 1998; Stirt questionnaire, 1998; and Straka questionnaire, 1998; all in Wood Turning Center Archives. The relationship between production work and creative work is also stressed in Terry Martin, "Gentle Strength: The Work of Betty Scarpino," *Woodwork* 61 (February 2000): 24–30.

53   The Museum of Contemporary Crafts mounted regional shows in the following years: Far West—1961; Central States—1962; and Eastern States—1963. Other popular events that showcased turners' work included the New York State Fair, the San Francisco Art Festival, and the Bucks County Guild of Craftsmen. A review of *Craft Horizons* in these years fleshes out much of this activity.

54   R. J. Christoforo, "Wood Lathes: How to Buy 'em, How to Use 'em," *Popular Science* 208, no. 2 (February 1976): 93.

55   See Bob Berger, "The Short Story on Wood-Turning Lathes," *Mechanix Illustrated* 69, no. 541 (June 1973): 106–107, 143–44.

Circular Logic: Wood Turning 1976 to the Present

Glenn Adamson

Fig. 1. Participants at the fourth Wood Turning Symposium, 1978, watch E. N. Pearson demonstrate spindle turning in the George School Shop.

Fig. 2. Instructors at the fourth Wood Turning Symposium, 1978. Left to right: Jake Brubaker, Albert LeCoff, Stephen Hogbin, Frank E. Cummings III, Dale Nish, C. R. (Skip) Johnson, E. N. Pearson, and Alan Stirt.

Fig. 3. David Ellsworth, Albert LeCoff, and *Fine Woodworking* editor John Kelsey discuss Bruce Mitchell's prizewinning entry in the "Turned Object Show" at the 1981 Wood Turning Symposium.

The invention of the wood turning field can be dated to 1976, the year of the first Wood Turning Symposium. The event brought wood turners together to share ideas and techniques at the woodshop of the George School near Philadelphia.[1] Throughout the twentieth century, there were hundreds of amateur practitioners in America, and a smaller number of craftspeople who made a living from their wares. But previous to the symposium, there was little communication between turners, who had not yet organized themselves around a national or even regional medium-oriented institutional base, as metalsmiths, potters, and glassmakers had done. In the absence of such an overarching structure, even the most accomplished of professional turners were not able to easily attract the attention of museums, writers, or serious collectors.

But all that changed with the 1976 symposium, which was attended by fifty turners from across the northeastern states. The event had an impact despite the fact that the organizers, turner Albert LeCoff, his twin brother Alan LeCoff, and the George School shop manager Palmer Sharpless, did not propose a radical new agenda for turners. In fact, their ideas about turning closely mirrored the existing state of affairs. They made no distinction between professionals and hobbyists in the organization of the symposium, for that distinction did not yet exist in a concrete way. Nor did they focus particularly on the production of vessel forms, which would become the virtually exclusive focus of professional turning in subsequent years.[2]

The symposium was novel, then, not for its vision of the future of the wood turning field, but for its suggestion that there could be a wood turning "field" at all. Previously, most woodworkers had thought of the lathe as one tool among many in the well-equipped woodworking shop, no more or less important than a bandsaw or a router. The event at the George School suggested for the first time that turning was sufficiently important to qualify as a separate division within the crafts, on a par with the larger and more established media categories of ceramics, fiber, metal, and glass. In fact, the 1976 symposium galvanized turners much as the founding of the Glass Art Society (GAS) and the Pilchuck Glass School in 1971 had done for glassmakers.[3] The initial symposium was followed by eight biannual gatherings, each of which was attended by fifty participants and five instructors (Figs. 1–2).[4] The series culminated with a tenth and final symposium in 1981, attended by 150 people and accompanied by the first survey exhibition of the field (Fig. 3).[5]

Innovations of the Late Seventies:
The Natural Edge, The Hollow Vessel, and the Textured Mass

One of the most important effects of the George School symposia was their establishment of two leaders for the new field, David Ellsworth and Mark Lindquist. Both were among the most technically proficient turners then active, and both had a level of personal ambition that matched their ability. At a time when most turners were still developing basic skills or making the difficult transition from slowly scraping the wood to cutting it quickly with a gouge and skew chisel, the walls of Ellsworth's vessels seemed impossibly thin. His vessels had a delicate elegance unrivaled by any of his contemporaries, and matched in the history of the field only by Californian Bob Stocksdale (see 14–17). Lindquist's work was equally impressive, but it could not have been more different. He shared his father Melvin's taste for sculptural, textured vessels (see 24, 32–35); and instead of cutting the wood on the lathe with precise

Mark Lindquist
52 *Silent Witness #1, Oppenheimer*
1983
Walnut, pecan, elm
H 85 × D 22
Collection of Margaret A. Pennington

Lindquist's reflection on Robert Oppenheimer, the inventor of the atomic bomb, takes the form of an abstracted mushroom cloud. The composition was inspired by the sculptures of Constantin Brancusi (Fig. 4), who also saw the base as integral to the overall composition. But in Lindquist's sculpture, the crowning component is a vessel form with a rough exterior and fluted interior. By placing this element atop a sculptural pedestal, Lindquist offers an unapologetic metaphor for the craftsman's elevation to the status of artist. When it was first shown at the 1985 Arrowmont conference exhibition "Woodturning: Vision and Concept," the piece provoked a controversy because of its enormous scale, abstract forms, unfinished texture, and high price tag—and also, perhaps, because of its metaphorical content.

gouge-work, Lindquist wielded a chainsaw with expressionist abandon.

Lindquist and Ellsworth both published their key technical innovations early on, inspiring turners across the country.[6] They also participated enthusiastically in the field as teachers and workshop demonstrators during the late 1970s and early 1980s. In addition to their contributions to the George School events, Ellsworth began a woodworking program in 1974 at Anderson Ranch in Colorado, while Lindquist initiated a wood turning shop in 1979 at the Haystack School of Crafts in Maine. Lindquist also went on to teach at the Worcester Craft Center in Massachusetts, and both taught at the Arrowmont School of Arts and Crafts in Tennessee. Yet the two turners led the field mainly by the example of their own work. Both were well acquainted with the field of ceramics, which by the late 1970s had already made a good deal of headway in the areas of gallery and museum recognition. Lindquist and Ellsworth wanted to do the same for wood turning. To this end, they pursued several of the avenues taken by studio potters, including the emulation of an Asian ceramic tradition that made no distinction between the semantic categories of "art" and "craft."[7] Like such American ceramists as Peter Voulkos and his followers, Lindquist and Ellsworth advanced the idea of craft as a species of formal sculpture. In effect, they insisted that if there was to be a new field of wood turning, it needed to break out of its parochial mentality. In this respect, they paralleled figures in other emerging craft media during the late 1970s who attempted to place their work in a fine arts context, such as glass blower Dale Chihuly and blacksmith Albert Paley.

Lindquist was particularly determined in his efforts to win the approval of the fine arts world. Each of his pieces was unique, most had titles, and all were subjected to rigorous standards of quality control before being sold or displayed. Beginning with the first American Craft Council Fair at Rhinebeck, New York, in 1972, Lindquist showed his work in craft fairs across the country. Over time, he developed elaborate art gallery-style booths that contrasted dramatically with the usual informality of the regional craft sales of the time. These strategies paid off in 1978, when he was the youngest of four turners included in "The Art of the Turned Bowl," the first exhibition devoted exclusively to wood turning, at the Renwick Gallery of the Smithsonian Institution.[8] In addition, Lindquist explicitly adopted the formal tropes of sculpture. As early as 1971, he dedicated one of his works to the woodcarvings of Paul Gauguin, and in the 1980s, he executed a series of monumental turnings based on the forms of the modernist sculptor Constantin Brancusi (Fig. 4; 52).[9]

Ellsworth, meanwhile, initiated a new area of formal experimentation for the field by developing a process called hollow turning. Previously, faceplate turning (in which one end of the workpiece is affixed to the lathe) had been limited to open platter and bowl forms. Ellsworth's innovation was to turn the exterior of a piece of wood to the shape of a vessel, bore a cylindrical hole into the center of the piece, and then use a bent-shaft tool to open out an interior volume that matched the exterior profile (53).[10] This technique paved the way for an escalation of skill and nuance, so that the vessel was elevated from a functional object to a fragile, impressive object for display.

One formal device that Lindquist and Ellsworth shared was the manipulation of the preexisting flaws and holes of their raw material. Interest in these features of wood was commonplace in the wider field of woodworking, stemming largely from the work of George Nakashima in the 1950s (Fig. 5).[11] But the turning process breathed new life into the

Fig. 4. Constantin Brancusi (1876–1957), *Yellow Bird*, 1919, yellow marble, limestone, and oak. Yale University Art Gallery, Collection of the Société Anonyme, bequest of Katherine S. Dreier, 1952.30.1.

Fig. 5. George Nakashima (1905–1990), New Hope, Pennsylvania, *Minguren I Table*, 1965, English oak burl, English oak, East Indian laurel. Collection of Dr. and Mrs. Seymour Lifshutz.

David Ellsworth
53 *Vessel*
1979
Brazilian rosewood
H 2 ¼ × Diam 8 ¾
Incised on underside: Ellsworth
1979 Brazilian rosewood
Collection of the Artist

David Ellsworth's enclosed and thin-walled vessels revitalized the lathe-turning field, directing it away from the classical open bowls popular at the time. His first explorations into hollow vessels were executed in milled exotic woods, often bought from lumber suppliers. These early attempts had wide mouths to permit the entry of the tool. Over time, Ellsworth challenged himself to make the entry hole smaller and smaller while varying the shape of the vessel itself. This was made possible by the use of a bent-shaft cutting tool of his own manufacture. The opening on this vessel has been pushed to the limit, allowing just enough room for the tool to hollow the interior. By reversing the form and reattaching it to the lathe with a "jam chuck" or "bucket chuck" after the interior had been hollowed, Ellsworth was able to shape the base. In this case, the bottom of the piece is a continuous curve, so that the vessel can be freely rotated with a spin of the hand.

compositional possibilities of wood's irregularity, as the natural valleys of the wood were translated into bold gaps in the finished vessel. Though Lindquist and Ellsworth shared this approach, they employed it to contrasting aesthetic ends. Lindquist abandoned the exotic hardwoods used by most early turners in favor of spalted domestic woods such as maple, elm, and cherry, and he often left much of the vessel surface in its natural state. The thick walls of his work revealed the depth of natural cracks and bark inclusions (54). Ellsworth, meanwhile, chose pieces of wood, often of an exotic species, with clearly demarcated areas of decay or color variation (55). More delicate and exacting than Lindquist, he played the graphic, random line of the natural edge against the smooth, regular surface of the vessel. The resulting composition of positive and negative space had the beneficial side effect of demonstrating Ellsworth's skill, as the thinness and evenness of the vessel walls could be fully revealed (56).

Another key contributor to the field in the late 1970s was Utah turner and educator Dale Nish. The George School symposia inspired Nish to hold similar conferences annually at Brigham Young University in Provo, beginning in 1978 and running nineteen consecutive years thereafter. Nish was also a prolific writer, and a series of books he published between 1975 and 1985 exposed the work of leading professionals and helped many isolated turners master basic skills.[12] His turnings proved to be an important milestone in the field as well. He developed the use of a particular "flawed" wood, worm-eaten ash, into a signature style of softly modeled pieces (57). Nish's work was hailed in the woodworking press as a quintessential statement of the predominance of sculptural form over utility: "if you can accept mere existence as function enough, you can turn (and find beauty in) any bit of wood, no matter how worm-eaten, bug-infested, rotten or scabrous."[13]

The idea of privileging form over function was taken to its logical conclusion by another key participant in both the George School symposia and the Provo conferences, Del Stubbs. Originally from the West Coast, Stubbs's roots were in myrtlewood production turning.[14] As a result of this extensive training, he amazed conference participants with his skill despite his youth. By the early 1980s, he achieved an unparalleled level of control on the lathe, turning his vessels down to the thickness of fifteen thousandths of an inch (58, 59). Though Stubbs represented the apex of sheer technical facility in the field, his primary concern was not the demonstration of skill. He cared more about the nuances of form, delighting in the way that the play of light or the touch of the hands would reveal the perfect gradation of a gentle curve. For Stubbs, the discipline of turning at the absolute limits of the wood's ability to hold together was a form of physical meditation, akin to the Eastern practices of yoga and *tai chi*.

By the middle of the 1980s, many turners were aware of the innovations of the leaders in the field, and several began to experiment with the inventions of what might be called "the George School generation." The natural edge and the hollow vessel held a particular fascination. Hap Sakwa turned delicate bowls with everted, natural-edge rims and deep, natural cracks (60). Rod Cronkite, who was introduced to turning by Dale Nish, hit upon a formal strategy that maximizes the potential of burl woods to produce an exciting natural edge. From the neck down, his works are straightforward Ellsworth-style hollow vessels, but they are topped by overhanging accretions of Lindquist-like sculptural burl (Fig. 6). Retiree Ed Bosley also came into contact with the idea of the hollow

Fig. 6. Rod Cronkite (b. 1954), *Winged Vessel*, 1989, maple burl. Whereabouts unknown; photograph, Wood Turning Center Archives.

Mark Lindquist
54 *Nehushtan*
1982
Cherry burl
H 14 × Diam 15
Inscribed on underside: Mark Lindquist/
cherry burl/Nehushtan
Collection of Robert A. Roth

Nehushtan is a virtual catalogue of
Lindquist's techniques of the late 1970s
and early 1980s. Though its burl rim
and enormous bark-lined crack demonstrate his continued reverence for the
natural state of the material, comparison with the early, comparatively
restrained *Meditating Vessel* (37) shows
that he has moved decisively in the
direction of manipulating the wood to
his own expressive ends. Lindquist used
a chainsaw to create several patterns on
the vessel surface, including a series of
horizontal grooves, a band of curved
slashes, a contrasting band of more
shallow curved incisions, and vertical
fluting of the interior. The regularity
of these patterns is achieved with

Lindquist's own indexing system,
similar to that of an ornamental lathe,
by which the piece can be rotated at
regular intervals of a few degrees. Each
time the piece is shifted, Lindquist cuts
the surface with the chainsaw.

David Ellsworth
55 *Vessel*
1979
Desert ironwood
H 6 ¾ × W 6
Incised on underside: Ellsworth/
1979/desert ironwood
Wood Turning Center, Anonymous Loan,
1995.01.01.051L

This is a classic example of Ellsworth's
utilization of the natural openings in
wood caused by rot or insect damage.
Turning away from milled lumber
bought from suppliers, he resorted to
unprepared material in log form. This
gave him more to work with in the
overall design of the vessel. Ellsworth's
use of wood in its natural state was also
pragmatically motivated, because lumber companies considered it to be a
lower grade and therefore charged less
for it. Eventually, however, such material has become so sought after by turners that it is no cheaper than milled
stock. This turning is oriented with
the rotted-out core of the log running
horizontally. The hollowing tool has
entered through a natural opening, the
contours of which are preserved in the
vessel mouth. Thus, natural voids are
exposed through two sides and the top,
in a remarkable display of sensitivity to
process and material.

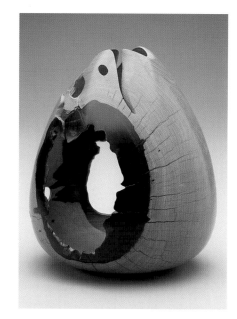

55

David Ellsworth
56 *Bowl*
1985
Broadleaf maple burl
H 11 × W 8 x D 15
High Museum of Art, Atlanta, Georgia,
Purchased with funds from the Special
Friends of the Decorative Arts, 1985.274

In this vessel, Ellsworth has pushed
himself to the limits of what the English
craft practitioner and scholar David Pye
called "the workmanship of risk." A
natural-edged rift extends three-fourths
of the way around the form, exposing
the fact that the walls of the vessel
are turned to a thickness of ¹⁄₁₆ inch.
Despite its fragility, the piece was
reversed and remounted on the lathe
so that its bottom could be turned
smooth. Ellsworth is working at a very
large scale here, at the outer extremes
of the technical capabilities of his tools
and lathe. A year after making this
piece, he would decide that, like others
in the field (Ed Moulthrop, Stephen
Hogbin, and Mark Lindquist), he
needed a larger lathe to accomplish
his goals. He therefore acquired a
custom-designed Thompson lathe that
provided greater stability and dimen-
sional capability.

56

Dale L. Nish
57 *Bowl*
1981
Wormy ash
H 3 1/16 × Diam 11 1/8
Burned on underside:
DALE L. NISH 1981/ASH
Collection of David Ellsworth

After seeing David Ellsworth and Mark Lindquist using decayed and otherwise damaged material, Dale Nish (jokingly, at first) decided to make a piece from thoroughly rotten wood. He settled on ash that had been eaten by boring insects. By turning and then sandblasting it, he produced a nonfunctional but surprisingly beautiful surface in which holes course along the grain lines in the wood. Gratified with these results, he went on to work consistently with borer-riddled ash, calling the series *nagare* (Japanese for "drifting"). Perhaps more than any other turner, he has become widely identified with his particular material. For Nish, the move away from traditional, functional objects translated directly into acceptance into craft galleries and museums. This piece is particularly effective because the wood is only half worm-eaten, so that the impact of the decay on the material is easily understood. It was displayed in the 1981 "Turned Object Show."

Del Stubbs
58 *Rippled Edge Form*
1984
Red eucalyptus
H 3 × Diam 6
Yale University Art Gallery,
Gift of Archer M. Huntington, BA 1897,
in memory of Arabella D. Huntington,
by exchange, 1999.63.1

59 *Curled Form*
1983
Madrone
H 2 3/8 × Diam 5
Yale University Art Gallery,
Gift of Archer M. Huntington, BA 1897,
in memory of Arabella D. Huntington,
by exchange, 1999.63.2

Del Stubbs was one of the most skilled turners and educators to emerge in the wood turning field in the late 1970s. Driven to push himself to the absolute limits of the craft, he turned a series of open bowl forms with incredibly thin walls, in some cases measuring only a few thousandths of an inch thick. He accomplished this feat by shining light through the wood to show the varying thickness of the wall as it was turned to shape. He also wet the piece as it was being turned by holding a wet sponge or towel against the opposite side of the wall. This made the paper-thin wall flexible enough to withstand the pressure of the cutting tool without breaking apart. The wet wood's resiliency was such that he could actually fold the bowl in his hand and then dry it under a lamp bulb, as is seen in *Curled Form.* Sometimes Stubbs displayed his finished pieces under a strong light to emphasize their translucency, a strategy later employed by Ron Kent (see 108); these pieces, however, have lost most of their translucency as they have aged.

Hap Sakwa
60 *Bowl*
1979
Wild lilac burl
H 4 ⅝ × Diam 10 ⅛
Inscribed on underside:
Hap Sakwa/9/79 / Wild Lilac
The Society for Contemporary Crafts,
Pittsburgh, Pennsylvania

At the beginning of his career, Hap
Sakwa used the turned vessel to capture
the simple beauty of natural floral
forms. This open form is typical for
Sakwa, and in fact all of his lilac bowls
have this everted rim shape. It conveys
a sense of fragility by virtue of its
thin walls, delicate natural edge, and
crevices running towards the center of
the bowl. The piece's refinement is
augmented by a small turned base that
gently lifts the bowl into the air. Sakwa
has also chosen a wood with a pronounced color contrast between the
sapwood and the heartwood that highlights the natural edge of the rim.

Edward J. Bosley
61 *#2 Canyon Sunset*
1987
Redwood lace burl
H 9 ⅞ × W 14 ⅛ × D 12 ¾
Inscribed on underside:
E. J. Bosley/1987/Redwood Lace/Burl
Collection of Ron and Anita Wornick

Edward Bosley was involved with turning as an avocation, bringing to the
craft his experience as an engineer for
the space division of General Electric.
Often his work reflects his memories of
travels through the Southwest, in this
case, a sunset in the Grand Canyon. As
he was turning the form, he realized
that the natural edge ran through it,
creating a crevasse. Taking advantage of
the figure of the wood, he left part of
the exterior intact while hollowing the
interior. As Bosley describes it, "I had
arrived at a bifurcating form of turning
that is a combination of an open bowl
form and a vessel hollowed out through
a small opening. This allowed me to
retain more of the natural surface of
the burl and exposed more of the interior features of the burl, grain patterns
and voids in a new and interesting way."

vessel through symposia. In 1987, he achieved a breakthrough with what he called "bifurcated turnings," in which the natural edge was extended from the lip into an additional decorative bowl shape, intersecting a typical hollow vessel form (61).

Todd Hoyer's work is another captivating extrapolation of Ellsworth's combination of the hollow vessel and the natural edge. Unlike other turners working in this vein, Hoyer infused his pieces with emotional content through bold texturing and scorching. A cavernous vessel he made in 1986 (62) could be a tortured, mannerist response to Ellsworth's earlier vase (see 55), while his *Peeling Orb* reduces the vessel/edge relation to a sphere and a serenely waved dorsal fin (63). Hoyer's most arresting pieces to date are arguably his *X Series* vessels of 1991 (64). With their stark graphic forms and burned ribs, they demonstrate that the hollow vessel continues to be a fertile area for expressive exploration.

As turners across the country enthusiastically adopted the hollow vessel, many others looked instead to Lindquist's fundamental idea, the textured mass. In direct opposition to the thin-walled shells produced by Ellsworth, Lindquist often preserved the shape of the raw piece of wood (65). An early exponent of this idea was Robyn Horn, whose *Geodes* similarly feature minimal transformation of the material. Often, she turns only part of the surface of her pieces, creating a contrast between smooth, worked surface and organic, unturned bark (66). Gradually, she added other textures by burning, scratching, or carving the wood. For Horn, the steady action of these processes is itself a metaphor for the passage of time. Her later *Millstone* pieces convey the feeling of ancient, well-worn objects of use (67).

Horn's fellow southern turner Stoney Lamar shares this acute sensitivity to turning's temporality. From 1984 to 1985, he worked as an assistant in the Lindquists' studio in New Hampshire. Lamar was particularly taken by his teachers' idea of preserving the basic form of the raw material. But unlike the Lindquists, he transformed his pieces through multiple-axis turning, in which the piece is mounted and turned several times at different angles (68). As Lamar has written, the marks of the cutting tool on the surface "capture in the static form the sense of movement that only I got to see while it was spinning on the lathe."[15] Lamar gradually became less interested in creating new variants on the vessel form and more intrigued by the lathe's potential to make figural sculpture (69).

A final turner who might be mentioned in connection with Ellsworth and Lindquist is Michael Peterson, whose work plays the hollow vessel against the textured mass. Sometimes, Peterson makes light, thin-walled pieces that follow in the Ellsworth tradition of echoing interior and exterior shapes (70). But he also creates heavy, biomorphic, handheld sculptures with a tremendous range of textures (71). By bleaching, carving, and sandblasting a variety of materials, from wood burls to grassroot tree, he evokes the simple grandeur of desert and mountain landscapes.

At the same time that Lindquist and Ellsworth were beginning to affect the field, other turners were contributing in a more independent fashion. Alan Stirt and Bruce Mitchell, two self-reliant craftsmen living on opposite coasts, each developed a distinctive, homegrown style of carving. Stirt began as a self-taught production turner (see 50), and his mature works are like giant extrapolations of his earlier small, fluted bowls. Despite their similarity to his relatively humble production wares of the 1970s, however, the quality, the scale, and the regularity of the carving on

Todd Hoyer
62 *Palo Verde Bowl, "Gourd Series"*
1986
Mexican blue oak
H 7 ¼ × W 9 ½ × D 8 ¼
Incised on underside:
MEXICAN/BLUE OAK/TH [conjoined]
Collection of Wendy Evans Joseph

Todd Hoyer uses wood from the desert surrounding his home in Bisbee, Arizona. He turns the log while it is still green (unseasoned), causing the wood to distort and develop surface checking. Often, he wraps his pieces in cloth or even buries them in order to slow the drying process and create an even rate of shrinkage. In this case, however, Hoyer took advantage of the variable drying speeds of the end and side grain to create a stretched "football" shape that accentuates the color variation of the rotten oak. In what seems like a mannerist reaction to David Ellsworth's use of natural voids in the wood, Hoyer centered the piece on an enormous, bark-lined cavity.

Todd Hoyer
63 *Peeling Orb*
1987
Mesquite
H 14 ½ × W 13 ¼ × D 8
Inscribed on underside: TH-Mesquite
Collection of Ron and Anita Wornick

This piece developed from Hoyer's *Wing* series, a technically challenging body of work in which he daringly turned large, off-center chunks of wood taken from the trunk of the tree. For *Peeling Orb*, Hoyer replaced the extended wing forms of the other pieces in the series with a vertical fin. In an artificial emulation of the distortion caused by wood movement, the fin curves back and forth as it rises from the spherical mass. It ends in a natural bark edge that indicates the original circumference of the tree trunk from which the piece was turned. With its deep, roughly turned grooves, bark inclusions, and lack of finish, *Peeling Orb* captures the raw immediacy of the turning process.

Todd Hoyer
64 X Series
1991
Cottonwood
H 13 ¾ × Diam 9 ⅝; H 12 × Diam 12;
H 13 ¼ x Diam 8 ½
Incised on underside of each:
COTTONWOOD/TH [conjoined]
Wood Turning Center, Gift of Fleur Bresler,
Robyn and John Horn, Albert and Tina
LeCoff, Arthur and Jane Mason, and Connie
Mississippi, 1998.04.23.001.a.b.c.G

In the early 1990s, Hoyer moved away from his investment in the evocative potential of wood and began to make more abstract, less material-oriented work. This tripartite sculptural grouping is typical of his new direction. Each of the processes used in making the group is emotionally charged, from the turning of deep grooves into the vessel walls, to the scorching of the interior and the ribs between the grooves, to the cutting of the pieces with a chainsaw. The resemblance of the iconography to the Christian cross further

evokes ritual and death. The set might also be interpreted as a dramatic rejection of the beauty of the hollow vessel, as if the aesthetic appeal of the softly ribbed forms had been "cancelled" by the violent action of the chainsaw.

Mark Lindquist
65 *Captive #6B*
1987
Spalted maple burl
H 23 × W 13 ½ × D 17
Incised on underside: (BOTTOM)/Mark
Lindquist/1987/Captive #6B/Maple Burl
Collection of Donald and Kate King

Mark Lindquist's *Captives* translate a classical sculptural conceit into the language of wood turning. Like Michelangelo's late *Dying Slaves*, the series features turned forms that only partly emerge from raw material. The interior surface pattern of the trapped bowl is an exploration of the visual potential of chainsaw "plunge cuts." Lindquist had originally used this technique to quickly remove a core of wood from the interior of his vessels, so that the core could later be used to make another, smaller piece. Noticing the striking pattern of radiating cut marks that resulted from this process, he refined the plunge cut and used it as a texturing device. The back side of *Captive #6B* is turned with a pattern of concentric circles that are centered on the point where the faceplate was attached to the lathe.

Robyn Horn
66 *Natural-edge Geode*
1988
Redwood burl
H 12 × W 16¼ × D 10
Yale University Art Gallery,
a partial gift of Robyn and John Horn
and a partial purchase funded by Ruth
and David Waterbury, BA 1958,
2000.55.1

Robyn Horn began her career making hollow vessels in the style of David Ellsworth, but rapidly moved on to a more massive style in which the wood is barely transformed from its natural state. In her *Geode* series, developed under the influence of ceramist Graham Marks and sculptor Isamu Noguchi, the shape of the piece is determined by the natural contours of the burl. The work's rough exterior contrasts with the smooth polish and circular grooves on the interior and face. Like an actual geode, the form feels as though it has been cracked open to reveal its interior beauty.

Robyn Horn
67 *Slashed Millstone*
1996
Ebonized redwood burl
H 21 ¼ × D 7
Collection of John and Robyn Horn

Horn's fascination with antique mill-
stones led her to develop a series based
on their strong, utilitarian forms. In
this example, she has ebonized and
textured a mass of redwood burl to
emulate the surface of worn, ancient
stone. A square hole in the center
echoes the axle shaft that was used to
drive the millstone on its axis, perhaps
referring poetically to the origins of
the work on Horn's own lathe. The slash
that crosses the central negative space
was made by a chainsaw and was her
first use of the tool to create a pictorial
effect. Together, the circular form,
square piercing, and horizontal slash
are a concise essay in geometric composition. A small base lifts the object
slightly from the ground and lends it
an air of refinement.

Stoney Lamar
68 *Firebird*
1989
Cherry burl
H 10 ½ × Diam 13
Inscribed in ink on underside of rim:
Stoney Lamar/Cherry Burl/7/89
Collection of John and Robyn Horn

Firebird, from Stoney Lamar's *Dance and Movement* series of the late 1980s, is indebted to the massive burl vessels of Melvin and Mark Lindquist. The piece is composed of an interior vase form and a textured collar that cascades from the rim to become a set of legs. The result is a rhythmic, off-kilter composition in which a traditional vessel is swallowed up inside an abstract sculptural frame. Lamar fashioned the concentric grooves by remounting the piece on the lathe several times and cutting shallow marks into the surface. These geometric accents contrast with the organic roughness of the bark-riddled cherry burl.

Stoney Lamar
69 *Hat Dance*
1993
Granadillo burl
H 24 ½ × W 14 × D 5
Incised on edge of base: Stoney Lamar
Collection of John and Robyn Horn

Hat Dance combines elements of Stoney Lamar's figural *Torso* series with the more rigid compositions of his *Geometric* series. The dynamic, architectonic shape refers to the human body in its overall twisting form and vestigial feet. The piece is willfully imperfect, with wormholes, cracks, and rough spalted areas playing against the purity of the form. Lamar's interest in the wood is also manifest in his delicate management of the contrast between the decayed light sapwood and the more polished dark heartwood. Like his earlier *Firebird*, the piece was challenging and dangerous to execute. Lamar remounted it on the lathe multiple times, and much of the turning was done with the bulk of the piece's weight off-center.

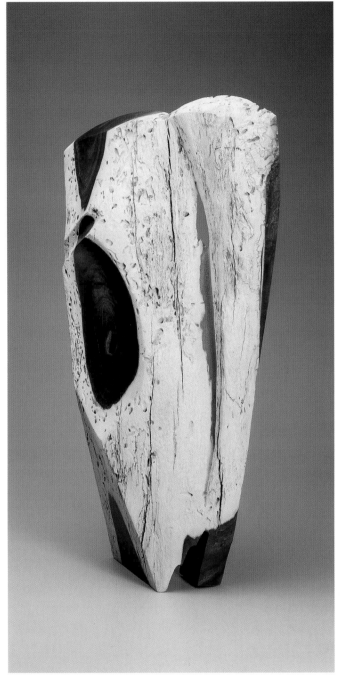

69

69

Michael James Peterson
70 *Two Canyon Mesa*
1989
Bleached and sandblasted box elder burl
H 5 × Diam 14 ¼
Inscribed on underside: MJ PETERSON
'TWO CANYON MESA' BOX ELDER BURL 1989
Collection of John and Robyn Horn

In Michael Peterson's interpretation
of the hollow vessel, both the shoulder
and the rim are fashioned from the
knobby surface of a chunk of box elder
burl. The result is a shape with a sloping top reminiscent of a mountainous
desert landscape, quite unlike the
rounded spheres of David Ellsworth.
Also unlike Ellsworth, Peterson has
used a fairly wide mouth opening. In
conjunction with the spacious natural
gaps in the vessel walls, the mouth gives
the vessel a feeling of permeability
and yields a view of the matte, unfinished surface of the interior. The
textures and colors of the box elder are
enhanced by the processes of bleaching
and sandblasting; but, unlike some
other turners who use such dramatic
surface treatments, Peterson is interested
in complementing the texture of the
natural wood rather than competing
with it.

Michael James Peterson
71 *Seashell*
1991
Grassroot
H 3 ¼ × Diam 8 ⅝
Incised on underside: MJP/91
Collection of John and Robyn Horn

In the 1990s, Peterson moved into a new
body of work featuring heavy carving
that interacts with the figure and texture
of a range of unusual materials. The
massive solidity of these pieces disguises
their origins in Peterson's hollow vessels
of the late 1980s, which have profiles
with similar sharply defined shoulders.
In this example, a vessel made from
grassroot is embellished with a series of
diagonal curved ribs that play against
a series of internal rays radiating from
the center of the wood. The ribs suggest
a handprint and thus beckon the touch
of the viewer. The sensuality of the
piece culminates in another appealing
tactile element, a biomorphic mouth
with softly rounded lips. The sculptural
direction announced in this body of
work eventually led Peterson to move off
the lathe; he now makes most of his
pieces exclusively through hand carving.

his monumental bowls of the mid-1980s make them powerful sculptural statements (72). The same can be said of Bruce Mitchell's expressive, chunky forms, which are comparable to Lindquist's both in their carving and their dependence on found, unprocessed woods (73). He studied the use of the chainsaw with the independent Bay Area furnituremaker J. B. Blunk; not only Mitchell's style, but also his conscious distance from the rest of the field descended from a mentality of "back to the land" self-sufficiency, inherited from the previous generation of California craftspeople.[16] Both Mitchell and Stirt have continued to work at a distance from urban culture.

The Challenge of Self-Definition: Polychrome and Paint

With the organizational thrust provided by the Pennsylvania and Utah conferences, and the formal innovations of Lindquist, Ellsworth, and their contemporaries, the early 1980s saw an explosion in the wood turning population. What had been primarily a broad-based hobbyist pursuit finally became a full-fledged subset of the professional studio craft movement. In order to stand out in this new competitive climate, turners had to be more than excellent craftspeople; they had to have a well-defined, easily identifiable style. As in the glass and ceramic fields, the vessel was the centerpiece of such invention. Often, turners created standard open or hollow vessels and enlivened them with carved, painted, or textured decoration. Others challenged the vessel format itself, piercing walls, putting pieces in stands, or assembling turned elements into sculptural forms.

In pursuing these strategies of surface embellishment, turners were taking part in a broader wave of postmodernism that swept the crafts field in the early 1980s. This was a stylistic, often superficial postmodernism with roots in the post-Pop design climate typified by design firms such as Memphis and Swid Powell. Color was the key to this period style (Fig. 7). Startlingly bright paint jobs were embraced not only by ceramists such as Peter Shire, but also by furnituremakers such as Mitch Ryerson (Fig. 8), Tom Loeser, Ed Zucca, and Alphonse Mattia. In large part, the use of paint in the context of woodworking was an attempt to direct attention away from the fussy details of technique, which had been such an obsession in the late 1970s, and place the emphasis on design concept instead.[17]

Ironically, this radical design aesthetic entered turning through a time-honored process, that of polychromatic lamination. By constructing a glued-up block out of layers of woods of contrasting colors, and then turning that block on the lathe, vessels of many small pieces could be made relatively quickly. This technique had a long history before its widespread embrace in the 1980s. Americans such as Thomas Nicosia and Howard Whipple had practiced lamination processes of varying degrees of complexity on a hobbyist basis in the 1940s (see 25 and 2), and amateur turners had been making polychrome vessels in Europe for centuries.[18] Treatises on polychromatic turning were commonly published in England throughout the twentieth century.

Yet the resurgence of laminated work in the early 1980s owes more to a period interest in Native American basketry than it does to an awareness of this turning tradition. The first issue of *Fine Woodworking* in 1975 suggested that turners look to lamination as a way of "reinterpreting in wood the designs of the American Indian," and many were to follow this lead.[19] Of the turners who tried their hand at basketry designs, the

Fig. 7. Carmen Spera, *Sky*, 1984, painted wood, as shown in Loris Calzolari, *Phoenix: An International Exhibition of New Design Works* (Toronto, 1984). Spera's painted bowl epitomizes the ornamentalism of early 1980s design.

Fig. 8. Mitch Ryerson (b. 1955), *Wheel Chair*, 1983, painted wood. Private collection; photograph courtesy of Mitch Ryerson.

Alan Stirt
72 *Fluted Bowl*
1985
Butternut
H 7 × Diam 19 ½
Inscribed on underside:
Al Stirt '85 / Butternut
Wood Turning Center, Anonymous Loan,
1995.01.01.228L

Alan Stirt has explored various texturing techniques on his bowls since he began working on a production basis in the 1970s (see 50). Gradually, as the field shifted towards one-of-a-kind pieces, he began to vary his work more and emphasize the unique character of each of his pieces of wood. In 1985, Stirt received an extraordinary large and figured butternut log from fellow wood-worker David Holzapfel (husband of turner Michelle Holzapfel—see 106, 107), who challenged him to do something "special" with it. The result was *Fluted Bowl*, his largest piece to date. Though Stirt normally used a hand chisel to flute his bowls, he decided to try using an air-powered chisel for this project. The new tool allowed him to execute the flutes more freely. He also charted new terrain by leaving a wide border of unfluted wood around the rim of the bowl. The piece was unveiled at the 1985 Arrowmont conference in the exhibition "Woodturning: Vision and Concept."

Bruce Mitchell
73 *Tide Pool*
1985
Curly redwood burl
H 9 ¾ × W 23 ¼ × Diam 24
Inscribed on underside: Tide Pool/Bruce Mitchell-1985-curly redwood burl
Collection of Martha and Pat Connell

Bruce Mitchell began woodworking as a maker of expressive, massive furniture carved with a chainsaw out of monolith-ic chunks of wood. He preserves this direct sculptural approach in his turned vessels, which combine lathe work with extensive hand carving. This example was fashioned from a piece of redwood recovered from a flood site. The finished piece bears much of the character of the driftwood in its natural state, from its natural-edge gaps to the white circular barnacle markings across the flat rim. Chiseled grooves rake across a portion of the exterior walls. These raw, muscular edges contrast markedly with the curly figure of the smoothly turned interior.

most faithful to the Native American model was Lincoln Seitzman. Early in his career, Seitzman realized the potential of the pre-planning inherent to the lamination process. Unlike most types of turning, in which the design can be invented and modified while the workpiece is on the lathe, complex polychromatic work must be mapped out in advance. The success of Seitzman's work is premised on such preparations, which he sums up as "an accurate drawing and a practical sequence of operations to build it"; he estimates that he spends 90 percent of his time on planning and preparation and 10 percent actually turning.[20] This approach has permitted him to execute designs based on the complicated weaves of a variety of baskets (74). In contrast to Seitzman's carefully assembled pieces, Max Krimmel demonstrated that glued-up blocks could also be a way of introducing random composition to the turned vessel. By fusing wood scraps into large platters, Krimmel approximated the startling effects achieved by some turners who used paint in the early 1980s (75). In retrospect, his platters look like deconstructed versions of Seitzman's work. Krimmel soon abandoned the technique for a more classical body of work in turned alabaster.

Between Seitzman's order and Krimmel's chaos lie the vessels of Bud Latven and Addie Draper.[21] Working in the same shop for several years in the mid-1980s, the two turners charted a course of consistent and ingenious improvisations on the basic polychromatic basket form. From the beginning of these experiments, their compositions were considerably more free and improvisatory than Seitzman's (76). The two soon began to experiment with more drastic effects, such as inlays that cut across the pattern of the vessel's construction, and metal stilts that pierce the vessel walls (77). Latven has continued these investigations in the 1990s, removing whole blocks from his finished vessels in order to make abstract sculptures (78).

Like Seitzman, Michael Shuler views polychromatic turning as a logistical problem, akin to engineering. He creates relatively small works of astounding internal detail through a complex process of segmented turning.[22] Often, Shuler uses the contrast between two woods to achieve decorative effects of remarkable beauty (79). His aesthetic is a happy marriage of older, organic "form and figure" sensibilities with the rigor of the lamination process. The same is true of Virginia Dotson, perhaps the most well known and successful of the polychromatic turners of the 1980s. Dotson learned her lamination technique from Rude Osolnik; and her smooth, precise forms are indebted both to Bob Stocksdale and to the early organic furniture of Wendell Castle. Her artistic persona is also patterned on a well-established precedent, that of modernist American painter Georgia O'Keeffe. Like O'Keeffe, Dotson lives in the Southwest and derives her primary inspiration from the desert landscape (80).

In retrospect, it is clear that polychromatic turning was a way of opening the wood turning field to new possibilities in the area of color, pattern, and graphic design. Even "form and figure" oriented turners such as Fletcher Cox (81) and Philip Moulthrop (82) were willing to turn to lamination, because it did not run counter to the attachment to wood and skill that had traditionally anchored the craft. Polychromatic turning requires the turner to be sensitive and skilled in handling the material. A poorly made assembly that does not take dryness, grain orientation, and relative shrinkage into account can easily split apart due to wood movement. Yet the emphasis that polychrome naturally placed on the vessel surface was pregnant with revolutionary potential, as can be seen

Lincoln Seitzman
74 *Petrified Sewing Basket*
1993
Cherry, wenge, imbuia
H 6 ¾ × Diam 13
Burned on inside of foot:
LINCOLN SEITZMAN #198
Collection of Robert M. Bohlen

Throughout his career as a wood turner,
Lincoln Seitzman has concentrated
on "Basket Illusions," which combine
the precision of well-designed lamination structures and the palette and
patterns of Native American basketry.
As his understanding of the technical
possibilities of polychromatic turning
progressed, he developed ever more
complex basket forms and weaves, as
well as illusory shadows. *Petrified Sewing
Basket*, for instance, incorporates 2,800
individual pieces of wood, and its
execution required ten separate mount-
ings on the lathe. Its form marked a
new direction in Seitzman's work, as it
was based on an Indonesian basket.
It also introduced a new element in his
technique, as it combines the segmented
lamination typical of his earlier work
with three steam-bent wooden hoops
(on the lid, base, and the midpoint of
the vessel).

Max Krimmel
75 *Makowenaplege*
1987
Various woods
H 2 × Diam 37
Inscribed in wax pencil on the underside:
#47 Makowenaplege/Max Krimmel [script]
Collection of Garry K. and Sylvia Bennett

Max Krimmel's unique style of poly-chromatic turning was accomplished by turning shallow, wall-hung platters from wide, flat blocks of glued-together scrap woods. Each wood fragment is separated from its neighbors by thin layers of dark veneer that vary in thickness. The rim is turned from segments of a contrasting wood that are glued onto the top of the block.

Using this technique, Krimmel was able to quickly achieve bold compositions of well-organized chaos. This example, the largest he ever made, was executed on a 1950s Craftsman lathe that he modified to turn at large scale.

Addie Draper
76 Hollow Vessel
1986
Wenge, holly, padauk, ebony
H 4 × Diam 6 ¼
Incised on underside: Addie/Draper/'86
Collection of John and Robyn Horn

Working collaboratively in the same studio in the mid-1980s, Addie Draper
and Bud Latven developed a technique
of precise polychromatic lamination.
The passion for technical perfection
shared by both artists is evident in the
finish of the exterior and interior of
their forms. Draper employs the vessel
as a three-dimensional canvas, using
exotic woods as a palette of contrasting
colors and textures. An irregular composition of lines plays freely across the
surface of orderly lamination lines. The
overall form, with its wide shoulders
and narrow mouth, is a witty reimagina-
tion of the Ellsworth-style hollow vessel.
Draper has made the piece in two sections and joined them, however, rather
than turning the interior through the
tiny opening at the top of the vessel.

Bud Latven
77 *Tightwire #15*
1989
Macassar ebony, silver, tulipwood
H 13 ½ × Diam 6 ⅜
Incised on underside of rim: Latven/89
Collection of Fleur Bresler

After several years of close collaboration with Addie Draper, Bud Latven broke through to his own unique style in the late 1980s. Typical of this developmental period in his career is his *Tightwire* series, which he pursued from 1987 to 1992. This example, from 1989, displays Latven's superb craftsmanship and sense of design. The lamination and turning of the delicate flaring walls are finely executed, and the vessel is balanced on two silver rods whose steel cores pierce the rim. On a metaphorical level, the precariousness of the composition calls into question the vessel's ability to stand on its own, perhaps announcing a move in Latven's own work towards a looser, more sculptural sensibility (78).

Bud Latven
78 Sudden Impact
1994
African bubinga, African ebony, avonite
H 11 × Diam 15 ¼
Collection of Ann Draper

Here Latven literally and metaphorical-ly deconstructs the vessel into its con-stituent elements. Just previous to the making of this piece, Latven had been using blocks of plastic to complement the exotic woods of his brick-laminated pieces. This inspired him to cut some of the blocks out of the piece after it had been turned, opening the door to a play between positive and negative space. *Sudden Impact*, like all of Latven's work, was designed on paper prior to its construction, accounting for its cool, precisely mathematical quality. But it is

also dynamic in its suggestion of a vio-lent disruption of the form, as the title implies. It was the first in a series of pieces in which Latven explored per-mutations on hyperbolic and parabolic curves, in a steady departure from the parameters of the vessel.

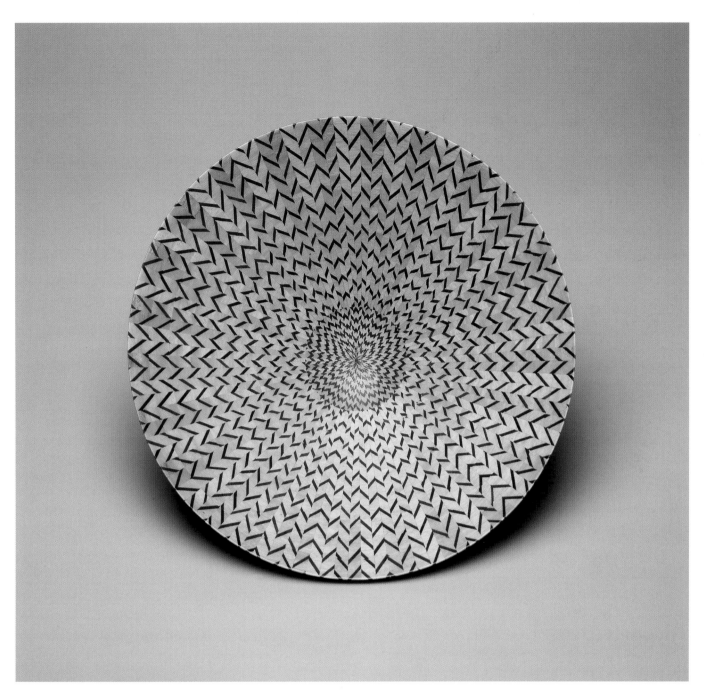

Michael Shuler
79 *Bowl*
1989
Satinwood, vermilion
H 4 ¾ × Diam 11 ⅝
Inscribed on underside:
Mike Shuler #458 1989
Collection of Fleur Bresler

Michael Shuler's extraordinarily complex approach to polychromatic turning is equal parts graphic design and engineering. He begins by gluing 104 small wedges of wood into a disc, each wedge radiating from the center like a piece of pie. The disc is then cut into multiple rings, which are then stacked and glued into a hollow cone, which can be turned into a bowl. The process is repeated for the bottom of the bowl with fewer wedges, producing a variation in the overall pattern. This elaborate assembly results in a dense composition of small, brick-like rectangles of wood. Shuler experiments endlessly with the initial set-up of the wedges in order to vary the patterns in the final form, like the intersecting parabolic curves in this bowl. He also uses colored glue, which is preserved in the final piece as a lattice of thin lines delineating the edges of each piece of wood.

Virginia Dotson
80 *Cross Winds*
1989
Wenge, maple
H 5 ⅝ × Diam 13 ⅛
Inscribed on underside: Virginia
Dotson/1989/Wenge/#89040
Collection of Ron and Anita Wornick

The design and construction of Virginia Dotson's complex, multilayered work are primarily accomplished prior to the turning process. After carefully planning the linear patterns that will appear in the final object, she glues together a block of layered woods. She then cuts the block into sections, reorients the sections, and reglues them into a new block, which is mounted on the lathe and turned. The construction of *Cross Winds* is more complex than that of Dotson's earlier explorations, which required fewer rearrangements of the laminated blocks. The result is an allover design of lamination lines that evokes, but does not replicate, the grain pattern of a solid wood. For Dotson this naturalism suggests the cross-bedding lines left in sandstone by ancient winds.

Fletcher Cox
81 *Drop Bop #1*
1982
Zebrawood, mahogany, purpleheart
H 2 1/16 × Diam 13 3/4
Inscribed in ink on underside: F COX 82
Collection of Hank and David Ingebretsen

Fletcher Cox was influenced by inlaid clay bowls made by local Mississippi potters like Carolyn Brice Brooks. These inspired him to begin making patterned polychrome assemblies based on techniques explained in Frank Pain's instructional text *The Practical Woodturner.*

This body of work developed into a series that explored the illusion of three-dimensionality, initially an unintentional side effect of combining light and dark woods. *Drop Bop #1* was the first of a series of plates in which plugs of different diameters were inlaid in a regular pattern. Shown at the 1985 Arrowmont conference exhibition "Woodturning: Vision and Concept," it was among the most widely seen polychromatic works of the mid-1980s.

from the career of the maverick Schenectady craftsman Giles Gilson.

Gilson was among the first turners to seriously engage with the possibilities of imitating basketry, extending the geometric language of previous laminated turning into the realm of figural iconography (83). But he soon became preoccupied with the possibility of rejecting considerations of the wood altogether. He had little respect for the inherent characteristics of the wood so prized by the other innovative turners of his generation; he valued the material only because it was relatively inexpensive and easily worked. Indeed, Gilson did not present or conceive himself as a "wood turner," but as a designer who just happened to use a lathe. He divided his time between turning and the design of airplanes, industrial products, and racing cars. Accordingly, he had no compunctions about covering his vessels with a shell of automobile lacquer. Like the furnituremakers of the day, he used an opaque finish because it concealed technique and material and emphasized his graphic design sensibility (84). Gilson clearly enjoyed the indignant attention his work received, and he articulated his oppositional stance with intelligence and wit.[23] His 1989 vessel *Point of View*, for example, contrasts a brilliant sky-blue interior with a conventionally "woody" exterior (85). With its faked bark inclusion and punning title, it is a subtle satire of mainstream wood turning.

Gilson was by no means the only turner to employ paint in the early 1980s. One of the first to do so was the ever-inventive Stephen Hogbin, who used color to enliven his experimental figurative works of the early 1980s (86). Hap Sakwa adopted paint in 1983, in a dramatic rejection of his early, refined, natural-edge bowls (see 60). When he began using paint, delicacy went out the window. His new work was intentionally garish, even kitschy, in its palette, and turned in awkwardly heavy shapes (87). For Sakwa, wood turning eventually became too limiting, and he moved into freewheeling sculptures that had little to do with craft; but his sense of humor was shared by Canadian turner and furnituremaker Michael Hosaluk. Sometimes satirical, sometimes ambiguously ritualistic, Hosaluk uses paint as a means to suggest narrative content (88). In this respect, he has a close colleague in Pennsylvanian Mark Sfirri, who is a master of multi-axis turning (89). Since 1992, Hosaluk and Sfirri have collaborated on a number of whimsical pieces, and Sfirri has also made several lighthearted works in cooperation with painter Robert G. Dodge (90).

Of course, not all of the turners employing paint in their work have used color to aggressive or humorous ends. Some have seen in paint a way of emulating the abstract linear or geometric compositions of the graphic design world. Wayne and Belinda Raab, for example, adapted their knowledge of abstract painting to the construction of vessels in which form and color are closely intertwined (91). And Addie Draper made a transition from polychromatic assembled vessels to simple painted forms that stress linear design (92). Eventually, Draper became a full-time painter and abandoned turning entirely.

Other turners have resisted the tendency to use paint as a way of departing from tradition, and have instead tried to wed color to the aesthetic values of the 1950s and 1960s. Foremost among this group is Bay Area turner Merryll Saylan. Even in her earliest turnings, Saylan had been interested in the way that form and texture interact with color, an interest rooted in her respect for Japanese ceramics and turnings (93). Later in her career, she preserved the subtlety of this early work in a series

Philip C. Moulthrop
82 *Mosaic Bowl*
1994
White pine cross sections, epoxy, sawdust
H 11 × Diam 19 ½
Incised on underside: PCM [within oval]/
PHILIP MOULTHROP/WHITE PINE MOSAIC/
Pinus strobus/3921
Yale University Art Gallery,
Gift of Ruth and David Waterbury, BA 1958,
in honor of Patricia E. Kane, 2000.93.1

In the *Mosaic* series, his best-known body of work, Philip Moulthrop emulates the "spheroid" form so associated with his father Ed (see 38); but he has invented a process that radically alters the visual impact of the piece. Moulthrop begins with a spheroid form turned from a solid piece of wood (often a cracked or otherwise undesirable vessel). He covers the surface of this blank with a layer of epoxy mixed with sawdust. He then sets cross sections of pine branches into the epoxy and lets the entire construction dry.

Finally, he turns the piece to shape, cleaning the outside profile to a smooth finish and hollowing the interior (thus eliminating the original blank from the final piece). The resulting "mosaic bowl" sets the natural wood graphically against a stark black background.

Giles Gilson

83 Interpretation #3
1981
Black-dyed veneer, birch, holly, padouk,
purpleheart, mahogany, ebony, maple, East
Indian rosewood, amaranth, black flocking
H 5 ¾ × Diam 7 ⅞
Inscribed on underside:
Interpretation/#3/Giles/Gilson/9/'81
Collection of Dr. Irving Lipton

Giles Gilson approaches the turning
process like an engineer, fabricating
each element of his work with fore-
thought and precision. In creating this
bowl, one of a series of vessels dealing
with the imagery of the Hopi Indians,
Gilson employed a variety of polychromatic lamination techniques. He
spent a great deal of time preparing
and executing the pictorial inlays,
taking into account the curving profile
of the exterior wall in laying out the
composition. In this piece, Gilson also
experimented with a technique called
flocking, in which small bits of fiber
are adhered to the wooden surface.
The lower part of the inside of the bowl
is covered with black flocking, adding
weight and density to the interior
volume. The *Hopi* series was the first
instance of figural imagery in Gilson's
career and in the turning field as
a whole, and brought attention both
to polychromatic technique and to
narrative themes.

Giles Gilson
84 *Sunset*
1987
Lacquered basswood and aluminum,
black flocking
H 12 ¼ × Diam 24
Inscribed on underside: GILES GILSON;
aluminum engraved: Giles Gilson 4/87
Renwick Gallery of the Smithsonian
American Art Museum,
Gift of George Peter Lamb and Lucy Scardino
in Memory of Natalie Rust Lamb, 1995.100.8

Sunset is the largest of a series of lacquered vessels executed by Gilson in
the mid-1980s. It is constructed of
laminated basswood and covered with
a pearlescent, translucent lacquer;
developed by the automotive industry,
it changes color as one moves around
the object. The graphic design that
wraps around the form is also taken
from car design, an interest of Gilson's
since the 1960s. This hot-rod imagery
is enhanced by an applied aluminum
rim, also fabricated by Gilson. The black
flocking lining the interior provides a
marked contrast to the gleaming exterior.

Giles Gilson
85 *Point of View*
1989
Cocobolo, holly, ebony, walnut, elder, paint
H 6 × Diam 8 ½
Inscribed on underside: Gilson/4/89
Collection of Ron and Anita Wornick

Gilson's unique sense of humor is evident in this satire of the "form and figure" turners' obsession with the natural beauty of wood. On close inspection, one realizes that the "natural edge" of the opening in the vessel wall overlaps two different woods that have been laminated together. Though it looks convincing, the edge is at least partly artificial. The title is also a clever piece of double entendre that refers both to the single "window" of the composition and to Gilson's skeptical attitude towards the sacred cows of turning.

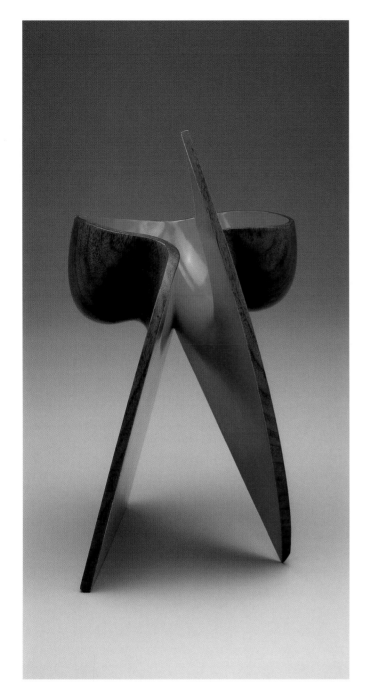

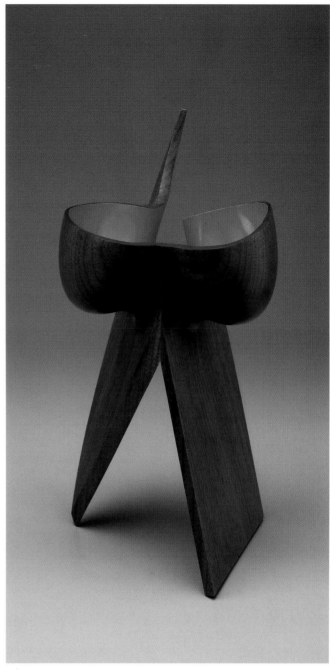

Stephen Hogbin
86 *Walnut Bowl of Walnut*
1981
Walnut, paint
H 9 ¹⁵/₁₆ × W 5 ¼ × D 7 ¼
Incised on outside of one leg: SH [conjoined]
Wood Turning Center, Anonymous Loan,
1995.01.01.081L

Like many of Hogbin's earlier pieces from the 1970s, *Walnut Bowl of Walnut* comes from a single turned form that has been cut apart and reassembled. The construction of this piece, however, marked a new level of complexity in Hogbin's career. The original turning was a bowl with a wide, flat rim reaching out into space. Hogbin cut this form into two sections along a curve, cut away most of the rim, and then rejoined the two sections at an angle. Finally,

he painted the interior in order to accentuate the shape. The finished "walking bowl" has a playful, figural quality quite unlike the vessel form from which it was generated. Hogbin chose this piece to represent his work in the "Turned Object Show" in 1981.

Hap Sakwa
87 *Torus*
1988
Poplar, maple, lacquer
H 6 ⅜ × Diam 13 ¾
Inscribed on underside in red ink:
Hap Sakwa/1988/TORUS
Collection of Garry K. and Sylvia Bennett

By the mid-1980s, Hap Sakwa began to distance himself from his early concerns with form and figure (see 60) by producing a body of satirical painted pieces. In the case of *Torus*, he may also have been targeting Ed Moulthrop's series of "spheroid" vessels (see 38). Sakwa has emulated the round shape of a Moulthrop, and he has even used spin painting to make a mock technicolor version of the mineral streaking that Moulthrop found in tulip poplar wood.

The kitschy paint job entirely hides the wood underneath, except on the bottom, where the unpainted surface is exposed to reveal that the piece is actually glued up from planks.

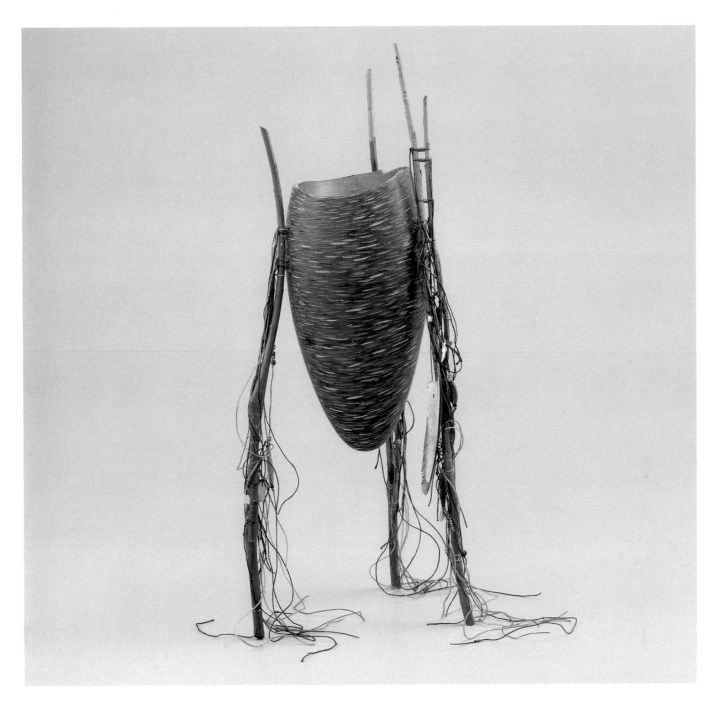

Michael Hosaluk
88 *Tribal Gathering*
1991
Elm, willow, linen thread, copper leaf, paint, beads
H 20 × W 8 × D 8
Incised on underside: MH [conjoined]/91
Collection of Julian H. Fisher

By the late 1980s, turner and furniture-maker Michael Hosaluk was one of the leaders in the use of paint, mixed media, and found objects in woodworking. In this case, he has attached long strands of multicolored linen and beads, evoking aboriginal ritual objects he had seen on a trip to Australia in 1988. The piece's spindly legs also owe something to Hosaluk's travel experience, the choice of willow having been inspired by the work of a basketmaker

he met while teaching at Arrowmont School of Arts and Crafts in Tennessee. The surface is periodically interrupted by cuts made with a hand-carving tool, each one painstakingly painted by hand. The dazzling coloristic effect is complemented by the interior, which is lined in copper leaf.

Mark Sfirri and Robert G. Dodge
90 *Secretaire*
1989
Lacewood, purpleheart, plywood, acrylic
paint, gold leaf
H 62 × W 51 × D 20
Burned on proper left side of the proper
right drawer under the hinged top:
Mark Sfirri 1989/Robert G. Dodge
Private Collection

From 1987 to 1989, Sfirri and painter Robert Dodge collaborated on several pieces of furniture and objects. Their most extravagantly decorative production was this *Secretaire*, a cartoonish but knowing takeoff on historical furniture styles. The four turned legs of the piece are quartered from a single, multi-axis turned spindle and then shaped with hand cutting. At first, these look like regular weight-bearing legs, but they are actually applied decorative turnings, as is evident from the fact that they end several inches from the floor. The facade of the piece is composed of weird curves and patterns that break up the rectilinear shapes of the wood into an explosion of abstract design.

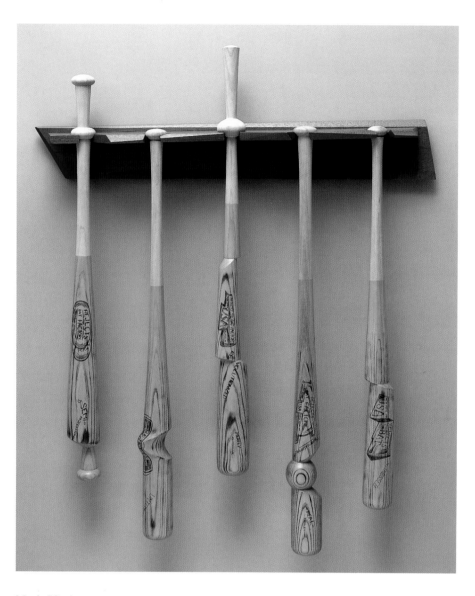

Mark Sfirri
89 *Rejects from the Bat Factory*
1995
Ash, mahogany
Each bat: L 36 × Diam 3;
Rack: H 5 ½ × W 36 x D 4 ½
Collection of John and Robyn Horn

Building on years of experience as a furniture and object maker, Mark Sfirri humorously exploits the wide range of possibilities of multi-axis spindle turning in *Rejects from the Bat Factory*.

Some of the bats feature off-center turning, in which the barrel looks as if it has been broken and misaligned; others have large dents and spherical displacements that suggest an encounter with a particularly hard fastball; and one bat is outfitted with a handle at both ends. The bats are turned from ash, the same wood that is used to make professional baseball bats. The eccentric angles on the mahogany rack, on the other hand, are inspired by the cubist furniture of Wharton Esherick, the father of studio furniture.

90

90

Belinda and H. Wayne Raab
91 *Vase: Red with Blue Squares*
1986 (repainted 1988)
Walnut, curly maple, acrylic lacquer
H 25 ³/₈ × W 6 ¹/₂ × D 5
Inscribed in black ink on underside:
Wayne Raab/1986–1988
Wood Turning Center, 1995.01.01.195

This multi-axis turned vase exemplifies the mid-1980s taste for boldly painted surfaces. The geometric vocabulary has its ultimate origins in the minimalist paintings Wayne Raab made as a graduate student in the early 1970s. Here the vessel is treated as a canvas in the round; the wooden substrate is totally inaccessible underneath the layer of sprayed acrylic lacquer. At the base, the form is circular, but it graduates into an oval at the top. This development in the cross section is mirrored by a vertical shift in color from red to blue. The work's complementary relationship of two-dimensional and three-dimensional design is completed by a series of five painted squares that dance up each side of the vase towards the square opening in the top.

Addie Draper
92 *Airbrushed Vessel #4*
1987
Holly, paint
H 2 ⅛ × Diam 8 ⅛
Inscribed in black ink on underside:
Addie/Draper/'87
Collection of Fleur Bresler

In 1986, after several years of making
polychromatic vessels with abstract patterns composed of exotic woods, Addie
Draper started to paint directly on the
surfaces of her turnings. This plate is
one of a series of shallow dishes and
vessels that combine delicately concave
or angular forms with linear geometric
designs. At this point in Draper's
career, her focus had shifted definitive-
ly away from the lathe and towards
graphic design. The wood underneath
the paint is entirely obscured. Yet
Draper is still clearly concerned with
dynamics of turning. The form of this
piece is elegant, and the painted
image's converging lines relate to the
convexity of the interior. Soon after
executing this work, Draper abandoned
turning to become a full-time painter
on canvas.

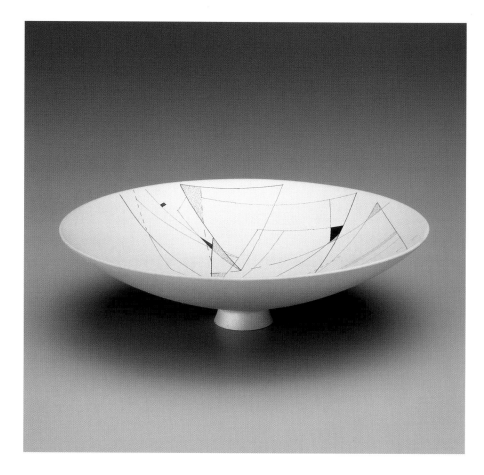

Merryll Saylan
93 *Rice Bowl Set*
1976
Laminated bird's-eye maple
Container: H 8 ¾ × Diam 8;
Bowls: H 4 × Diam 4; Paddle: L 8 × W 2 ¼
Arizona State University Art Museum,
Gift of James and Joanne Rapp, 90.222–223

Although Merryll Saylan was an experienced woodworker by 1976, these rice bowls and server were among the first objects she made on the lathe. They are inspired by Eastern concepts of food presentation and ritual, which Saylan had recently experienced on a trip to Japan. The forms of the bowls, in particular, are close relatives of Asian ceramic and lacquer shapes, and the entire set is designed to fit into a presentational box. Though the pieces are laminated from several boards of maple, the forms have a round organicism and are meant to feel comfortable in the user's hand. These qualities, as well as an overall simplicity of form, anticipate concerns that have lasted throughout Saylan's career. The same year that it was made, the rice bowl set was exhibited in the exhibition "California Design '76" in Los Angeles.

of colored platters. Often, she used dye or bleaching instead of paint to achieve a deep, painterly effect. Though her pieces retain little of the original color of the material from which they are made, they nevertheless recreate the depth and richness of natural wood (94).

After Saylan had taken the shock value out of painted wood, John Jordan began to create similar painted and textured works in the hollow vessel idiom (95). Like Saylan, he was interested both in the natural quality of the wood and in the way that it could be enhanced or transformed through surface effects. His recent lobed vessels are often so subtly affected by bleaching and carving that their exteriors seem to be covered with an organic skin (96). Other established turners, such as David Ellsworth and Alan Stirt, have recently turned to paint as a counterpoint to, or enhancement of, the sensual and visual appeal of the wooden surface (97 and 98).

Michael Chinn and Michael Graham also experimented with surfaces and materials in the 1980s. Their work, like that of the polychromatic turners, is strongly marked by a penchant for engineering and industrial design. In the late 1970s, Chinn and Graham met in Long Beach, California, where Chinn was studying with Frank Cummings (see 43). Both shared with Cummings an interest in using the lathe as a way of generating unique solutions to formal design problems, an attitude that hearkens back to the patternmaker's use of the lathe in industry. Chinn is best known for his *Tri* series of cleverly juxtaposed, uninflected geometric shapes (99). Graham, following in the footsteps of Stephen Hogbin, has created a series of innovative sliding boxes fabricated almost entirely on the lathe (100).

The Arrowmont Conference and its Consequences

In 1985, the field of wood turning began to undergo another series of dramatic shifts. As in 1976, the catalyst for change was a conference, this time organized by Sandra Blain, director of the Arrowmont School of Arts and Crafts in Gatlinburg, Tennessee, with David Ellsworth and Mark Lindquist. In sharp contrast with the casual atmosphere of earlier symposia, the Arrowmont conference featured a lavish display of work by top turners, and many hobbyists were disgruntled. In the wake of the seismic changes in the field during the 1980s, they were concerned about the consequences of the field's rapid professionalization. A review of the conference published in *Fine Woodworking* pointed out that "the rank-and-file turner had come to Arrowmont to learn about turning, not to worship at the shrine of art."[24]

As a result of this disparity between the interests of hobbyists and those of professionals, two organizations eventually emerged from the cauldron of the 1985 conference. The first was the American Association of Woodturners (AAW), the plan for which was proposed at Arrowmont by an amateur turner, Dick Gerard of Indianapolis; the second was the Wood Turning Center (WTC), based in Philadelphia and headed by Albert LeCoff. The AAW was, and has continued to be, a grassroots organization of local chapters focused primarily on the needs of amateur turners. Its publication emphasizes technique, project ideas, and opportunities to learn through workshops and conferences. Though a few professionals such as David Ellsworth, William Hunter, and Merryll Saylan have taken leadership roles in the AAW, it is mainly a hobbyist group.[25] The Wood Turning Center, by contrast, is concerned with the promotion of professional work being done on the lathe. Its publication, *Turning Points,*

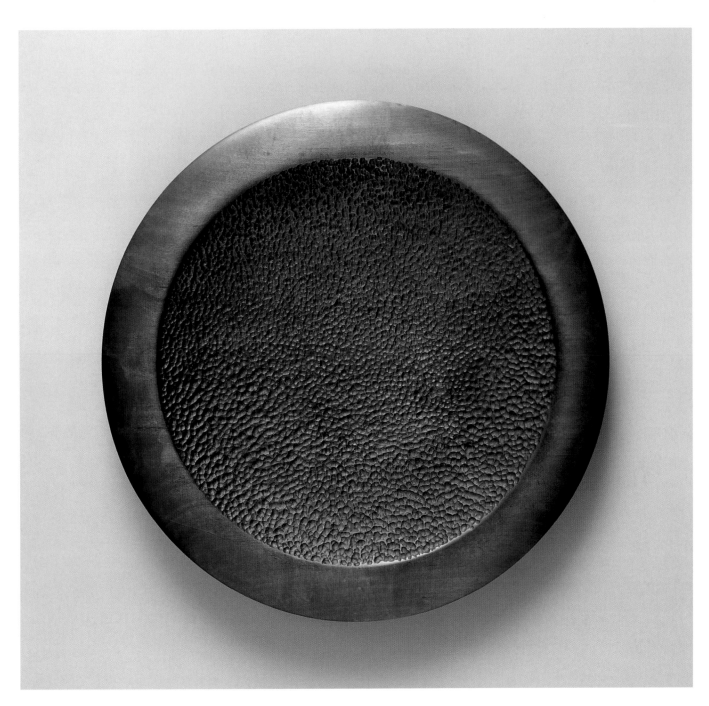

Merryll Saylan
94 *North Seas*
1988
Maple, fiber-reactive dye, tung oil finish
H 2 ¼ × Diam 20 ½
Incised on underside in script:
Merryll Saylan/Calif./Maple/1988
Collection of Donald and Kate King

In the mid-1980s, Saylan began to use dyes, bleaching, and other gentle surface treatments to color the surfaces of her simply shaped wooden platters. This piece, among the first of her colored and textured works, emerged from technical difficulty Saylan experienced in applying dye to a wooden surface. The sanding lines in the wood absorbed more of the dye, resulting in a scratchy looking surface. The solution to this dilemma was provided when a friend, furnituremaker Gail Freidell, suggested doing something to the surface to hide the marks. This idea led to the use of carving tools, in this case a handheld dremel tool that powers a small rotating cutter. What had begun

as a problem became an asset, as Saylan exploited the difference in the absorbencies of rough and smooth wood to create subtle color contrasts with a single dye. She also worked with the reflection of light off the wood surface by varying the direction of cuts. These techniques allow her to combine the richness and textural complexity of wood with the palette of a painter.

John Jordan
95 *Black Textured Jar*
1993
Dyed box elder, fossil inlay
H 13 × Diam 9
Inscribed on bottom: John Jordan '93
The Arkansas Arts Center Foundation
Collection, 96.23.2

John Jordan's work is premised on finely detailed turning, strong classical shapes, and subtle surface textures. This lidded jar, one of a series of six, is among his more formal and ornate pieces. It was one of Jordan's first uses of dye, which obscures the natural color of the wood but preserves something of its matte texture. The leaf pattern on the shoulder is chisel carved, and the remainder of the surface is covered with small hammer marks reminiscent of metalworking technique. The lid is embellished with a series of turned beads and a cap of fossil inlay.

John Jordan
96 *Lobed Vase*
1998
Box elder
H 8 ½ × Diam 10 ¾
Inscribed on bottom: John Jordan '98
Burton Creek Collection

Jordan has recently continued his taste-ful explorations into the hollow vessel with a series of lobed and textured vases. In form, coloration, and texture, this body of work takes its inspiration from rocks and undersea life. This example profits from the use of a spec-tacular piece of box elder, a pale wood that is sometimes found with a natural red mineral "stain." The appeal of the

surface is further enhanced by a soft texture executed with a wire brush. Wood movement has brought the piece slightly out of round, contributing to an overall feel that is looser and more organic than Jordan's earlier work.

David Ellsworth
97 *Hemisphere with Orange*
1991
Scorched ash, red dye
H 8¾ × W 13 × D 10¼;
H 5¼ × W 8 × D 7; H 2¾ × W 4
Largest piece inscribed on bottom: Ellsworth
1991/"Hemisphere with Orange"
Collection of Jane and Arthur Mason

David Ellsworth began scorching and painting his vessels in 1990 with the *Solstice* series. Although this startling departure from his previous work did not end his unpainted explorations into the subtle nuances of turned form (see 124), it did signal a new looseness in Ellsworth's approach to the material. Previously, he had allowed the wood itself to guide him to the final shape of the piece; here, he is willing to create compositional effects through the relatively arbitrary means of applied color. The emphasis on surface design

rather than form was especially pronounced in the first pieces in the series, which were perfectly spherical. This particular set, however, balances Ellsworth's new interest in color with his longstanding sculptural interests. This is emphasized by the arrangement of different vessels into a group that encourages the comparison of similar forms (see also 121).

Alan Stirt
98 *Pine Needle Plate*
1996
Maple, paint
H 2 ¾ × Diam 6 ⅜
Incised on underside: AL Stirt '96
Collection of Fleur Bresler

While teaching a workshop in New
Zealand in 1993, Alan Stirt was encouraged by Michael Hosaluk (88, 126) to
begin painting his forms. Stirt responded by converting his long-practiced
carving into a sgraffito technique, in
which abstract geometric designs are
thinly chiseled through a layer of black
paint. The flat, high-contrast effect is
reminiscent of a block print. To match
this new direction, Stirt chose a shallow
bowl form with a wide brim that afforded room to explore the design. This
platter format was one he had used for
several years in a series of textured
"ceremonial vessels." *Pine Needle Plate*
was one of the first in which he cut the
rim to follow the pattern on the bowl,
further emphasizing the graphic character of the piece.

Michael Chinn
99 *Tri-10,000*
1988
Purpleheart, Indian ebony, aluminum
H 3 ½ × W 9 × D 6 ⅛
Wood Turning Center, 1995.01.01.029

Michael Chinn's work has evolved stylis-
tically from bowl-like curved containers,
to vertical-walled cylindrical vessels, to
cone-based geometric assemblies. This
body of work stems from his graduate
work with Frank Cummings in the
late 1970s in Long Beach, California.
There, Chinn was struck by the precise
action of a compound table attachment
for the Rockwell lathe, an apparatus
that converts the lathe into a milling
machine. He saw artistic possibilities in
the regularity of this device and adopted what he calls a "machinist's visual
language based on the straight-line
path of metal lathe tool bits." *Tri-10,000*
is typical of this style. Deceptively simple looking, the composition is actually
a ballet of interacting forms and architectonic structure. Its smooth wooden
diagonals revolve dynamically around a
stable central square made of textured
aluminum, producing a balance of
contrasting shapes, materials, colors,
and textures.

Michael N. Graham
100 *Circle/Square #15/35*
1987
Basswood, paint
H 4 ¹/₈ × W 9 × L 18
Incised on underside: (four petal blossom)
#15/35©1987 M Graham
Wood Turning Center, 1995.01.01.068

Michael Graham began his woodworking career in the 1970s making organic, hand-carved boxes. In the 1980s, he made a transition to works such as *Circle/Square #15/35*, which features painted surfaces and hard geometric designs. This piece also typifies Graham's interest in using the lathe to solve functional design problems: in this case, the construction of a radial (curved) sliding drawer. Attracted to both the efficiency and the flexibility of the

lathe, Graham followed in the steps of Stephen Hogbin by exposing the basically geometric character of turned volumes by cutting them into sections and rejoining them. All parts of this box are turned except for the caps on each end.

reviews exhibitions and books and is a forum for discussion of ideas about turning; and its exhibitions, beginning with "Lathe-Turned Objects: An International Exhibition" in 1988, have defined new directions in the field. In addition, the Center's collection of objects from the last three decades constitutes a canon that has played a key role in shaping the sensibilities of the recent generation of private collectors. The division between the AAW and the WTC has had a dramatic impact upon the field. Other craft organizations, such as the National Society for Education in the Ceramic Arts, or the Society of North American Goldsmiths, simultaneously serve professional and amateur constituencies. In the wood turning field, however, a wide gulf exists between hobbyists and "lathe artists." This separation has resulted in a particularly intense spirit of innovation and technical accomplishment among the field's leaders; but at the same time, professionals sometimes disdain the amateurs that were once the lifeblood of the craft.

Alongside the institutionalization of the wood turning scene came an increasing interest in collecting the work of prominent figures in the field. Before the mid-1980s, only a handful of collectors, notably Dr. Irving Lipton in Los Angeles and Edward (Bud) Jacobson in Tempe, Arizona, had paid attention to the field. In 1985, however, Jacobson arranged "The Art of Turned-Wood Bowls," an exhibition of his collection at Arizona State University, which subsequently toured to the Renwick Gallery. Unlike earlier turning shows, Jacobson's exhibition was accompanied by a lavish catalogue with color illustrations. It demonstrated that a collector could focus exclusively on bowl turning and yet amass a group of objects of great depth and variety.

In the years following the Jacobson show, the first significant wave of collectors of wood turning emerged. Among the key figures in this generation are Jane and Arthur Mason, Anita and Ron Wornick, Dorothy and George Saxe, Fleur and Charles Bresler, Ruth and David Waterbury, Don King, and Robyn and John Horn.[26] These patrons created an interest among galleries and museums, resulting in a generally more competitive field. The few established galleries that had been carrying wood turnings since the 1970s, like Clyde Jones's Highlight Gallery in Mendocino, California, Jan Peters and Ray Leier's del Mano Gallery in Los Angeles, Joanne Rapp's Hand and the Spirit Gallery in Scottsdale, Arizona, and Rick and Ruth Snyderman's galleries in Philadelphia, expanded their roster of turners and began to publicize their shows more effectively. New galleries began to carry the work of wood turners at this time as well; a particularly prominent addition was Martha Connell's gallery in Atlanta.[27] Though the opportunities for professional turners to make a living from their work had never been greater, the pressure to create impressive tour de force pieces increased exponentially.

Super-Objects: High Skill in the Late Eighties

Thus, by the late 1980s, new intellectual, aesthetic, and technical demands were being placed on professional turners by large-scale institutional transformations. The craftspeople were obliged to respond by raising the level of their commitment. In the main, this meant the development of what are called "off-lathe" processes, in which the plain turned vessel could be enhanced by burning, bleaching, sandblasting, cutting, or texturing. Of course, the idea of pairing lathe turning with carving was not unprecedented; the combination can be traced back at least to the rope-twists and finials of Baroque furniture. More recently, in the vessel

William Hunter
101 *Autumn Flutes*
1982
Vinhatico
H 2 1/8 × Diam 10 9/16
Incised on underside: #293 AUTUMN FLUTES
VINHATICO Hunter '82
Arizona State University Art Museum,
Gift of Edward Jacobson, 90.27

In 1979, William Hunter developed an approach to carved vessels that was originally inspired by the spiral patterns on ornamental turnings (see 26, 112). The first series in this vein, of which this is an example, featured densely packed carved flutes. A number of technical developments enabled Hunter to execute these forms, chiefly the use of a disc sander to shape the spiral grooves as the piece was slowly hand-rotated on the lathe. He also employed rotary files and a horizontal drill press in roughing out the form.

These pieces were always made from dense exotic woods that offered a beautiful figure and enabled him to maintain clean carved lines. *Autumn Flutes*, the largest piece from this period of Hunter's work, was featured in Edward Jacobson's 1985 exhibition and publication "The Art of Turned-Wood Bowls."

tradition, California woodworkers such as Frank Cummings, Bob Stocksdale, Jerry Glaser, and Bob Trout (see 43, 16, 23, and 44) had shown the potential of this tradition in the 1960s by texturing their work with chisels, bandsaws, and carving tools. But a more extreme notion of "off-lathe" work emerged in the 1980s with the use of allover carving, a demonstration of the turner's skill and investment in the vessel.

The most prominent practitioner of carving as a virtuoso performance is undoubtedly William Hunter. In 1980, he began a series of spiral-carved bowls whose elegance and high degree of craftsmanship garnered national attention (101). Since that time, Hunter has developed his carving skills, sometimes creating spiral open-work effects, and sometimes taking advantage of the color and figure of precious exotic woods (102). In his increasing elegance and reverence for finish, which contrasts so starkly with the rough, natural pieces made early in his career (see 36), Hunter exemplifies the trend towards technical perfection.

Another leading carver is Ron Fleming, who has developed a style of densely detailed, finely wrought vegetal carving that extends across the entire vessel surface. Fleming worked as a commercial illustrator for many years before he began turning professionally, and his work exhibits a strongly graphic sensibility that contrasts with Hunter's more sculptural bent. Though turning is still important to Fleming's work as a determinant of form, only a tiny percentage of his time is actually spent on the lathe.[28] Like Hunter, he has been among the leading figures in the use of exotic woods, but he has also shown a flair for transforming less exalted materials into impressive displays of technique and nuanced form (103).

Such lavish carvings can be described as "super-objects," a term coined by ceramic historian Garth Clark to describe the extraordinary technical refinement of low-fire wares by Ron Nagle and Ken Price in the late 1960s and early 1970s. The super-object impulse in ceramics was also expressed in hyper-realist objects by Marilyn Levine, Robert Hudson, and Richard Shaw, in which ceramic was made to imitate leather, paper, wood, and other materials.[29] The term super-object could also be applied to trompe-l'oeil carved furniture of the 1970s by Wendell Castle and Fumio Yoshimura (Fig. 9), or to the extraordinary bentwood creations of Michael Jean Cooper.[30]

In both of these cases—ceramics during the late 1960s, and furniture during the 1970s—a craft medium was coming into its own and receiving unprecedented attention from national art and craft institutions. The impulse to lavish time and skill on individual objects was, in part, a response to these pressures. The same dynamic was at work in the turning field in the late 1980s. By this time, the standard of accomplishment for young turners was extremely high, and the demonstration of skill was the most obvious route to institutional attention. In addition to the painstakingly carved work of Hunter and Fleming, hyper-realist objects came into vogue. Michael Brolly, for example, simulated natural forms exclusively through the use of the lathe, adapting Stephen Hogbin's fragmental turning techniques to representational ends (104). Furnituremaker Craig Nutt has created an equally inventive body of trompe l'oeil work using his considerable skills as a woodcarver. Many of his works derive their humor from the ridiculously literal transposition of traditional furniture's "vegetal" ornamentation (105).

Perhaps the most intriguing variant of the super-object impulse in wood turning is seen in the work of Michelle Holzapfel, another turner widely known for her accomplished carvings (106). Holzapfel's carved

Fig. 9. Fumio Yoshimura (b. 1926), *Typewriter*, 1972, various woods. Philadelphia Museum of Art, Gift of Mr. Benjamin D. Bernstein.

William Hunter
102 *Unfolding Lilies*
1990
Pink ivory, ebony dust, epoxy resin
H 10 ⅛ × Diam 8
Incised on underside: FOR SPECIAL FRIENDS,
BRUCE & MARINA WITH LOVE BILL/#1000/
"UNFOLDING LILIES"/ WM. Hunter
[script]/'90
Collection of Bruce and Marina Kaiser

From his first craft show in 1970, Hunter saw how strongly the public reacted to exotic woods, and he has continued to work with them throughout his career. *Unfolding Lilies* is made from a particularly large and strongly colored sample of South African pink ivory, a desirable and expensive wood. In addition to its beautiful color, pink ivory exhibits chatoyence, a shimmering three-dimensional luster that appears in the figure. A final stunning feature is the star-like cracking of the wood pith, which Hunter has filled with a mixture of ebony dust and resin to preserve the flawless polish of the surface. The piece is embellished with a free composition of undulating art nouveau-like vine forms. The recesses that define these vines are amazingly shallow, leaving little room for error in the carving.

Ron Fleming
103 Earth Offering
1992
Buckeye burl
H 9 × W 23 × D 20
Inscribed in black ink on underside of one
leaf: Ron Fleming
Collection of Susan and Neil Kaye

Ron Fleming's work has evolved from turned vessels with carved rims to pieces in which decoration encompasses the entire form. *Earth Offering* developed from a series of "suspended" vessels in which a bowl is lifted up on carved leaf forms. This form is unusual in the series in that it is cantilevered, as if the smoothly polished bowl were in the process of rising from a pile of roughly textured leaves. After turning a vessel with a smooth interior and bottom and a roughly turned curved wing, Fleming hand carved the exterior, in some cases piercing the wall to create negative space. In executing the leaves, he largely followed the figure of the wood so that the ornament seems to grow naturally from the material.

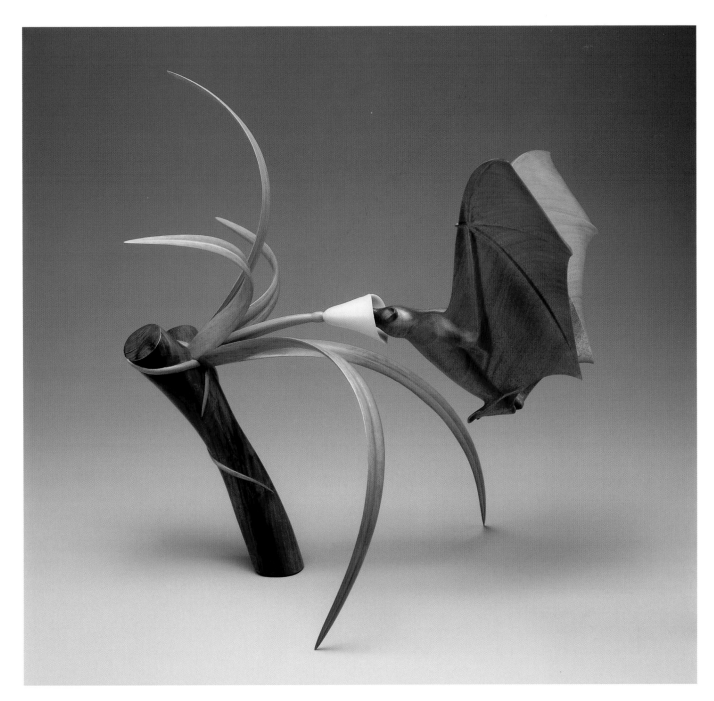

Michael J. Brolly
104 *Our Mother Hangs in the Balance*
1992
Mahogany, walnut, holly, brass, various
veneers
H 18 × W 12 × D 16
Collection of Dr. Irving Lipton

Inspired by Stephen Hogbin to "break out of the circle," Michael Brolly makes figural works through the recombination of sections cut from circular turnings. His technical virtuosity with this technique of reassembly is such that it becomes difficult to believe that the piece's components are actually fashioned on the lathe. The wings of the bat in this example, for instance, were built up from a circular platter form and then hand-carved. For Brolly, constant experimentation with lathe technique goes hand-in-hand with the development of a personal world of symbols, characters, and figures. This process is epitomized in *Our Mother Hangs in the Balance*, which Brolly sees as addressing political and environmental concerns: "This bat's three-inch brass tongue holds it in the flower. [If it is] Removed, the bat—and the tree which supports the plant—fall down, a symbol of the interconnectedness of all things and all actions." The piece was included in "Conservation By Design," a 1993 exhibition that was intended to draw public attention to the problem of rainforest depletion.

105

Michelle Holzapfel
106 *Oakleaf Bowl*
1989
Maple burl
H 6 15/16 × Diam 14
Incised on underside: Michelle Holzapfel/
Marlboro, Vermont/May 1989/maple/burl
Museum of Fine Arts, Boston,
Gift of Mr. and Mrs. William White Howells,
1989.328

As a child, Michelle Holzapfel was attracted to her father's metal lathe and the spiny brass shavings flying from the cabinet door pulls he turned on it. Holzapfel still turns on her father's lathe. Unlike a hand-turning lathe, the cutting tool of a metal lathe is held in a sliding tool rest. The cutting process is accomplished by rotating gear handles, which move the cutting tool on an "x" and "y" axis. With dexterity, Holzapfel is able to use the lathe freehand to create compound curves. The elegance of form that she achieves with this technique is evident in *Oakleaf Bowl*, one of a series of monumental vessels based on classical architectural ornament. Holzapfel took most of her cues for the layout of the carved composition from the natural voids, cracks, and grain lines of the wood.

Craig Nutt
105 *Radish Salad Bowl*
1998
Unidentified wood, paint
H 56 × W 21 × D 21
Inscribed on leg: Nutt 98
Renwick Gallery of the Smithsonian
American Art Museum,
Gift of the James Renwick Alliance, 1999.5

Craig Nutt has been making sculptures, furniture, and vessels incorporating turned and carved vegetable forms since the mid-1980s. He uses the lathe as a roughing-out tool to create components that can later be shaped by hand, painted, and assembled. Nutt's work tends towards broad humor and exaggeration, here conveyed by brighter-than-life colors, the absurd scale of the radish, and the punning fit between the imagery of the piece and its ostensible purpose. The leaves that crown the piece are removable and can be used as salad servers, while the lid may be inverted and used as a functional salad bowl.

work exhibits a broader range of forms and interests than either Hunter's or Fleming's. Perhaps because she encountered the work of Melvin and Mark Lindquist early in her career, she has always preferred thick-walled vessels of monumental, almost architectural, proportions. But Holzapfel, like Brolly and Nutt, was also interested in trompe l'oeil as a means of introducing content into her work. A key example is her early masterpiece *Domestic Violence II*, which addresses social issues even as it pushes the boundary of craft technique (107). Holzapfel's piece is clearly a statement of technical mastery, but it is also a feminist manifesto, in which the supposedly masculine skills of the woodcarver are used to explore the psychology of female domestic life. By virtue of this contrast of technique and theme, the piece implicitly addressed the marginalized position of women in the wood turning field itself, which tended towards macho displays of skill. One of the most welcome developments in the field since Holzapfel began her career has been the emergence of a generation of women turners in a field long dominated by men.[31] Holzapfel's efforts to establish herself in a male-dominated field finally came to fruition in 1990, when she became the first and only turner to be shown in Peter Joseph's prestigious New York City furniture gallery.

Though carving was the most important of the super-object tendencies of the late 1980s, it can be placed into a broader context of work in which other types of advanced craftsmanship and fine materials are showcased. One variant is the phenomenon of translucent turning, an idea that had already been suggested by Del Stubbs's thin-walled vessels (see 58 and 59). This strategy was adopted by Hawaiian turner Ron Kent, who uses naturally translucent, sap-rich tropical woods such as Norfolk pine (108). Like other super-objects, Kent's vessels benefit from off-lathe process; he oils his vessels as many as thirty times to make them luminous. But in his case, the tie to the work's institutional surroundings is more overt. To attain its full impact, his work depends on proper presentation, ideally a museum pedestal with a strong light above.

Presentation was also important for Frank Cummings, who had been an exponent of the California texturing tradition in the 1960s and 1970s (see 43). Cummings hit upon a format that symbolizes the meaning that carving had for turners in the 1980s. By mounting his pieces on a delicate band of lacework, and by adding a curving band of hand-carved filigree to the lip, Cummings marked the edges of his vessels as transitional spaces (109). Here, decoration serves to frame the object for aesthetic contemplation, not use.[32] Cummings often enhances this effect by adding a ring of precious stones to his pieces and placing his objects in handmade presentational boxes.

The apex of the super-object trajectory in wood turning was not achieved until the 1990s, in the work of technical and stylistic innovator Hugh McKay. Like Del Stubbs, McKay was trained in the West Coast myrtlewood tradition. After a hiatus from the lathe and a series of investigations into contemporary sculpture, he resumed turning in 1989. Though carving is a key ingredient in McKay's super-objects, his real forte is multi-axis turning, in which a piece is remounted and turned on the lathe multiple times. Other turners have focused on this technique, notably Mark Sfirri and Stoney Lamar. But McKay has made multi-axis turning an end in itself, pushing it to its technical limits in such works as *Pentapot*, composed of five hollow vessel forms carved into a single piece of wood (110). Even more extreme is the magisterial *Heart*, which is turned on several axes, exhaustively carved, and inlaid with soapstone

Michelle Holzapfel
107 *Domestic Violence II*
1987
Assorted hardwoods, acrylic
H 29 × W 18 × D 14
Burned in a circle on one end of the spool:
MICHELLE HOLZAPFEL • MARLBORO.VT. JAN.
1987•
Yale University Art Gallery, 1999.41.1

Domestic Violence II was a crucial milestone, not only in Holzapfel's career but in the development of the wood turning field as well. Up to this point, Holzapfel had been making pleasing, yet quite tame, turned and carved representations of domestic objects. But she was dissatisfied with these works — as she puts it, "deeply irritated by their passive niceness." *Domestic Violence II* was an abrupt departure into the more trenchant territory of feminist protest art. It speaks to the dominant culture's ongoing disregard for the difficulties of domestic life, the day-to-day struggle to fulfill responsibilities to family, community, and self. A whirlwind of domestic objects is sucked into a funnel in a dynamic, even menacing, array. The execution of the piece took many weeks, largely because of the elaborate trompe l'oeil carving reminiscent of the work of English baroque craftsman Grinling Gibbons.

Ron Kent
108 *Translucent Bowl*
1991
Norfolk pine
H 7 ¹¹/₁₆ × Diam 21 ⁵/₁₆
Yale University Art Gallery,
Gift of the Artist, 1994.59.1

Ron Kent used many different woods
after he began turning in the late 1970s,
but when he discovered the characteristics of the Norfolk pine local to
Hawaii, it became his wood of choice.
Ever since, his work has exploited
the dramatic spalting and exciting knot
patterns of this easily accessible material.
Kent has become particularly well
known for his emphasis on its translucency, which he amplifies by soaking the
wood in vats of oil before he turns it.
This is the largest and most spectacular
example of a series of works Kent
produced in the early 1990s, in which a
"floating" flared bowl form rests on a
small foot. The difficulty of making the
form is clear from the great disparity
between the enormous rim and the thin
stem that connected the piece to the
lathe. Nonetheless, Kent was able to turn
the vessel walls evenly from rim to base.

Frank E. Cummings III
109 *Lacework Vessel*
ca. 1980
African blackwood, ivory, 18k gold
H 5 ³/₄ × Diam 3 ¹/₂
Inscribed on underside in black ink:
Frank E. Cummings III 198[?]
Collection of Dr. Irving Lipton

As he had done in the 1960s (see 43),
Cummings here uses the lathe to establish a form, and then extensively refines
it with hand carving. But where his
early work was rough and expressive,
the cool artifice and delicacy of *Lacework
Vessel* surpasses even the repetitive
perfection of ornamental turnings. The
vessel's foot is delicately fashioned into
a band of filigree fretwork. Another
register of ornament is painstakingly
carved into the rim, curving back and
forth in a wave pattern. Fine gold rods
that frame squares of ivory are set
into tiny holes drilled into the top and
bottom edges of a groove in the wood,
completing the effect of refinement.
Pieces like this one launched Cummings
into a new body of work featuring
precious stones, in which turning
reaches new heights of preciousness.

Hugh E. McKay
110 *Pentapot #2*
1996
Madrone burl
H 16 ½ × W 18 × D 15
Incised on underside: Hugh E. McKay*/
Pentapot #2/1996
Collection of Dr. Irving Lipton

In the mid-1990s Hugh McKay developed his own tools and techniques to create a series in which multiple hollow vessels are turned from a single solid block of wood. To make these pieces, McKay first turns the interior of one pot with a specialized tool fitted with an adjustable cutting tip. He then shapes the exterior of the pot form by rotating it against a sliding router jig system, also of his own design. McKay then takes the piece off the lathe, remounts it, and repeats the process for each of the other four vessel forms. Finally, he finishes the intersections of the five forms with carving tools. The resulting "connected vessel" can be seen as a major milestone in the tradition of technical innovation begun by David Ellsworth's introduction of the thin-walled hollow vessel in the late 1970s.

Fig. 10. Ornamental lathe owned by Frank Knox, Holtzapffel Lathe Company, London, England, 1853. Photograph, Wood Turning Center Archives.

and lead (111). With its extensive investment in both lathe technique and off-lathe processes, McKay's work embodies the high standards that contemporary turners must meet in order to succeed.[33]

Ornamental and Decorative Turning

Allied to the super-object trend in the 1980s was a resurgence of interest in the practice of ornamental turning, in which a specialized lathe is used to create small, densely decorated objects. Unlike the lathes that most wood turners use, ornamental lathes are machine tools (Fig. 10). They were originally developed in industries that required extreme precision, such as horology (clock making). A variety of indexing systems and carving tool bits connected to the ornamental lathe permit the creation of regular patterns in the surface of a circular wooden blank. Thus, to use English turner and craft theorist David Pye's terms, the "workmanship of risk" common to most craft processes is replaced by the "workmanship of certainty."

Until recently, all serious ornamental turning has been done on vintage lathes, most of which were manufactured by the English Holtzapffel Lathe Company beginning in 1794. Frank Knox, one of the first Americans to take up ornamental turning on a hobbyist basis (see 26), claimed that fewer than 300 such lathes were extant worldwide. Another observer has guessed that the number of usable lathes is under one hundred.[34] This factor of rarity, along with the rigorous demands of executing a pattern with hundreds of miniature cuts, lend this subdiscipline of turning a preciousness similar to that of hand-carved super-objects.

It was not until the 1980s that ornamental turning became popular in this country. Unlike Knox, the present generation of ornamental turners is fully integrated into the wood turning field; they sell to the same collectors and show in the same venues. Nonetheless, ornamental turners remain a breed apart. They have their own organization, separate from the American Association of Woodturners, and as a group they tend to be concerned with the history and connoisseurship of the extraordinary lathes they use. Furthermore, perhaps because of the ornamental turning tradition's involvement with ivory, gold, and exotic woods, their work tends to be jewel-like and relatively conservative in form. Jon Sauer and Dale Chase exemplify these traits of the ornamental turning community. Both work in a refined, precise style in which design and execution take precedence over expressive breadth. Sauer is known mainly for his graceful spiral-turned bottles (112), while Chase's layered "window boxes" are a particularly ingenious and technically accomplished use of the ornamental lathe (113).

A few turners have incorporated the regularized cutting action of ornamental turning to their work on standard lathes, which are often equipped with basic indexing plates that allow the workpiece to be rotated and fixed at intervals of five or ten degrees. John Diamond-Nigh relied on such a system to produce his serene sculptural pieces, which were inspired by the work of David Pye (114 and Fig. 11). On a grander scale, many of Mark Lindquist's pieces are made through an automatic process of his own invention, by which a chainsaw is pushed into the wood at standard intervals (115; see also 54, 65). And, in a different vein, Steve Paulsen emulates the effects of an ornamental lathe with "chatterwork," a demanding technique in which a tool is allowed to bounce rapidly across the surface of the rotating workpiece. Paulsen's decorative sensibility is delicate, but like true ornamental turnings, his pieces assert the primacy of technical finish (116).

Fig. 11. David Pye (1914–1993), *Double Bowl*, ca. 1970, wood. Wood Turning Center; photograph by John Carlano.

Hugh E. McKay
111 *Heart*
1993
Madrone burl, cast lead, soapstone
H 19 × W 22 × D 24
Incised on underside: Hugh E. McKay/
"Heart"/Madrone Burl/1993
Collection of Susan and Neil Kaye

Inspired by the mixed media sculpture
and jewelry of René Lalique and the
metalwork of Albert Paley, McKay's
monumental *Heart* is a combination of
a bewildering number of techniques
and materials. He began with the root
structure of the madrone burl, preserving the roots as a design element by
using multi-axis turning to shape each
root separately on the lathe. McKay

then exhaustively textured the exterior
with power and hand-carving tools.
Finally, he inlaid cast lead and carved
soapstone arches into the root ends.
The result is an exercise in baroque
ornamentation and contrasting textures
in which the piece's origins on the
lathe are practically erased. Yet *Heart*
retains its connection to the hollow
vessel tradition by virtue of its narrow
mouth and large interior volume.

Jon Sauer
112 *Red Spiral Bottle*
1993
Dymond wood, blackwood
H 5 × Diam 1 ½
Incised in script on underside: Jon Sauer/
P+1#93–42/Blackwood/Dymondwood
Collection of Dr. Irving Lipton

Jon Sauer made this bottle shortly after
he acquired a spiral-turning apparatus
for his Holtzapffel ornamental lathe.
This tool cuts a groove laterally across
the cylindrical workpiece as it revolves,
resulting in a single spiral flute that
wraps around the entire bottle. Sauer
added color contrast to this effect by
boring out the center of a cylinder of
dymond wood (an artificial material
resembling an exotic wood) and insert-
ing a smaller cylinder of blackwood.
In the finished piece, the blackwood is
revealed by the deepest spiral cut.
Sauer drew the composition together
further by cutting holes into the
dymond wood walls and inlaying circular
pieces of blackwood.

M. Dale Chase
113 *Best Box '94*
1994
African blackwood, pink ivory
H 1 ¾ × Diam 2 ¾
Incised on rim on one half: Chase
Yale University Art Gallery,
Gift of Ruth and David Waterbury, BA 1958,
in honor of Patricia E. Kane, 2000.93.2a–b

Initially, Dale Chase became involved with turning as an avocation. His profession, neurosurgery, taught him hand-eye coordination and an extraordinary attention to detail. Now he turns full-time on ornamental lathes, using complex cutters of his own design, which are manufactured by the master machinist and ornamental turner Walter Balliet. In this piece, Chase combined lamination of contrasting woods with an internal design made with an ornamental lathe. The wood layers are exposed through the turning process to make a three-dimensional decorative pattern. In his previous work, Chase had been primarily concerned with "sensuality," particularly with the way the boxes fit in the palm of the hand. In *Best Box*, however, the design is more about the visual pattern created from exotic woods. The pink ivory is among the most valuable of exotics, and the blackwood is a particularly splendid sample; Chase says that he "would have paid a fortune for more chunks of blackwood so fine." This interest in fine materials continues in Chase's current work, which is made exclusively of gold and silver.

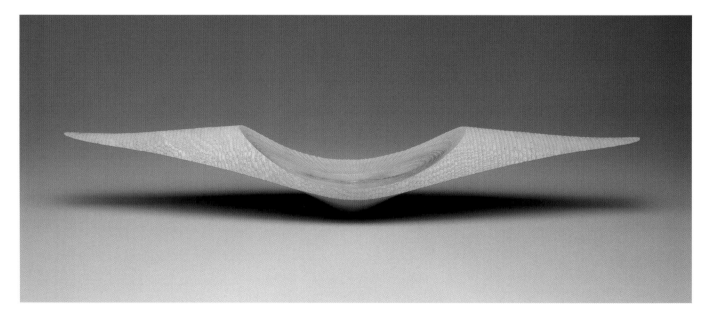

John Diamond-Nigh
114 *Untitled*
ca. 1985
Birch
H 3 ¼ × W 4 ¾ × D 23 ½
Wood Turning Center, 1995.01.01.039

John Diamond-Nigh made wood sculptures using bowl forms for inspiration, methodically developing a body of work that explored the concave and the convex, the convergence of geometries, fluted textures, and the subtlety of untreated wood surfaces. He reached his zenith in woodworking with this piece, one of his last works before he gave up turning to pursue landscape architecture. The piece was turned between centers lengthwise, like a spindle turning, and textured while it was still mounted on the lathe. Then it was mounted crosswise, like a propeller, and a bowl shape was cut into the wood from the front and the back. The result is an elegantly elongated sculpture with an assortment of converging curves.

Mark Lindquist
115 *Analog #1*
1993
Spalted pecan
H 30 ½ × W 38 ½ × D 19 ½
Inscribed on underside inside the ring:
Mark Lindquist 1993
Lindquist Studios Archive Collection

Throughout his career, Mark Lindquist's choice of raw materials has always been in harmony with his sculptural intent (see 37, 54). In this recent work, he combines his concern for wood with a new interest in figuration. The crotch of a pecan tree has been inverted, creating a form that gives the impression of a body striding across the floor. The legs rest on turned supports reminiscent of Japanese sandals, which lift the massive shape slightly off the ground. The enormous size of *Analog #1* is typical of his work from the early 1990s, which was achieved using a huge lathe and tools controlled by robotics. The spalted figure of the wood plays dramatically against a complex adaptation of Lindquist's earlier "plunge cut" work, here transformed into a descending spiral of delicate, knife-edged planes.

Stephen Mark Paulsen
116 *Precolumbian #2*
1981
Ceanothus burl, ebony
H 6 ⅝ × Diam 1 ½
Inscribed on underside: SM Paulsen/1981
Wood Turning Center, Anonymous Loan,
1995.01.01.1801.

Stephen Paulsen does not use an ornamental lathe, but he achieves densely
textured effects reminiscent of ornamental turning through the technique
known as "chatterwork," in which the
turner allows his cutting tool to bounce
very slightly off of the surface of the
workpiece as it spins on the lathe.
Usually, this is seen as a sign of poor
tool control, but Paulsen is able to skill-
fully control the rhythm of the tool
strikes against the surface to create regular decorative patterns. *Precolumbian
#2* exhibits chatterwork on the top and
underside of the lid. The bottle retains
much of the quality of the original
wood blank from which it was turned,
from the natural opening halfway up
the shaft to the square outcropping at
the top (which preserves the original
dimensions of the wood block). Paulsen
has turned decorative cuts into the cor-
ners of these square forms, giving the
piece the severe geometric appearance
of a Mesoamerican temple structure.

The Nineties: Reframing and Deconstructing the Vessel

When one looks beyond technique, it is clear that all super-objects raise the fundamental question of the status of the crafts. Is wood turning a high-style decorative art, as might be implied by Stephen Paulsen's tableaux of ornamental vessels (117)? Or is it a species of formal sculpture, as Mark Lindquist and David Ellsworth have argued since the 1970s? As the field expanded in the late 1980s and came increasingly into contact with craft museums, collectors, and galleries that patterned themselves after fine arts institutions, the question of the proper context for turnings became more and more difficult to ignore. Increasingly, turners would direct their attention towards the logic of the museum pedestal that had begun to govern their craft.

The first turner to explore this conceptual terrain was Steve Loar, in the mid-1980s. Like Giles Gilson's slightly later *Point of View* (see 85), Loar's *Bowl for the Coastal Tribes* exhibited skepticism towards the traditional values of turning (118). Though its centerpiece is an exquisite spalted bowl, the exterior is sandblasted and painted in a Gilson-like disregard for the inherent qualities of the wood. More importantly, the piece features three flat, stilt-like legs that lift the bowl form into the air, ambiguously symbolizing the exalted status of the vessel in the professional turning field. Later, Loar would abandon the vessel for collaborative sculpture, suggesting perhaps that the artistic identity of the craftsperson has as much to do with community as with personal vision (119).

Loar's introspective turn was ahead of its time, but many young turners have taken up the issues he articulated. In 1989, both Christian Burchard and Michael Hosaluk reprised Loar's idea of elevating the vessel on a scaffold-like stand (120; see also 88). Two years later, Burchard (along with Robyn Horn, Stoney Lamar, John Jordan, and David Sengel) participated in a class entitled "Woodturning: Off the Ground" that Loar taught at the Arrowmont School of Arts and Crafts (Fig. 12). The class was expressly intended to provide professionals with a way of conceptually distinguishing their work from that of hobbyists. As Loar explained, "while not *everyone* can turn a bowl, the last ten years have shown that many people certainly can. How to make your work personal and unique becomes a question for many of us, once we begin to master the basic woodturning techniques. One way which is being explored is to somehow get the bowl higher up."[35] The gesture of elevating the vessel form announces its status as an object of aesthetic contemplation.

Fig. 12. Christian Burchard at Steve Loar's 1991 workshop at the Arrowmont School of Arts and Crafts, Gatlinburg, Tennessee.

In the wake of the 1991 class, Burchard continued to explore the theme of aesthetic framing. Instead of exalting a single vessel through presentation, he began to execute roughly spherical vessels that provide visual accompaniment for each other (121). In effect, the "frame" has been displaced from the scaffolding of his earlier work to the more subtle device of comparative grouping. Because each object is seen in relation to other, similar objects, Burchard is able to highlight the variations in form caused by wood movement (which varies depending on the size of each spheroid). Burchard's baskets are typical of the best work of the 1990s in that they redirect the viewer's attention away from exterior issues of status and towards nuanced, craft-based self-analysis. In many cases, today's turners revisit commonplace forms but infuse them with a metaphorical content by using carefully calibrated process and ornament (122 and 123).

Mark Lindquist and David Ellsworth have recently brought a similar reframing to bear on their own early work. Lindquist's *Analog #1*, for example, amplifies some of his earliest formal insights (see 115).

Stephen Mark Paulsen
117 *A Collection of Goblets, Chalices, and Spirit Vessels from the Seventeen Peoples of the Eight Inner Worlds*
1987
Wenge, mahogany, buckeye burl, ebony, kingwood, pink ivory, cocobolo, macadamia nut, wild lilac burl, tagua nut, antique ivory, olive, boxwood, pernambuco, manzanita, arariba, 18k and 22k gold
H 10 ½ × W 17 × D 3 ½
Wood Turning Center,
Gift of Dr. Irving Lipton, 1995.01.01.178G

This piece is one of a series in which Paulsen designed wall box settings for his miniature decorative turnings. The theme of the contained chamber was inspired by the example of treasure troves uncovered on archaeological digs. The frame is constructed from bricks of aged buckeye burl that imitate the color and marbling of stone, while the background of the "tomb" is covered in gold leaf. Some of the pieces are raised on pedestals, and the entire arrangement is placed behind glass and surrounded by a lavish, handmade frame. This elaborate context seems appropriate for the precious grouping of small-scale containers in exotic woods, which range from a chatterwork platter to fantastically tiny goblets.

Steve Loar
118 *Bowl for the Coastal Tribes*
1985
Spalted maple, veneered plywood, enamel and latex paint
H 12 ⅝ × W 16 × Diam 12
Collection of David Ellsworth

Bowl for the Coastal Tribes is a study in contrasts, from the distinction between the painted edges and the veneered faces of the plywood legs, to the vivid opposition of the burl in the interior and the sandblasted and painted exterior. Yet the work is most interesting for its foreshadowing of things to come. The figurative, almost cartoonish lines of the vessel's supports give the piece the appearance of a communal ceremonial utensil, suggesting the narrative bent that Loar's work would soon take. Furthermore, the raising of the bowl on asymmetrically arranged, stiltlike legs anticipates similar strategies that would be taken by Christian Burchard, Michael Hosaluk, and others in the late 1980s (see 88, 120).

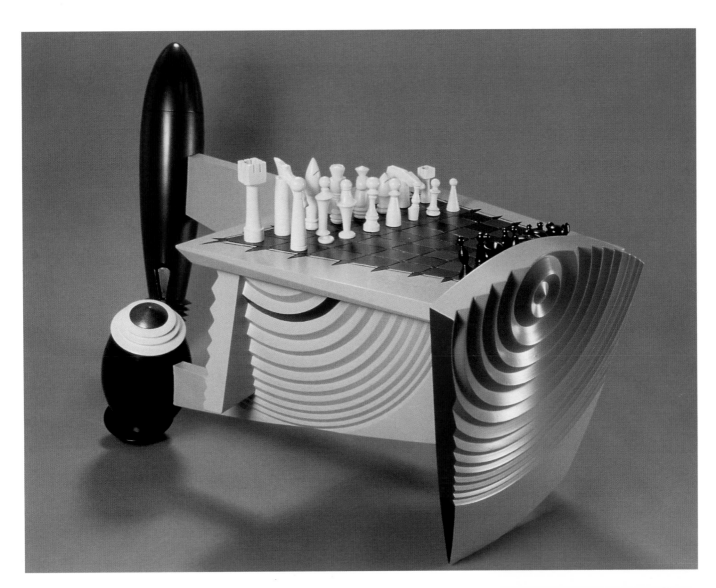

Michael Hosaluk, Mark Sfirri, Steve
Loar, Graham Carson, and class
119 *Chessed Table*
1997
Unidentified wood, paint
H 28 × W 54 × D 24
Inscribed in black ink on underside
of table with the names of the instructors
and students
Private Collection

Chessed Table is the result of a recent
collaboration between two classes at the
newly expanded woodworking studio
at Arrowmont School of Art and Crafts.
Michael Hosaluk and Mark Sfirri, who
have a history of collaborating with
each other, produced the table from
a large turned platter form with deep
concentric grooves cut into it. This
platter was cut up to form components
of the structure, which was embellished
with smaller turned elements made by
Hosaluk and Sfirri's students. The table
was then given over to Steve Loar, who
has a history of composing work from
scraps made by other artists. With
the help of his assistant Graham Carson,
Loar determined and applied the final
surface treatment, which uses color to
highlight the smaller marginal elements
in the composition. The finished product demonstrates both the collaborative
spirit in the wood turning field and
the continuing importance of informal
workshops as educational opportunities
for developing craftspeople.

Opposite side

Christian Burchard
120 *A Nest for Raven*
1991
Madrone burl, dyed beech, linen thread,
maple dowels
H 29 × W 12 × D 12
Incised on one leg near base: A Nest for
Raven, Christian Burchard [script] 1991
Collection of Louise Brown Albert

Though he was trained as a furnituremaker, Christian Burchard found his
true calling after teaching himself to
turn. Here, he combines a natural-edge
vessel form with a constructed base, to
contrast the natural and the manmade.
This disparity is emphasized by the
difference between the organic, modu-
lated surface of the madrone burl
and the linear geometry of the frame,
which is stained a velvety black. The
sculptural quality of the vessel is further
accentuated by its distortion, the result
of turning the burl while it was still
wet, or unseasoned. Burchard also began
to question the exalted status of the
hollow turned form by elevating the
turning within a construction of sticks,
a gesture that would eventually lead
to his serial basket forms of the 1990s.

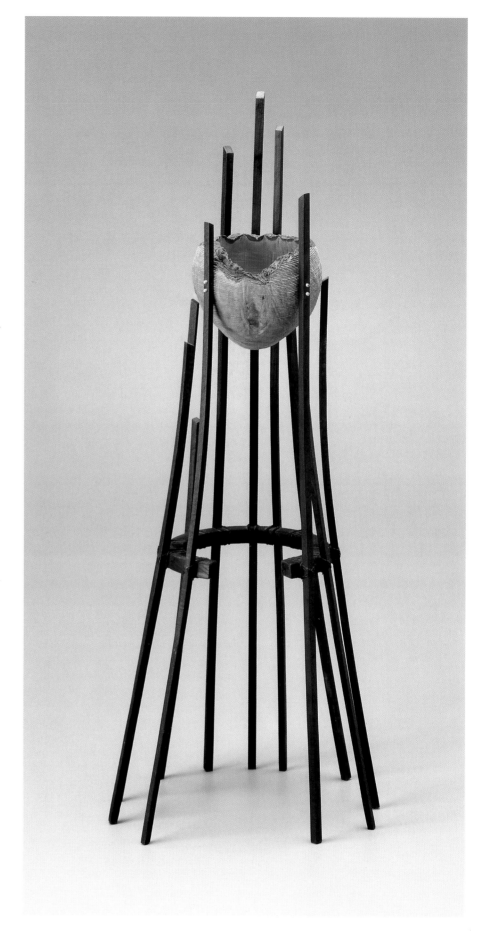

Christian Burchard
121 Set of Baskets
1998
Madrone burl
Diam ¼ to 10
Larger baskets inscribed on underside in
black ink: C BURCHARD *or* Christian Burchard
[script] *and* MADRONE BURL/"BASKETS";
smaller baskets inscribed in black ink: C.B.
Yale University Art Gallery,
purchased with a gift from David Waterbury,
BA 1958, and Ruth Waterbury,
1998.19.1.1–.21

Burchard's *Basket* series, of which there
are several versions, is an essay on the
relationships among multiple distorted
vessels. By turning burl wood to thin
dimensions while it is still wet (unseasoned), Burchard encourages drastic
wood movement. The lightness of
the baskets plays against the sense of the
weight, gravity, and materiality of the
wood, as the different size of each form
makes it warp in a different way. The
resulting variations imbue the whole
set with a playful group character, like
a gathering of individual but related
family members.

Merryll Saylan
122 *Tea Set*
1997
Box elder, paint
H 6 × Diam 6 (cup); Diam 5 ⅛ (saucer);
L 6 ⅛ × W 1 ⅜ × D ⅞ (spoon)
Inscribed in black ink on underside of saucer:
Merryll Saylan/ITE '97 BOX ELDER
Wood Turning Center,
Gift of the Artist, 1997.12.01.005G

Tea Set, made during Merryll Saylan's
residency at the Wood Turning Center's
1997 International Turning Exchange,
was an early piece in her current series
of still-life sculptures. In form, the work
closely follows the shape of a standard
domestic tea cup, saucer, and spoon.
But its slightly inflated size, painted
surface, and full contours announce
the piece as something more than
functional. In its serene evocation of
the intimacy of domestic ritual, *Tea Set*
is a quietly insistent meditation on
the dignity of everyday experiences.
It also continues a line of thinking
Saylan began in the 1970s by focusing
intensely on the humane essence of
a humble vessel form (see 93).

David Sengel
123 *Tea Cup*
1996
Pearwood, black paint, thorns
H 3 ³/₁₆ × Diam 5 ¼
Incised on underside of saucer: Sengel '96
Collection of Phyllis and Sidney Bresler

David Sengel's *Tea Cup* is an interesting
counterpoint to Merryll Saylan's nearly
contemporary *Tea Set* (122). Like Saylan,
Sengel has transformed the everyday,
familiar tea cup into a deeply emotional
object. But while Saylan has emphasized
the warmth and peacefulness of tea as
a domestic ritual, Sengel's cup is dark
and disturbing. Thorns bristle from the
areas that are touched most often:
the handle, the vessel wall below the
lip, and the saucer brim. An unrelieved
coating of black matte paint adds to
the sense of menace. Yet *Tea Cup* can
also be seen as having more ambiguous
spiritual and personal overtones. The
thorns, sent to Sengel by fellow turner
Robyn Horn, remind one of Christ
on the cross, and their use may have
been inspired by Sengel's father, who is
a Presbyterian minister. In this light,
the untouchable cup may be seen as a
deeply felt image of loss, or perhaps
a symbol of personal sacrifice.

His long-standing concern with raw material is visible in the use of a muscular, anthropomorphic tree form as the exterior of the work, while the inside of the piece is a breathtaking elaboration of Lindquist's early use of the chainsaw as a texturing tool. David Ellsworth's recent series of "dancing pots" is also marked by a sensitivity to the behavior of wood. Through the agency of wood movement, the vessel becomes an animated, active form that seems caught in mid-stretch. The wood is treated as a living medium rather than as a static material (124).

Virginia Dotson, Michael Hosaluk, and William Hunter have also mined their early styles for fresh sculptural ideas. Dotson's *Elements* series (125), Hosaluk's *Family* (126), and Hunter's *Converging Helix* (127) do not depart radically from the previous investigations of each artist. Yet all three turners have loosened up considerably. Their recent work exhibits both a willingness to break from the circularity and symmetry of earlier forms, and a keen sense of how the power of the vessel form can be abstracted and extended into space. This predilection for free-form composition is shared by many turners who have emerged in the 1990s, including Betty Scarpino, whose elegant plate-stands literally frame and extend the circular shapes of her painted and textured turnings (128).

Lindquist, Ellsworth, Dotson, Hosaluk, and Hunter continue to arrive at fresh insights because they are able to balance the traditional attachment to "form and figure" ideals with a challenging, self-critical attitude towards sculptural content. This is the dynamic that has driven the field for the past twenty-five years, and it continues to be important in the wood turning scene of today. Partly this is because of the unique layering that is possible in a craft community that continues to honor its elder statesmen, such as Bob Stocksdale (129). But the current generation of turners also includes individuals like Dan Kvitka (130), Derek Bencomo (131), and spooncarver Norm Sartorius (132), who continue to explore the beauty of well-figured wood transformed with sensitivity and skill.

The most promising developments of the 1990s, however, are more evocative of the attitude of the painter-turners of the 1980s, who looked to developments in design and the fine arts for new sources of vitality. Los Angeles wood turner Connie Mississippi, for example, comes from a contemporary sculpture background. Her *Black Hole* addresses the traditional concerns of turning even as it charts new aesthetic territory (133). By reconceiving the interior of a vessel form as a series of stages, Mississippi symbolizes the temporal quality of gradually pushing a tool into a spinning mass of wood in order to make a hollow interior. One keenly senses the time and labor that have gone into the excavation of the piece; its layers, like the strata of an archaeological dig, are the record of Mississippi's engagement with the form. Another provocative contribution to the field is Gord Peteran's *Untitled So Far* (134). Peteran is not a turner, but a furnituremaker involved with the Canadian contemporary art scene. Despite appearances, his piece, a found spindle turning wrapped in red leather, is not an attack on turning. Rather, it interacts with the history of turning in a thoughtful way, suggesting that the traditional values attached to wood, such as color and tactility, can easily be displaced. The leather wrapping the piece retains the warmth of the wood even as it conceals the wood from view.

The continuing dialogue between such symbolic approaches to lathe-turned objects, on the one hand, and contemporary "form and figure" turners on the other, suggests that wood turning has come full circle even as it has matured into a distinct craft discipline. Before 1976,

David Ellsworth
124 *Lunar Pot*
1996
White oak with spalted sapwood
H 10 × W 9 × D 10
Incised on underside: 1996/Ellsworth [script]
"Lunar Pot"/White Oak
Collection of Gayle and Andrew Camden

In his recent work, David Ellsworth
has continued to explore the design
potential of wood orientation. In
the early 1990s, he moved away from the
use of exotic and figured materials to
plainer woods from his own backyard.
But if the inherent beauty of the figure
and color of special woods is absent,
Ellsworth compensates by subtly manipulating the internal dynamics of his
local, common material. Here, the form
has been fashioned from unseasoned
wood, which distorts during the drying
process. The result is a swollen oval
shape that accentuates the color contrast
of the heartwood and sapwood (see
also 62). In an additional innovation,
Ellsworth reacts to the cracking of the
drying wood by bridging the cracks
with wooden "stitches" that graphically
interact with the rays emanating from
the center of the log.

Virginia Dotson
125 *Elements Series #1: Air*
1998
Pau marfim plywood, paint
H 4 ⅞ × Diam 16 ¾
Collection of the Artist

Air is typical of Virginia Dotson's recent work, which continues her earlier exploration of laminated layers of wood as a metaphor for natural forms. Like the other works in her *Elements* series, *Air* symbolizes one of the four fundamental elements that compose the world (a myth that dates back to ancient Greek physics). For Dotson the spiral form of the piece, made by cutting voids into the bowl form, represents a whirlwind of air "coalescing into wind and weather." The atmospheric effect is enhanced by Dotson's choice of

material, a high-quality dense plywood desirable for its consistency and subtle patterning. By turning through the layers of the vertically laminated plywood, a pattern of concentric circles is established. Selective bleaching and the negative spaces cut into the form create the illusion of circles spiraling out from the central void.

Michael Hosaluk
126 *Family*
1998
Wood, acrylic paint
H 6 × W 24 × L 24
Each piece incised: Hosaluk
Collection of the Artist

Michael Hosaluk's *Family* is a deceptively simple-looking sculptural grouping of hollow containers. To construct each box in the set, Hosaluk began with a series of turned cylinders of different diameters. He cut out the center of each cylinder longitudinally and at an angle. The halves were then reglued, resulting in a series of truncated cones that are football-shaped in section. The ends of these pieces were then sliced off, also at an angle, and the forms were glued together in a chain, resulting in a twisting, snakelike hollow box.

Finally, the interior was textured with a small power tool called a dremel, and the whole piece was painted with a black acrylic gesso. The central joint of each piece is left unglued, so that the piece can be opened and used as a container; the two halves can also be rotated 180 degrees with respect to each other, changing the overall shape. Hosaluk also intends the whole group to be rearranged periodically, so that the piece is fully interactive.

William Hunter
127 *Converging Helix*
1999
Cocobolo
H 10 × W 18 × Diam 23
Incised on side of larger element: #1414
"CONVERGING HELIX" Wm. Hunter [script]
1999
Collection of David and Nancy Trautenberg

William Hunter's career has long been premised on the virtues of his extraordinary hand carving (see 101, 102). In 1989, he began cutting all the way through the walls of his vessels in order to create open-work spirals, vegetal forms, and other abstract sculptural compositions. This process of creating form through subtractive carving has been taken to its logical conclusion in Hunter's current work, of which *Converging Helix* is an outstanding example. The turned vessel shape is nothing but a distant memory, pre-

served in the roughly circular embrace of two interlocked arcs. Hunter's choice of an exotic hardwood is partly pragmatic, as the material must hold a crisp edge in order to emphasize the quality of the carving. But he has also carefully selected his wood because of its attractive color and pattern. Despite his recent departure from the vessel, then, Hunter continues to anchor his work in the "form and figure" tradition.

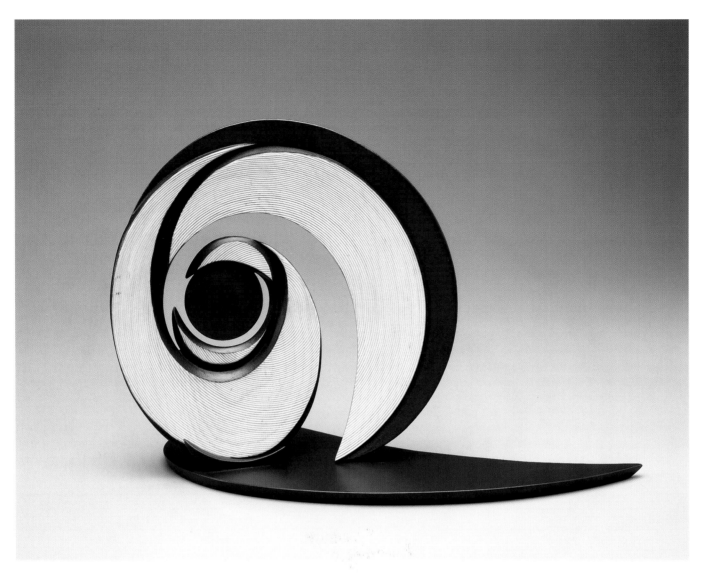

Betty J. Scarpino
128 *The Most Indirect Route*
1997
Turned, carved, bleached, and ebonized
maple, with lacquer and graphite
H 15 × W 3 × D 12
Incised in script on upright element:
Betty J. Scarpino 1997; incised in script
on base: Betty J. Scarpino 1997 "The Most
Indirect Route"
Yale University Art Gallery,
Gift of Ruth and David Waterbury, BA 1958,
in honor of Patricia E. Kane, 2000.93.3

Betty Scarpino uses her experience as
a furnituremaker and wood sculptor to
create sculptural frames that display
her turned, carved, and painted plates
in a vertical format. *The Most Indirect
Route* is one of the most effective of this
group of "Altered Plates." A flat stand
leads gently into a black arc encircling
the bottom of the plate, which is in
turn echoed by a series of curves that
spiral into a black circular center.
The effect is that the plate seems to be
composed entirely of compositional
framing elements. Scarpino's use
of paint, inspired by the example set
by Merryll Saylan, is restrained and
intended to complement rather than
overwhelm the color of the natural
wood surface. Similarly, though she
extensively carves the plate form after
turning it, the composition emphasizes
the centrifugal energy of an object
made on the lathe.

Bob Stocksdale
129 *Bowl*
1987
Oak
H 3 × W 10 $^{15}/_{16}$ × D 9 $^{9}/_{16}$
Burned on underside: Oak/from/
England/Bob/Stocksdale/1987
Wood Turning Center, 1995.01.01.237

Throughout most of his long career, Bob Stocksdale turned his bowl and platter forms with an absolutely uniform wall thickness. Then, in 1985, he was inspired by the bowls of Irish turner Liam O'Neill, which had a uniformly thick wall with a wide, flat rim. Stocksdale emulated this last feature, but varied O'Neill's design by swelling the vessel wall into a wide lip. This way, he was able to have a light, thin-walled bowl that was topped off by a flat rim. This example of Stocksdale's new technique also features a shallow, undulating shape derived from the outside edge of the log. The subtle irregularity of the lip complements the oak's figure, which exhibits a shimmering illusion of three-dimensional depth.

Dan Kvitka
130 *Hollow Vessel*
1997
Amboyna burl
H 6 × W 13
Incised on underside: KVITKA #91/
AMBOYNA/1997
Collection of Kenneth Spitzbard

Dan Kvitka is one of the outstanding current exponents of the "form and figure" tradition that has been at the heart of the wood turning field since its earliest days. To a large degree, Kvitka's concerns are those of the thousands of craftspeople who pursue wood turning as an avocation; he looks for well-figured wood and tries to convey the beauty of the wood in the final form of the piece. What sets Kvitka apart from the many turners who pursue this goal is the enormous scale of his pieces, the fine quality of the woods that he turns, and his distinctive, geometric shapes. These simple forms invariably feature broad areas of flat or gently sloping surface across which the figure can play freely. The "flaw" or break in the wall of this vessel is unusual in Kvitka's oeuvre: typically, he brooks no imperfection in his material.

Derek A. Bencomo
131 *Pacific Rim Series:*
Gift from the Rain Forest
1999
Kamani
H 15 × W 18 × D 12
Incised on underside: DEREK '99/MAUI HI/
KAMANI/WOOD
Collection of Robert M. Bohlen

Hawaiian turner Derek Bencomo mar-
ries traditional "form and figure"
concerns with the explosive compositional potential of multicenter turning.
In this technique, the workpiece is
remounted several times on the faceplate
of the lathe so that it can be turned
at different positions (see also 86, 110,
111). Multicenter turning often results
in an illustrative, even mechanical
effect; but in Bencomo's hands it is a
way to rough out a smoothly flowing,
organic form. As is typical of many
turners of the 1990s, he finishes the
form extensively with hand carving so
that the circularity created by the
lathe is largely obscured.

Norm Sartorius
132 *Spoon from a Forgotten Ceremony*
1991
African blackwood
H 2¾ × W 4 × L 20½
West Virginia State Museum, Charleston,
Mu 92–20

Norm Sartorius has revived the craft of
spoon carving, making one-of-a-kind
decorative pieces whose shapes are
largely determined by the figure, shape,
and coloration of a particular piece of
wood. While none of Sartorius's pieces
are really functional, this spoon is
quite aggressive in its freedom from
pragmatic concerns, with two handles
meeting in a bowl. It was the first in
a series of two-handled pieces, each of
which was turned and carved from a
single piece of wood. He has since made
other designs incorporating turned
handles. *Spoon from a Forgotten Ceremony*
was thus the work that opened the
turning field to Sartorius, giving him
access to a new group of collectors and
exhibition opportunities.

Connie Mississippi
133 *The Black Hole*
1992
Laminated plywood, paint, rubber, nails
Diam 37 ⅜ × D 21
Collection of the Artist

Connie Mississippi can be taken as the antithesis of the "form and figure" turners of earlier decades. She uses plywood to build up her forms because it is easily obtained and infinitely expandable in dimension. For her, the importance of the material is that it be flexible and easily manipulated, not that it be inherently expressive. Here, she combines plywood with an even less organic material, black rubber. Yet the results Mississippi achieves are quite evocative, partly because of the very impersonality of her industrially fabricated materials, and partly because of the startling simplicity of her compositions. *The Black Hole* captures the infinite expanse of outer space with a series of textured, curved planes receding from a facade of "constellations" outlined in nail heads.

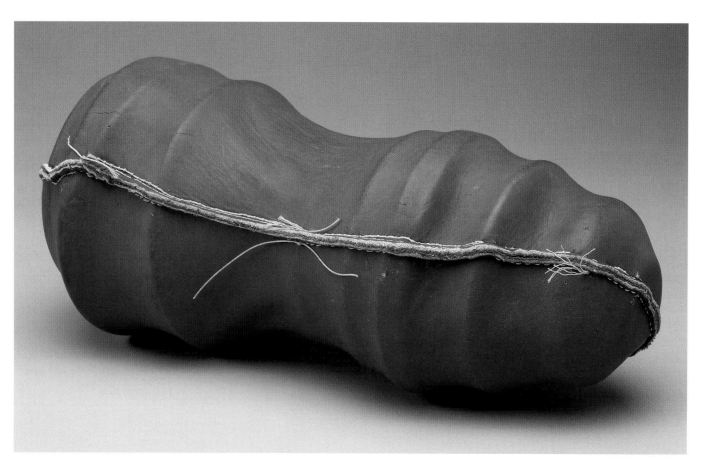

Gord Peteran
134 *Untitled So Far*
1996
Leather, wood, linen thread
L 14 × W 6 ½ × D 7
Scratched in leather on end: "PETERAN 1996"
Wood Turning Center,
Gift of Albert and Tina LeCoff,
1996.11.20.001G

Furnituremaker and sculptor Gord Peteran made *Untitled So Far* at the Emma Lake gathering in 1996. Organized by Michael Hosaluk, the event was one of an ongoing series in which wood turners, furnituremakers, and other craftspeople congregate in Saskatchewan to create collaborative work. Emma Lake products are usually as chaotic in spirit as the event itself; but Peteran participated in the goings-on with characteristic finesse, plucking a large spindle turning from a scrap heap and covering it with a hand-sewn sheath of red leather. This simple gesture revealed the latent sensuality of the cast-off piece's peaks and valleys, transforming an anonymous utilitarian turning into a mysterious, sexually charged object. As Peteran writes, *Untitled So Far* "by no means abandons traditional turning, but employs the intrinsic kinetic nature of the process as a catapult to convey something vital, something primal, something universal."

the lathe was only one tool among many in a woodworker's shop, and wood turning a means to an end rather than an end in itself. In the late 1970s, turners began to explore the possibilities of the lathe itself and to think about the formal possibilities of wood. In the ensuing decade, wood turning was relatively circumscribed, its concerns intrinsic to the dynamics of lathe and material. This trend culminated in the technique-oriented super-objects of the late 1980s. But alongside this general escalation of skill has grown a counter-current, in which an engagement with the status and the interior dynamics of craft has taken precedence over sensitivity to wood and technical facility. In retrospect, the painted works of the 1980s can be seen as the point of origin for this cooler, more intellectual strain. The satirical bent of such work was liberating, and currently formalism is gradually being displaced by a more broadly expressive, literate approach. Today, we may again be at a point where craftspeople envision lathe turning not as an end in itself, but as a means to the expression of ideas.

Notes

1   The first nine symposia in the series were held at the woodshop of the George School (a Quaker elementary and high school) in Newtown, Pennsylvania, from 1976 to 1980. See also note 5, below.

2   The organizers invited several production turners who were involved with architectural detailing, like Manny Erez, or furnituremaking, like Paul Eshelman, and even a musical instrument maker, Michael Hornpiper. See John Kelsey, "Turning Conference: Notes and Information on a Recent Gathering," *Fine Woodworking* 1, no. 3 (Summer 1976): 44–45.

3   GAS was formed at the Penland School of Handcrafts in North Carolina in 1971, the same year that the Pilchuck Glass School was founded as a craft-oriented commune north of Seattle. On the effects of these organizations in the glass world, see Suzanne Frantz, *Contemporary Glass* (New York: Abrams, 1989), 129–34; and Tina Oldknow, *Pilchuck: A Glass School* (Seattle: University of Washington Press, 1996).

4   See Richard Starr, "Last Was Best," *Fine Woodworking* 32 (January/February 1982), 61. Among the participants in the symposia were Jake Brubaker, Frank Cummings, Leo Doyle, David Ellsworth, Giles Gilson, Stephen Hogbin, Ray Huskey, C. R. (Skip) Johnson, Frank Knox, Melvin and Mark Lindquist, Ed Moulthrop, Thomas Nicosia, Dale Nish, Rude Osolnik, Del Stubbs, Alan Stirt, Bob Stocksdale, and Jack Straka.

5   The "Turned Object Show," juried by David Ellsworth and Rude Osolnik, was exhibited at the symposium at Bucks County Community College; it was then shown at the Richard Kagan Gallery and Ruth Snyderman's Works Gallery, located across the street from each other in Philadelphia. Both galleries were important early promoters of studio craft in wood, including both lathe turnings and furniture. Finally, the show traveled to the Greenville County Museum of Art in South Carolina and the Squires Student Center at Virginia Polytechnic State University. The exhibition was accompanied by a catalogue entitled *A Gallery of Turned Objects.*

6   The techniques of turning spalted wood (that is, wood figured by the intrusion of fungus) and creating hollow vessels were popularized not only through conference demonstrations but also by Lindquist's article "Turning Spalted Wood," *Fine Woodworking* 11 (Summer 1978): 54–59; and Ellsworth's "Hollow Turnings," *Fine Woodworking* 16 (May/June 1979): 62–66.

7   See Mark Lindquist, *Sculpting Wood: Contemporary Tools and Techniques* (Worcester, Mass.: Davis Publications, 1986), 216ff; and Robert Hobbs, *Mark Lindquist: Revolutions in Wood* (Richmond, Va.: Hand Workshop Art Center, 1995).

8   The other turners in the exhibition were his father Melvin Lindquist, Ed Moulthrop, and Bob Stocksdale. The prestige of the event was enhanced when the Metropolitan Museum of Art in New York acquired pieces by both Lindquists from the Renwick show for their permanent collection (see 33).

9   For more on Lindquist's interest in modernist sculptural precedent, see *Sculpting Wood*, ix, 178.

10   Melvin Lindquist and Ed Moulthrop had made some initial attempts to widen the interior volume with a straight scraper or gouge held at an angle through the vessel opening (see 32, 38), but Ellsworth was the first studio turner to employ a bent-shaft cutting tool.

11   On Nakashima, see Michael Stone, *Contemporary American Woodworkers* (Salt Lake City: Peregrine Smith, 1986); and George Nakashima, *The Soul of A Tree* (New York: Kodansha, 1981).

12   In 1975, Nish had authored *Creative Woodturning* (Provo: Brigham Young University Press), the first comprehensive book on lathe processes. The text impressed Albert LeCoff, who invited Nish to teach at several of the early symposia. Inspired in turn, Nish based his conferences in Utah on the informal model established at the George School. Nish also published a follow-up book, *Artistic Woodturning* (Provo: Brigham Young University Press, 1980), which included a section of color illustrations showing work by leading professional turners, most of whom Nish had met at the George School. See also Nish's final book, *Master Woodturners* (Provo: Artisan Press, 1985).

13   John Kelsey, "The Turned Bowl: The End of Infancy for a Craft Reborn," *Fine Woodworking* 32 (January/February 1982): 57.

14   Stubbs lived and worked in the craft-oriented community of Chico, California, and he had been an apprentice to Oregon myrtlewood turner Paul English.

15 Lamar questionnaire, 1998, Wood Turning Center Archives.

16 See my "California Spirit: Rediscovering the Furniture of J. B. Blunk," *Woodwork* 59 (October 1999): 22–31.

17 See Edward S. Cooke, Jr., "Wood in the 1980s: Expansion or Commodification?," in *Contemporary Crafts and the Saxe Collection*, ed. Davira Taragin (New York: Hudson Hills Press, 1993), 154.

18 Irving Fischman, "Checkered Bowls," *Fine Woodworking* 1, no. 1 (Winter 1975): 16–19.

19 Ibid.

20 Seitzman questionnaire, 1998, Wood Turning Center Archives.

21 For an explanation of Draper and Latven's technique, see their "Segmented Turning," *Fine Woodworking* 54 (September/October 1985): 64–67.

22 Michael Shuler, "Segmented Turning," *Fine Woodworking* 76 (May/June 1989): 72–75.

23 For a typically tepid response to Gilson's work, see John Perrault, "Turning Point," *American Craft* 47, no. 1 (February/March 1989): 30.

24 David Sloan, "Arrowmont Turning Conference: New Work, New Guild," *Fine Woodworking* 56 (January/February 1986): 64–66.

25 I am indebted to David Ellsworth, who was the first director of AAW, for information about the organization's formation and purposes.

26 In 1997, they joined with newer collectors to form an informational organization that promises to do much to support the expansion of the turning and furniture fields. See Alan Lacer, "Collectors of Wood Art: Strong Kickoff for a New Organization," *American Woodturner* 13, no. 4 (Winter 1998): 40–42.

27 Connell has been important in raising the institutional profile of the craft. In addition to her efforts to place wood turnings in museum collections and expand the circle of wood turning collectors, she has been an active curator and writer in the field. See, for example, her work on Rude Osolnik in "Grandmaster of Woodturning," *Turning Points* 10, no. 3 (Fall 1997): 15–18.

28 On Fleming's time-consuming process, see Bob Hawks, "Floral Visions," *Fine Woodworking* 99 (April 1993): 54–57.

29 Garth Clark and Margie Hughto, *A Century of Ceramics in the United States, 1878–1978* (New York: E. P. Dutton/Everson Museum of Art, 1979), 200–203.

30 On Yoshimura, see Susan Edmiston, "Fumio Yoshimura," *Craft Horizons* 31, no. 4 (August 1971): 22–25, 71; on Cooper, see my "California Dreaming: The Second Generation of Studio Furniture Making in Northern California," in *Furniture Studio One: The Heart of the Functional Arts*, ed. John Kelsey and Rick Mastelli (Free Union, Va.: The Furniture Society, 1999): 32–42.

31 The gender dynamic in the wood turning field has only recently become a topic of open public discourse, notably in a panel on women in wood turning at the 1997 World Turning Conference. The panelists were Holzapfel, Merryll Saylan, Betty Scarpino, and Connie Mississippi. See Merryll Saylan, "Women's Role in Woodworking," *Woodwork* 51 (June 1998): 65–67; and *Papers from the 1993 World Turning Conference* (Philadelphia: Wood Turning Center, 2000).

32 On this property of ornament, see Karsten Harries, *The Bavarian Rococo Church: Between Faith and Reason* (New Haven: Yale University Press, 1983), 246.

33 A telling document of McKay's technical approach is his detailed explanation of his own improvements to the standard hollowing technique pioneered by David Ellsworth; see Hugh McKay, "Articulated Hollowing System: Doing the Impossible Easily," *American Woodturner* 12, no. 2 (June 1997): 20–23.

34 Frank M. Knox, "Ornamental Turnery: The Hobby of Kings and Princes," *Antique Trader Weekly* (Dubuque, Iowa), October 1977; John Kelsey, "Ornamental Turning," *Fine Woodworking* 1, no. 4 (Fall 1976): 46.

35 Steve Loar, "Woodturning: Off the Ground," unpublished course description, 1991.

Wood: Its Properties in Relation to its Use in Turning

Graeme P. Berlyn and
Andrew D. Richardson,
Yale University
School of Forestry &
Environmental Studies

Wood has been a source of service and beauty for humans since long before the dawn of history. It provided fuel for fire and was among man's earliest weapons, in the form of clubs, spears, bows and arrows, and blow-guns; in war it served as shields and even armor. In addition, wood was used to make traps for animals and fish, and it was the basis for the earliest transportation, from sleds and snowshoes to dugouts and wheeled carts. It provided structural materials for housing, fences, and forts. Wood was fashioned into ladles, bowls, utensils, toys, and tools of many kinds, and even today it serves as a source of medicines and other chemical extracts. If wood's utility made it an indispensable resource for human survival, appreciation of its beauty in time resulted in myriad artistic uses as well: for example, carvings, totems, musical instruments, furniture, and religious artifacts. Certain woods ultimately proved more suitable than others for such uses. It is the purpose of this essay to provide some insights into the anatomy, chemistry, and formation of wood so that the reader might better understand the particular texture, figure, color, and physical properties that are the basis of its beauty as well as its utility.

Wood Anatomy

Tree trunks, or boles, stand erect and grow upward in order to collect the energy of the sun and convert it to chemical bonds through the process of photosynthesis. Certain useful aggregates of these chemical bonds we call food (e.g., fruit, nuts, vegetables, and root crops); others we call wood. A tree's utilization of air and light necessitates radial as well as vertical growth, so that the trunk does not buckle under its own weight. This accounts for the large sizes of tree boles, which are the source of boards and sections of wood that can be used in turning and in carving large objects such as totem poles. A simplified representation of a tree is shown in Fig 1. Examination of a cross section of a well-sanded or turned piece of wood, or of a stump in the forest, reveals much about both wood in general and also about the wood of that particular species. In many cases, you can identify the wood just by the characteristics of the cross section (Figs. 2, 3). In the center, there is usually a very small circle of lighter colored tissue that is called the pith. Around the pith are concentric layers of wood. In most temperate zone trees and in many tropical woods, these rings are annual increments—the layers of wood produced each year.

Although the transition to bark appears abrupt, in reality there is a layer of cells between the wood and the bark called the cambial zone, where the new wood and bark are formed each year (see 62). In each radial row of the undifferentiated cells of the cambial zone is a unique cell called a cambial initial. These initials constitute the vascular cambium. Each initial is surrounded by the daughter cells it has produced; those to the "outside" (toward the bark) will develop (differentiate) into phloem (food-transporting tissue), and those to the "inside" (toward the pith) will form xylem (water-transporting tissue) (Fig. 4). The initials and their derivatives collect carbohydrates and other growth substances from the leaves, and minerals and water from the roots. These materials are then used to construct the cells and cell walls that make up bark and wood. Close examination of a cross section of both bark and wood reveals that most cells are oriented longitudinally (lengthwise in relation to the tree bole), but there are radial lines, called rays, radiating out from the pith. The distance between these rays as well as ray size affect the appearance of wood and its ability to take a finish. Rays are especially visible in some oak species.

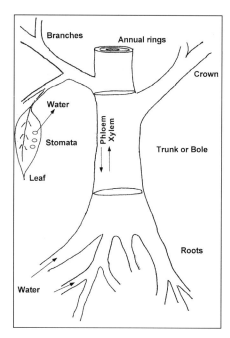

Fig. 1. A simplified tree, showing roots, trunk, crown, leaves, stomata, xylem, and phloem.

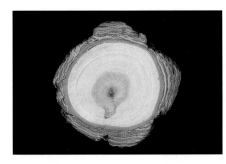

Fig. 2. Douglas fir (*Pseudotsuga menziesii*) root cross section, illustrating heartwood, sapwood, and corky bark. Note irregular heartwood probably due to wound response.

Fig. 3. Osage orange (*Maclura pomifera*) bole cross section, illustrating pith, heartwood, sapwood, and bark.

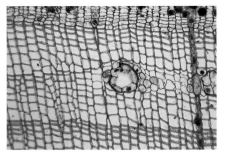

Fig. 4. The vascular cambium in white pine (*Pinus strobus*), with phloem on the top and xylem on the bottom.

The bark of a tree is actually a complex tissue consisting of an inner bark and an outer bark. The inner bark is composed of phloem tissue, which conducts food materials generally from the leaves to the rest of the tree, including the roots. The outer bark consists of dead phloem tissue (that was once part of the inner bark) and layers of cork tissue (periderm) that separate dead phloem from the inner bark. Formed by its own initials in the cork cambia (phellogen), cork tissue helps to protect the tree from insects, fire, fungi, water loss, heat, cold, and other stresses (Fig. 2).

In addition to the cross-sectional plane, wood also has two longitudinal planes: the tangential and the radial. If you imagine cutting off slices of wood tangential to the annual rings, the resulting view will be the tangential-longitudinal plane (Fig. 5). Here cells are seen in long view, interspersed with the cross-sectional view of the ray cells that appear in a linear group of vertically stacked cells that are one or more cells in width. The radial view is a bit more difficult to visualize. If you imagine cutting the cross section of a stump like an apple pie and then view the slice on its side, you see wood in its radial plane (Fig. 6). Here the rays appear in their cellular long view and are stacked up one on top of the other. The particular appearance of radially cut wood is also due to the contrast in many species of trees between the cell wall thickness of wood produced early in the growing season (earlywood) and the thicker cell walls of wood produced later in the growing season (latewood).

The wood around the pith is generally much darker than the wood in a band near the bark (see Figs. 2, 3). The dark wood is called heartwood and the light wood is called sapwood. Heartwood is composed almost exclusively of dead cells, while sapwood is about 90 percent dead on an area basis. It is the sapwood that functions in water transport, moving water into the roots from the soil, up the tree through the xylem to the leaves, and out of the leaves through the stomata in a process known as transpiration. Heartwood has no capacity for water transport. Its dark color comes from organic compounds called extractives, which are made in the rays as they die at the sapwood/heartwood transition points in the xylem. Extractives, including resins and gums, help to protect the tree and prevent rot. Different species produce different amounts and types of these extractive chemicals, and thus heartwood colors can vary in hue and intensity (Figs. 7, 8; compare 53, 124).

When wood is turned, carved, or sawn, its color and texture as well as the amount of each plane of view (cross, radial, tangential) exposed on the surface greatly affect its appearance. The different planes not only reflect light differently, they also absorb different amounts of varnish, oils, stains, and other wood finishes. These characteristics are a function of the anatomy of wood and its microscopic structure.

Softwoods and Hardwoods

If you look at a freshly cut or well-sanded cross section with a 10-power magnifying glass, it is possible to determine the tree's category (botanical group). In general, there are two main types of woods, softwoods and hardwoods. These terms are not perfect, as a few of the softwoods are actually harder than some of the hardwoods. For example, balsa wood is technically a hardwood, although it is much lighter than many of the so-called softwoods like pine and douglas fir. This is because the categories really refer to botanical groups, not weight or density of wood. The softwoods are conifers (cone bearers) like pine, fir, spruce, cedar, larch,

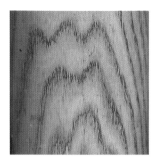

Fig. 5. Tangential-longitudinal section illustrated in a white ash (*Fraxinus americana*) baseball bat.

Fig. 6. Radial longitudinal section of douglas fir (*Pseudotsuga menziesii*).

Fig. 7. Heartwood in vermillion (*Pterocarpus dalbergiodes*).

Fig. 8. Heartwood in purple heart (*Peltogyne paniculata*).

hemlock, and douglas fir (see 108). The hardwoods, from which most wood turnings are fashioned, include the flowering trees of the group called dicotyledons. The familiar hardwoods include oak, maple, walnut, chestnut, hickory, basswood, beech, magnolia, poplars, and many tropical woods like mahogany (*Swietenia*), Spanish cedar (*Cedrela*), rosewood (*Dalbergia spruceana*), cocobolo (*Dalbergia retusa*), and teak (*Tectona*). Whereas conifers comprise only several hundred different species, dicotyledons consist of many thousands of diverse species.

Conifers evolved earlier than hardwoods, and their relatively simple wood structure reflects this. Softwood is primarily composed of a single type of long, spindle-shaped cell called a tracheid. Conifer tracheids are much longer than hardwood fibers and are thus especially useful for fine paper-making.

The texture of a softwood is determined by the tangential diameter of the tracheids, which is usually measured in the cross-sectional plane of the wood. Redwoods are the most coarse-textured of softwoods, while yew is among the finest textured. Coarse-textured woods absorb more stain, varnish, or paint than fine-textured woods and are less smooth in appearance.

The Samuel James Record Wood Collection, formerly held at Yale University, once contained over 55,000 samples representing some 12,000 genera and over 20,000 species, most of them hardwoods. The wood of hardwoods is much more specialized than that of conifers. Hardwoods of course have the same three planes of view, the cross-sectional, the radial, and the tangential. However, there are many different kinds of cells in hardwoods, resulting in much greater variations in appearance. Hardwoods also produce a greater variety of chemicals so that the variation in color as well as texture is much more extensive. Whereas softwoods are primarily composed of longitudinal tracheids that serve both for support and water conduction, hardwoods are distinguished by a greater division of labor. In addition to fiber tracheids that primarily provide support, a new kind of conducting multicellular structure evolved in hardwoods. Called vessels, these structures may be many times larger in diameter than conifer tracheids and therefore can conduct significantly greater amounts of water.

The thickness of the walls of the vessels as well as their shape vary, and their distribution in the wood also forms a characteristic pattern. On the basis of vessel distribution, hardwoods are separated into two general categories. In the first, known as ring-porous hardwood, the vessels that form early in the spring are large and form a band around the tree; the later-formed vessels are much smaller in diameter (Fig. 9). Exemplified by red oak, elm, ash, northern white oak, hickory, and American chestnut, ring-porous hardwoods are generally found in temperate regions. The second type of hardwood, termed diffuse-porous, exhibits no difference in the diameter distribution of earlywood and latewood vessels. Some woods like walnut and butternut are intermediate and so termed semi-ring porous (Fig. 10), while others are intermediate but tend to be more like the diffuse porous hardwoods and so are termed semi-diffuse porous.

Because of the vast number of species, each with their particular biosynthetic pathways, there is a great variety of color in the hardwoods. Even individuals of the same species will show variation depending on growing conditions; degree and type of insect, fungal, and mechanical damage experienced by the tree; as well as its own distinct genetic makeup.

Hardwoods also produce a larger variety of chemicals, so that the variation in color as well as texture is far more extensive than in softwoods. Heartwood can be a solid color or streaked in a cornucopia of colors (see 14). Heartwood is black in ebony (*Diospyros ebenum*), persimmon (*Diospyros virginiana*), African blackwood (*Dalbergia melanoxylon*), and in some individual trees of magnolia, among others (see 113). It is red in rosewood (*Dalbergia*), blue or blue-streaked in blue mahoe (*Hibiscus elatus*), dark chocolate in walnut (*Juglans nigra*), lighter chocolate in butternut (*Juglans cinerea*), and yellow in fustic (*Chlorophorea tinctorea*) and in the many yellow woods (e.g., *Enantia chlorantha*) (Figs. 7, 8).

The death of ray cells at the sapwood-heartwood boundary initiates the formation of heartwood. As the ray cells die, they undergo a surge in metabolism and synthesize many organic chemicals (extractives) and produce breakdown products of various sorts that initiate the formation of the hardwood heartwood. Starch and many minerals including calcium are transported away from the sapwood-heartwood boundary. Heartwood formation is an active process, but once formed it contains no reclaimable storage compounds and is not an active metabolic compartment of the tree. Thus, the heartwood is assumed to perform the purely mechanical function of support. However, it may also act as a reservoir for both water and mineral nutrients. Heartwood comprises the bulk of the wood of mature trees and has the characteristic color we associate with quality hardwoods. Thus much of the hardwood used in wood products is heartwood. It is also the most resistant to insect and fungal attack because of the organic chemicals deposited in it.

As is usual in biological phenomena, there is much variation in the expression of heartwood. Though average trees of the temperate and northern zones initiate heartwood in thirty to fifty years, some species, such as alder (*Alnus*), black gum (*Nyssa*), some maples (*Acer*), birch (*Betula*), and horse chestnut (*Aesculus hippocastanum*), do not typically show the characteristics of heartwood for a century or more. Some living ray cells may persist for many years. Other woods such as beech (*Fagus*), called ripewoods, have light-colored heartwood: ray cells die in the usual pattern, but the strongly colored extractives characteristic of heartwood are not produced. Wound heartwood (also called pathogenic, false, blackheart, or traumatic) can also form as a response to attack by fungi and insects. Normally this is easily identified by its patchy form, but the infection can spread and pathological heartwood may be superimposed over the normal pattern, giving unusual designs and coloration due to higher secondary chemical production. Tapping of sugar maple may cause this type of heartwood formation.

Figure in Wood

The beauty of wood has long been appreciated. The ancient Greeks and Romans prized the gleaming highlights of their tables made from root burls of "thuya" (*Tetraclinus articulata*). The three planes of wood are responsible for the mysteries of wood figure and reflectance. Figure is most dependent on grain alignment—the way in which the wood cells are arranged along the tree bole. The grain may be inclined, spiral, twisted, or interlocked (intermittent alternation of grain direction). In the latter, the changes in angle result in alternating spiral helices of the wood elements. Wood with interlocked grain is sometimes called roey wood or roe-grained in the trade, especially if the stripes are short. Straighter grain, finer texture, and thinner and more uniform cell walls

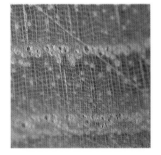

Fig. 9. Cross section of ring-porous pignut hickory (*Carya glabra*).

Fig. 10. Cross section of semi-ring-porous black walnut (*Juglans nigra*).

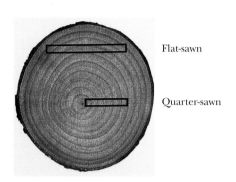

Flat-sawn

Quarter-sawn

Fig. 11. How a log is cut determines some of the properties of the resulting boards.

Fig. 12. Flat-sawn cherry (*Prunus serotina*).

result in smoother cutting properties. Conversely, interlocked grain, thicker and non-uniform cell walls, and coarse texture lead to brash and difficult cutting properties. The craftsperson must use appearance, feel, and cutting properties to select the right piece of wood for a given objective. A sharp pocket knife and magnifying glass augment the sensory capabilities in this regard.

Figure is also determined by texture, which is due to the diameter and cell wall thickness of the major structural components of the wood, primarily the vessels and fibers. This property also determines the density of wood and thus its weight, feel, and cutting properties. Density is also the key factor in the strength of the wood. Color and its variation are an integral aspect of figure. Its primary genesis is in the heartwood forming process as discussed above. Together these factors influence the way light is reflected and refracted by wood. As the light impinging on wood changes, so does the appearance of the wood. It is never constant, but always complex and variable with a richness of hue unequalled by other materials.

The final determinant of figure is the way wood is sawn or turned. There are two primary ways to cut wood into boards: flat-sawn and quarter-sawn (Fig. 11). Wood that is cut along the grain (tangential-longitudinal plane) is called flat-sawn. The darker latewood appears as inverted U- or V-shaped stripes across the board (Fig. 12). The trueness of the cut determines the distinctness, slope, and configuration of the stripes. If the surface of the wood is primarily derived from the radial-longitudinal plane, the wood is termed edge-sawn or quarter-sawn. The radial exposure of the rays may lead to distinctive lines called ray flecks, which are especially visible in maple and beech. The various ways in which a block of wood is mounted on the lathe can also result in different types of figures (Figs. 21–28 as shown on pages 158–159). Unusual patterns in grain can result from indentations, waviness, or bulges in cambial activity. The presence of interlocked grain leads to a distinctive ribbon or striped figure, which is quite common in tropical woods and also in many local species such as elm, sycamore, and gum (Fig. 13, see also 129).

Myriad different figures may arise from various combinations of spiral, wavy, and interlocked grain, resulting in broken stripes or various closely spaced stripes as in fiddleback (Fig. 14). The latter figure takes its name from the selection of fiddleback maple for the backs of violins by many of the master makers. The sounding boards were always made of straight-grained spruce. A combination of wavy and interlocked grain causes figure called broken stripe (Fig. 15) or bee's-wing (Fig. 16). When wavy grain predominates over the interlocked grain, the resulting figure is called mottled (Fig. 17).

Blister figure (Fig. 18) also originates with variations in the helical patterning of the wood elements (interlocked grain) combined with clumping of wood elements due to localized activity of groups of initials in the vascular cambium. If the clumps of wood elements are greater in extent across the grain (transversely), the result is quilted figure (Fig. 19). Bird's-eye figure is caused by axial distortion along the grain. Clumps of wood cells are laid down at right angles to the grain instead of the normal deposition parallel to the grain. This results in a pattern of conical-shaped dimples (Fig. 20). When logs are flat-sawn (tangential to the growth rings), these dimples look like birds' eyes. Most common in sugar maple (*Acer saccharum*), the trait can also be found in other maples like soft maple (*Acer saccharinum*), birch (*Betula* spp.), and white ash (*Fraxinus americana*). Bird's-eye figure in maple bestows a value over 250-fold greater

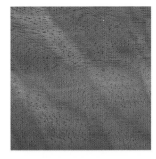

Fig. 13. Striped figure in satinwood (*Chloroxylon swietenia*).

Fig. 14. Fiddleback mahogany (*Swietenia*).

Fig. 15. Broken stripe in mahogany (*Swietenia*) as shown in R. Bruce Hoadley, *Identifying Wood: Accurate Results with Simple Tools* (Newtown, Conn.: The Taunton Press, 1990).

Fig. 16. Bee's-wing mottled figure in Ceylon satinwood (*Chloroxylon swietenia*) as shown in R. Bruce Hoadley, *Identifying Wood: Accurate Results with Simple Tools* (Newtown, Conn.: The Taunton Press, 1990).

Fig. 17. Mottled figure in planetree maple (*Acer pseudoplatanus*).

Fig. 18. Blister figure in bigleaf maple (*Acer macrophyllum*) as shown in R. Bruce Hoadley, *Identifying Wood: Accurate Results with Simple Tools* (Newtown, Conn.: The Taunton Press, 1990).

Fig. 19. Quilted figure in bigleaf maple (*Acer macrophyllum*) as shown in R. Bruce Hoadley, *Identifying Wood: Accurate Results with Simple Tools* (Newtown, Conn.: The Taunton Press, 1990).

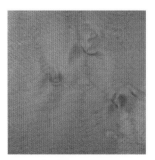

Fig. 20. Bird's-eye figure in sugar maple (*Acer saccharum*).

Fig. 21. An open form turned from the whole log with the pith at the bottom will have a concentric circular pattern. If the form extends beyond the bark, there will be a natural-edged bowl.

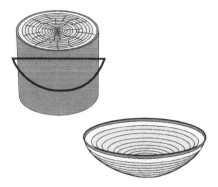

If the log is convoluted, the bowl form will have a scalloped edge.

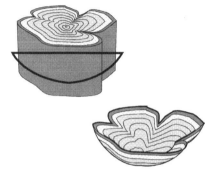

Fig. 22. Theoretically, a form turned with the vertical axis through the pith and the larger diameter through the sapwood will have a light ring around the widest portion, with a concentric circular grain pattern.

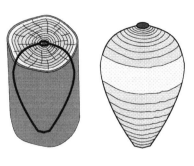

A vase form turned from a convoluted log will have openings along the sides where the wider portion of the form intersects the air.

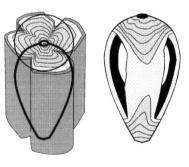

Fig. 23. Theoretically, a round form turned with the pith running horizontally through the form will have a light band running from the rim down and around the sides. The rings of the log will show as concentric circles on both sides of the shape.

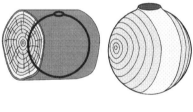

If this form is turned thin enough, the shrinking growth rings will force the pith outward into a football shape instead of cracking.

That same form, if extended through the log, will have a natural undulating rim surrounded by bark and sapwood.

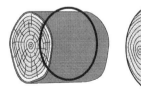

Fig. 24. An open form turned with the pith at the rim will display a hyperbolic pattern inside.

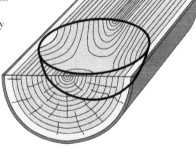

A bowl form in which the rim and bottom cut into the sapwood will show white patches at those points.

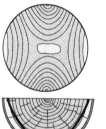

Boards in which the rings are not centered will have the pattern shift toward the pith side.

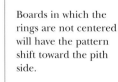

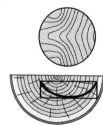

Fig. 25. If the log has a natural hole through the pith, a natural opening will be formed on each side of the vessel.

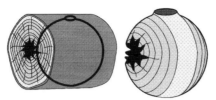

If a similar form is turned from a log that has rot in the center, there will be a naturally rotten edge on the vessel.

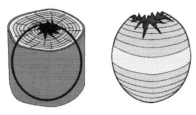

A tall vessel turned with the wider diameter overextending the hollow center and the outside edge will have a hollow opening extending through the vessel.

Fig. 26. A form turned from half a log with the opening at the sapwood will have a light spot highlighting the opening, surounded by an undulating grain pattern.

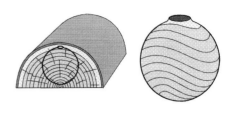

If that form is extended through the bark, a naturally undulating edge will be produced.

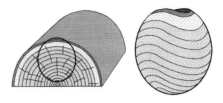

The same form turned from a log with a wide sapwood area will appear darker on the bottom and lighter on the top.

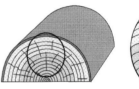

Fig. 27. Turning a form in which the diameter extends into the sapwood will show a sapwood patch at the widest portion, surrounded by concentric ovals to the other side.

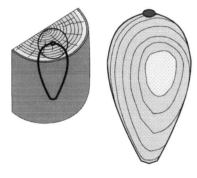

If that diameter overextends the bark, a hole will occur on the side at the widest portion, surrounded by the bark edge and sapwood.

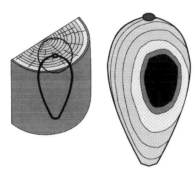

Fig. 28. Open bowls turned with the pith at the bottom will display a concentric oval pattern. The outermost rings will be broken due to the flat rim being cut through them. If the edges cut into the sapwood, a sapwood streak will show at each edge.

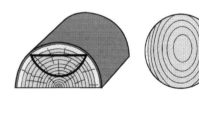

Bowls turned from boards where the pith is off-centered will create an off-centered pattern.

By extending the open form through the bark, an oval-shaped bowl with an undulating natural rim will be produced. All of the rings will be whole because none of them were cut off by the flat rim.

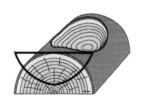

© Todd Hoyer

than the usual maple boards; so highly prized is this trait that a single tree may have a market value of up to $40,000 (1998 prices in Upper Peninsula of Michigan). Lodgepole pine (*Pinus contorta*) also has the dimples, and they are sometimes found in ponderosa pine (*Pinus ponderosa*). They are not as spectacular in these softwoods, however, because of the simplicity of the structure and the paucity of color. When trees fork, deviation of the xylem to the forks results in yet another unusual and highly prized grain pattern called crotch figure (see 115).

Wood that is attacked by rot or insects loses its structural integrity as the cell walls are partially digested and therefore cannot be used in situations where strength is at a premium. However, the incipient stages of attack may produce intricate and beautiful patterns in the wood that can be exploited in turned products where strength is not a problem. Pieces turned from decayed or bored wood may present unique and beautiful figures. In particular some white rot fungi (lignin digesters) leave dark layers in the wood; when the wood is cut or turned, these may form unusual patterns of irregular lines. This is sometimes called spalted wood or spalted grain (see 24). Likewise, many wood-mining larvae produce channels in the wood that may provide interesting appearances if the mining is not too intensive (see 57).

Summary

In this short and elementary introduction to the properties of wood that are important for its visual appearance and particular use in turning, we have examined how the basic anatomy of wood affects its properties. We hope that this primer will provide impetus to learn more, because the intelligent use of wood requires an intimate understanding of its biology and its physical and mechanical properties. To this end, a short bibliography is included to guide the reader's study of this fascinating and complex material called wood.

Bibliography
for the preceding essay

Baas, P., A. J. Bolton, and D. M. Catling, eds. *Wood Structure in Biological and Technological Research.* Leiden: Leiden University Press, 1976.

Berlyn, Graeme P. "Morphogenetic Factors in Wood Formation and Differentiation." In *New Perspectives in Wood Anatomy*, ed. P. Baas, 123–50. The Hague: Martinus Nijhoff, 1982.

—. "Trees." *Encyclopaedia Britannica.* 15th ed. Vol. 28: 903–13. Chicago: Encyclopedia Britannica, 1993.

Bramwell, Martyn, ed. *The International Book of Wood.* New York: Simon and Schuster, 1976.

Desch, Harold. E., and J. M. Dinwoodie. *Timber: Its Structure, Properties, Conversion and Use.* 7th ed. Binghamton, N.Y.: Haworth Press, 1996.

Hoadley, R. Bruce. *Understanding Wood.* Newtown, Conn.: Taunton Press, 1980.

—. *Identifying Wood.* Newtown, Conn.: Taunton Press, 1990.

Hough, Romeyn B. *The American Woods, Exhibited by Actual Specimens and with Copious Explanatory Text.* Vols 1–11. Lowville, N.Y.: 1888–1910.

Jane, Frank W. *The Structure of Wood.* 2nd ed. London: Adam and Charles Black, 1970.

Larson, Philip R. *The Vascular Cambium.* New York: Springer-Verlag, 1994.

Panshin, Alexis J. and Carl de Zeeuw. *Textbook of Wood Technology.* 4th ed. New York: McGraw-Hill, 1980.

Record, Samuel J., and Robert W. Hess. *Timbers of the New World.* New Haven: Yale University Press, 1943.

Tsoumis, George T. *Wood as a Raw Material.* Long Island, N.Y.: Pergamon Press, 1968.

—. *Science and Technology of Wood: Structure, Properties, Utilization.* New York: Chapman & Hall, 1991.

Zimmermann, Martin, and Claud L. Brown. *Trees: Structure and Function.* New York: Springer-Verlag, 1975.

Selected Portraits of the Artists

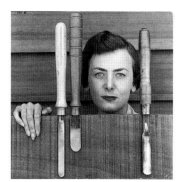

Joyce Anderson

Christian Burchard

Derek A. Bencomo

Arthur Espenet Carpenter

Edward J. Bosley

Michael Chinn

Michael J. Brolly

Virginia Dotson

Jacob E. Brubaker

David Ellsworth

Ron Fleming

Robyn Horn

Ron Kent

Giles Gilson

Michael Hosaluk

Frank Knox

Michael N. Graham

Todd Hoyer

Max Krimmel

Stephen Hogbin

C. R. (Skip) Johnson

Stoney Lamar

Michelle Holzapfel

John Jordan

Bud Latven

Portraits continue on page 178

Biographies
of the Artists

Joyce Anderson (1923–) received her undergraduate degree in philosophy from Dickinson College in Carlisle, Pennsylvania, and her MA in public affairs and regional studies from New York University. After college she worked as an economic researcher and writer. She and her husband Edgar (b. 1922) became craftsmen/designers as a lifestyle choice in 1948, preferring to be self-employed and working in their own space. Edgar taught Joyce the basics of turning. She continued to learn by experimenting, first making legs and spindles for her husband's fledgling furniture business, then expanding to bowls, plates, weed pots, and her favorite—platters. Being more interested in furniture than lathe art, she always approached the lathe as just one more tool that could produce certain shapes. Anderson is a Fellow of the American Craft Council and a founding member of the New Jersey Designer Craftsmen. Born in Plainfield, New Jersey, she currently resides in Morristown, New Jersey.
Selected Public Collections: American Craft Museum, New York; The Montclair Art Museum, N.J.; The Newark Museum, N.J.

Derek A. Bencomo (1962–) was born in Los Angeles and raised on the southern California coast. His interest in woodworking developed when he started buying restorable antique furniture for his own use. In search of a low-key lifestyle, he and his wife moved to Hawaii in 1984. His exposure to exotic woods and the history and quality of Hawaiian craftsmanship influenced Bencomo's decision to become a woodworker. He had to teach himself and as a result developed unique techniques and his own personal style. He teaches and welcomes visitors to his studio in Lahaina, Maui.
Selected Public Collections: The Detroit Institute of Arts; Fine Arts Museums of San Francisco; Hawaii State Foundation on Culture and the Arts, Honolulu; Renwick Gallery of the Smithsonian American Art Museum, Washington, D.C.; Yale University Art Gallery, New Haven

Edward J. Bosley (1917–), who holds a BS in mechanical engineering from the University of Wisconsin, started turning after he retired from the air and space industry. He renewed an earlier interest in wood by refinishing antiques and briefly creating free-form furniture. His youngest son, who had become interested in woodworking in junior high school, introduced him to the lathe. Bosley enhanced his artistic sensitivity by taking classes in oil painting and clay sculpture at the Pennsylvania Academy of Fine Arts, and he honed his wood turning skills at numerous symposia. Over a period of about ten years, turning for pleasure and artistic expression, he created a body of turned objects in both wood and stone, examples of which are in numerous private collections. Bosley, who has now given up turning, was born in Schenectady, New York, and resides in Exton, Pennsylvania.
Selected Public Collections: Wood Turning Center, Philadelphia

Michael J. Brolly (1950–) was introduced to the lathe while studying for his BFA (1981) at Kutztown University of Pennsylvania. As a child he had made things by hand that should have been turned on a lathe, so he was excited when he discovered the device. Brolly now supports his family through lathe turning. He treats his work as art, not craft, and tries to use the lathe differently in every piece to express personal life experiences. He has received numerous awards for his work and in 1996 was chosen to participate in the Wood Turning Center's International Turning Exchange in Newtown, Pennsylvania. Born in Philadelphia, Brolly now lives in Mertztown, Pennsylvania.
Selected Public Collections: The Detroit Institute of Arts; Kutztown University, Pa.; Los Angeles County Museum of Art; Wood Turning Center, Philadelphia

Jacob E. Brubaker (1897–1981), a Mennonite minister from Lancaster County, Pennsylvania, learned to turn from his father and grandfather, who had learned the craft from Joseph Long Lehn, a prolific Lancaster County turner. At the age of fourteen, Brubaker was employed by the Hubley Manufacturing Company where he would work intermittently as a designer and pattern-maker until 1950. In the late 1920s he established the short-lived Brubaker-Frank Novelty Company, a turning shop that specialized in polychromatic laminations and "ARTWOOD," primarily in the form of nut bowls and fruit bowls on stands. In 1975, Brubaker shared his passion for turning with hundreds of Vietnamese and Cambodian refugee children at Ft. Indiantown Gap, Pennsylvania, by bringing them Hubley toys and guiding their hands at the lathe.
Selected Public Collections: Wood Turning Center, Philadelphia

Christian Burchard (1955–) was born in Hamburg, Germany, and after extended travels apprenticed with a furnituremaker there. Although he admits that he was not really interested in the countless museums and churches that his mother, an architect, took him to, this childhood experience made a lasting impression. Burchard immigrated to the United States in 1979 and studied sculpture at the School of the Museum of Fine Arts, Boston, and at Emily Carr College of Art and Design in Vancouver. Today as a self-taught lathe artist he has a passion for wood and the immediacy of the turning process.
Selected Public Collections: The Detroit Institute of Arts; Fine Arts Museums of San Francisco; Mint Museum of Craft and Design, Charlotte, N.C.; Renwick Gallery of the Smithsonian American Art Museum, Washington, D.C.; Royal Cultural Center, Jedda, Saudi Arabia; Wood Turning Center, Philadelphia; Yale University Art Gallery, New Haven

Arthur Espenet Carpenter (1920–) is a graduate of Dartmouth College and a World War II veteran. He was buying and selling Asian art in his native New York City when he saw a turned bowl by James Prestini in a design exhibition at the Museum of Modern Art. Inspired by this object, he moved to San Francisco, bought a lathe, and started turning teak bowls. After a ten-year turning career, Carpenter switched to making furniture. In the early 1950s, he started selling his wares through his own retail business, Espenet Fine Woods. The artist lives in Bolinas, California, and works full-time as a furnituremaker, primarily fulfilling commissions. He has taught woodworking for San Francisco State University and the Baulines Craft Guild, as well as Anderson Ranch Arts Center in Snowmass Village, Colorado. Carpenter received a fellowship from the National Endowment for the Arts in 1976. In 1985 he was the Fulbright Lecturer in New Zealand and Australia and also received the California Living Treasure Award. Three years later he was made a Fellow of the American Craft Council.
Selected Public Collections: The Museum of Modern Art, New York; Oakland Museum of California

M. Dale Chase (1934–) has worked with wood since his early teens, but he was a neurosurgeon by profession before embracing wood turning in 1974. He received his BA in zoology from the University of California, Berkeley, in 1956 and his MD from the University of California Medical Center, San Francisco, in 1960. After purchasing a Holtzapffel ornamental turning lathe in the mid-1970s, he developed a series of ornamented jewelry boxes turned from exotic hardwoods and often inlaid with ivory, precious metals, and rare woods. Chase was born in Grand Rapids, Michigan, and resides in Penn Valley, California.
Selected Public Collections: Arizona State University Art Museum, Tempe; Wood Turning Center, Philadelphia

Michael Chinn (1950–) was born in Sherman, Texas. He studied crafts at San Jose State University and received his MFA in woodworking from California State University, Long Beach, where he taught three-dimensional design and general crafts for three years. Chinn was first attracted to lathe turning during a woodworking course taught by Leo Doyle in 1971. He embraced wood turning as an artistic medium in graduate school while studying with Frank Cummings and honed his skills during his first few years as a faculty member at Iowa State University. He headed the wood design program at that institution for fourteen years. Since 1995 he has been professor and chair of the Department of Art at Central Washington University in Ellensburg.
Selected Public Collections: Los Angeles County Museum of Art; Wood Turning Center, Philadelphia

Fletcher Cox (1948–) is a self-taught turner who has been a professional designer and craftsman in wood since 1974. He is an adjunct assistant professor at Mississippi State University School of Architecture and an adjunct professor at the University of Tennessee School of Architecture, Memphis Center for Architecture. He has lectured at several universities, including Tulane and the Graduate School of Design at Harvard. Numerous churches and public institutions in Mississippi have commissioned furniture and architectural elements from him. He received his AB in 1970 from Columbia College, Columbia University, New York City. Cox was born in Williamsburg, Virginia, and currently resides in Tougaloo, Mississippi.
Selected Public Collections: The Arkansas Arts Center Decorative Arts Museum, Little Rock; Mississippi Museum of Art, Jackson; Mississippi State Historical Museum, Jackson; Mobile Museum of Art, Ala.; Southern Highland Handicraft Guild, Asheville, N.C.; The White House

Frank E. Cummings III (1938–) was born in Los Angeles, California, and currently lives in Long Beach. He earned a BA in art from California State University, Long Beach, and an MA focusing on design and crafts from California State University, Fullerton. Teaching art, design, and crafts at the university level has been his passion for the past thirty years. He worked in the California State University system from 1969 to 2000 and was director of the honors program at California State University, Fullerton, as well as associate dean of the School of the Arts. Throughout the years he has accepted short-term positions in many states, as well as in several countries in West and Central Africa. Cummings served as consultant for the National Endowment for the Arts and the State Department on arts in America and Africa. In 1998 he made furniture and vessels for the motion picture, "How Stella Got Her Groove Back."
Selected Public Collections: Los Angeles County Museum of Art; Mint Museum of Craft and Design, Charlotte, N.C.; Renwick Gallery of the Smithsonian American Art Museum, Washington, D.C.; The White House; Wood Turning Center, Philadelphia

John Diamond-Nigh (1953–) is a native of Ft. Erie, Ontario, and currently resides in Elmira, New York. He holds a bachelor of humanities and master of humanities from Pennsylvania State University and is completing a master's degree in fine art, literature, and creative writing at Bennington College. He taught himself the basics of turning, but enhanced his carving skills by studying in Hania, on the Greek island of Crete. Diamond-Nigh's most recent interests are papermaking, making sculpture from paper, and writing poetry. Although he is not presently working with wood, many of the aesthetic ideals of his previous turnings are manifest in his current work. He teaches classes on subjects ranging from Picasso to African literature to French architecture and design at Elmira College. He has also been a visiting artist at Alfred University.
Selected Public Collections: Wood Turning Center, Philadelphia

Virginia Dotson (1943–) was born into a family of musicians in Newton, Massachusetts. She attended Wellesley College and discovered wood turning as an adult student at Arizona State University, where she earned her BFA in wood. At the first workshop she attended, the Southern California Woodturning Conference, Dotson worked with and discussed laminating with Rude Osolnik. She cites the stack-laminated furniture forms of Wendell Castle, the early plywood vessels of Rude Osolnik, and the lightness of Bob Stocksdale's bowls as direct influences on her own work. She now lives in Scottsdale, Arizona, and divides her time between producing laminated vessels inspired by the layered landscapes of the Southwest, and participating in various activities intended to educate the public about art, craft, and wood turning.

Selected Public Collections: Arizona State University Art Museum, Tempe; The Arkansas Arts Center Decorative Arts Museum, Little Rock; The Detroit Institute of Arts; Dowse Art Museum, Lower Hutt, New Zealand; High Museum of Art, Atlanta; Los Angeles County Museum of Art; The Mesa Arts Center, Ariz.; Mint Museum of Craft and Design, Charlotte, N.C.; Mobile Museum of Art, Ala.; Renwick Gallery of the Smithsonian American Art Museum, Washington, D.C.; The White House; Wood Turning Center, Philadelphia

Addie Draper (1952–) was born in Albuquerque and currently lives in Mountainair, New Mexico. She earned her BA in art and philosophy from the University of New Mexico, Albuquerque, in 1975. Since then her artistic interests have evolved through many stages. From 1975 to 1982 she focused on furniture design and construction. For the next ten years she worked on the lathe, often creating polychromatic forms, sometimes in collaboration with Bud Latven. Draper gradually approached the vessel form as a three-dimensional canvas and focuses her talents entirely on painting.

Selected Public Collections: The Albuquerque Museum; The Arkansas Arts Center Decorative Arts Museum, Little Rock; Mobile Museum of Art, Ala.; Renwick Gallery of the Smithsonian American Art Museum, Washington, D.C.; Wood Turning Center, Philadelphia

David Ellsworth (1944–), born in Iowa City, Iowa, first experienced turning when his junior high school woodworking instructor reluctantly let him try the lathe. He continued to turn through high school, then spent three years in the military and eight years in college studying architecture, drawing, and sculpture, receiving both bachelor's and master's degrees in fine arts from the University of Colorado in 1973. He started the woodworking program at the Anderson Ranch Arts Center in Snowmass Village, Colorado, in 1974, and the following year opened his first private wood turning studio in Boulder. During the 1970s Ellsworth designed a series of bent turning tools and developed methods for making the thin-walled hollow forms for which he is well known. He now makes and sells specialized tools and tutorial videos, writes and lectures extensively on turning, and operates the Ellsworth School of Woodturning at his studio in Quakertown, Pennsylvania. Recognition for his work has included grants from the Pew Foundation of Philadelphia and the National Endowment for the Arts. A founding member of the American Association of Woodturners, Ellsworth is its first Honorary Lifetime Member.

Selected Public Collections: American Craft Museum, New York; Arizona State University Art Museum, Tempe; The Arkansas Arts Center Decorative Arts Museum, Little Rock; The Contemporary Museum, Honolulu; The Denver Art Museum; The Detroit Institute of Arts; Fine Arts Museums of San Francisco; High Museum of Art, Atlanta; Los Angeles County Museum of Art; The Metropolitan Museum of Art, New York; Mint Museum of Craft and Design, Charlotte, N.C.; Mobile Museum of Art, Ala.; Museum of Fine Arts, Boston; Philadelphia Museum of Art; Renwick Gallery of the Smithsonian American Art Museum, Washington, D.C.; School for American Craftsmen, Rochester Institute of Technology, N.Y.; Sheldon Memorial Art Gallery, Lincoln, Nebr.; The White House; Wood Turning Center, Philadelphia; World Forestry Center, Portland, Oreg.

Paul W. Eshelman (1906–1977) developed his hobby of wood turning and formal education in industrial arts into a full-time career after leaving his first vocation as a music teacher. In 1972 he retired as associate professor of industrial arts from Millersville State Teachers College, where for twenty-five years he taught other woodworking teachers traditional turning techniques and styles. He was born in Elizabethtown, Pennsylvania, and graduated from Elizabethtown College. He earned an MA from Columbia University and also attended New York University and Temple University. He was president of the Pennsylvania Guild of Craftsmen from 1951 to 1953. In 1966 he received a national merit award from the American Craftsmen's Council.

Selected Public Collections: Wood Turning Center, Philadelphia

Ron Fleming (1937–) was born in Oklahoma City and currently works as a professional illustrator and wood turner in Tulsa. For many years he watched and helped his father and grandfather work in wood and now finds it to be a rewarding means of expressing his thoughts on the beauty and passages of nature. He is a self-taught wood turner, but his work has been strongly influenced by technical knowledge and ideas shared at wood turning symposia. In addition to his studio work, he periodically lectures and gives demonstrations. Fleming is an active member of the American Association of Woodturners and is currently serving on the board of trustees for the Wood Turning Center.
Selected Public Collections: The Arkansas Arts Center Decorative Arts Museum, Little Rock; Fine Arts Museums of San Francisco; The Detroit Institute of Arts; Kirkpatrick Center Museum Complex, Oklahoma City; Los Angeles County Museum of Art; Mint Museum of Craft and Design, Charlotte, N.C.; The Philbrook Museum of Art, Inc., Tulsa, Okla.; The White House; Wood Turning Center, Philadelphia

Giles Gilson (1942–), a native of Philadelphia, has acquired an eclectic education through numerous independent studies in fine art, music, design (including aircraft and automobile design), and philosophy. From 1968 to 1973 he had a full-time career as a jazz musician. He is a designer, consulting artist, technician, and maker of industrial models and prototypes for industry. In addition to being a studio artist, Gilson lectures and gives demonstrations on turning. He currently resides in Schenectady, New York.
Selected Public Collections: Arizona State University Art Museum, Tempe; The Detroit Institute of Arts; Los Angeles County Museum of Art; The Metropolitan Museum of Art, New York; Mint Museum of Craft and Design, Charlotte, N.C.; Mobile Museum of Art, Ala.; Renwick Gallery of the Smithsonian American Art Museum, Washington, D.C.; Schenectady Museum, N.Y.; Wood Turning Center, Philadelphia

Jerry Glaser (1919–) learned to work with his hands at a young age and turned his first bowl in 1933 as a junior high school student. While earning his BS in mechanical engineering from the Illinois Institute of Technology in Chicago, Glaser spent some time working in machine shops learning the properties of wood and metal and how to use various tools.

Most of his professional career was in the aerospace industry, working with the National Advisory Committee for Aeronautics, now NASA, as well as aerospace companies in California. He focused on the design and development of high-speed rotating machinery for aircraft systems. Glaser bought his first lathe in 1955 and began collecting books on wood turning and traveling to obtain exotic woods. As a designer he was inspired by a 1938 display of Scandinavian furniture and later by the work of Bob Stocksdale and Sam Maloof. He was a member of the Southern California Designer Craftsmen group. Now he makes tools for wood turners and sells them through Craft Supplies USA and other distributors. A native of Chicago, Glaser currently resides in Playa del Rey, California.

Michael N. Graham (1943–), a native of Stockton, California, graduated from the University of California, Santa Barbara, with a BA in theater arts in 1967. He is now a self-taught sculptor living in Laguna Hills, California.
Selected Public Collections: Los Angeles County Museum of Art; Renwick Gallery of the Smithsonian American Art Museum, Washington, D.C.; Santa Barbara Museum of Art, Calif.; Wood Turning Center, Philadelphia

Stephen Hogbin (1942–) was born in Tolworth, England. He immigrated to Canada in 1968 and currently resides in Wiarton, Ontario, overlooking Lake Charles. His first significant experience working with wood, though he did not use a lathe at the time, was in the late 1950s at Rycotewood College in Thame, Oxfordshire, England. Hogbin earned degrees in design from Kingston College and Royal College of Art. He became a wood turner in 1971 and throughout his career has been an instructor at numerous colleges and universities and has lectured for workshops around the world. He participated in residency programs in Australia in 1975–76 and in 1999. Hogbin writes extensively, curates exhibitions, and has been involved in public art projects. He is the author of the influential text, *Wood Turning: The Purpose of the Object.*
Selected Public Collections: Arizona State University Art Museum, Tempe; Canadian Craft Museum, Vancouver; Crafts Association of Victoria, Australia; Los Angeles County Museum of Art; Massey Foundation, Canadian Museum of Civilization, Ottawa; Melbourne State College, Australia; The Mendel Art Gallery, Saskatoon; Metropolitan Toronto Library; Mint Museum of Craft and Design, Charlotte, N.C.; Ontario Crafts Council; Parnham House, Dorset, England; Tom Thomson Memorial Gallery, Owen Sound, Ontario; Wood Turning Center, Philadelphia

Michelle Holzapfel (1951–) was born in Woonsocket, Vermont, and had a lot of exposure to tools and their uses while growing up. She learned needlework, including embroidery and lacemaking, and also made crude baskets, woven mats, and other forms that have profoundly influenced her turning over the past twenty years. She received advanced training in art history and techniques while in high school. Holzapfel began turning legs for her husband's burl-top tables in 1977, but soon changed to sculptural work after meeting Mel Lindquist. She received her BA from Vermont College/Norwich University in Brattleboro, Vermont, and currently resides in Marlboro, Vermont.
Selected Public Collections: Mint Museum of Craft and Design, Charlotte, N.C.; Mobile Museum of Art, Ala.; Museum of Fine Arts, Boston; Renwick Gallery of the Smithsonian American Art Museum, Washington, D.C.; Rhode Island School of Design Museum, Providence; Wood Turning Center, Philadelphia; Yale University Art Gallery, New Haven

Robyn Horn (1951–) became familiar with art at an early age through her mother, who was a painter. She majored in art at Hendrix College in Conway, Arkansas, and tried various artistic routes before her brother-in-law, who had recently studied with David Ellsworth, introduced her to the lathe. Horn does woodworking intermittently as she has other interests, including encouraging collectors of wood art. She is an Honorary Lifetime Member of the American Association of Woodturners and is past-president of Collectors of Wood Art. Horn was born in Fort Smith, Arkansas, and now resides in Little Rock.
Selected Public Collections: American Craft Museum, New York; The Arkansas Arts Center Decorative Arts Museum, Little Rock; Arrowmont School of Arts and Crafts, Gatlinburg, Tenn.; The Detroit Institute of Arts; Mint Museum of Craft and Design, Charlotte, N.C.; Mobile Museum of Art, Ala.; Renwick Gallery of the Smithsonian American Art Museum, Washington, D.C.; The White House; Wood Turning Center, Philadelphia; Yale University Art Gallery, New Haven

Michael Hosaluk (1954–) was born in Invermay, Saskatchewan. He first experienced wood turning as a ninth grader in shop classes and later developed his interest using his father's lathe. Hosaluk studied cabinetry and millwork at Kelsey Institute of Applied Arts and Sciences in Saskatoon. After attending Albert LeCoff's Tenth Wood Turning Symposium in 1981, he started holding wood turning conferences and workshops in Saskatoon, where he currently resides. He is the driving force behind the biennial Emma Lake Conference. Hosaluk lectures and gives demonstrations throughout the world several months of the year and devotes the rest of his time to turning and furnituremaking. He is a founding member of the American Association of Woodturners and is a Lifetime Member of the Saskatchewan Woodworkers' Guild. He has received numerous awards, including grants from the Saskatchewan Craft Council and the Canada Council for the Arts.
Selected Public Collections: The Arkansas Arts Center Decorative Arts Museum, Little Rock; City of Regina, Civic Art Collection, Saskatchewan; The Contemporary Museum, Honolulu; Craft and Folk Art Museum, Los Angeles; The Detroit Institute of Arts; Los Angeles County Museum of Art; Melbourne University, Australia; Mint Museum of Craft and Design, Charlotte, N.C.; Royal Ontario Museum, Toronto; Wood Turning Center, Philadelphia

Todd Hoyer (1952–) was born in Beaver Dam, Wisconsin, and raised in Phoenix, Arizona. He learned the basics of turning in junior high school but shifted to drafting in high school and college. From 1970 to 1976 he studied at Arizona State University, where he majored in manufacturing engineering and minored in design technology. After attending a wood turning conference in Provo, Utah, in the early 1980s, Hoyer began to focus seriously on wood turning as a vocation. In addition to creating lathe art in his studio in Bisbee, Arizona, he teaches for woodworking workshops and conferences.
Selected Public Collections: Arizona State University Art Museum, Tempe; The Arkansas Arts Center Decorative Arts Museum, Little Rock; The Detroit Institute of Arts; Los Angeles County Museum of Art; Mint Museum of Craft and Design, Charlotte, N.C.; Mobile Museum of Art, Ala.; Renwick Gallery of the Smithsonian American Art Museum, Washington, D.C.; Wood Turning Center, Philadelphia

William Hunter (1947–), born in Long Beach, California, is a full-time studio turner living in Rancho Palos Verdes, California. His career began in 1970 when he and a high school friend started turning gift items in his friend's garage to make extra money for college. He had his first craft show that year and has had no other job since. Rarely traveling to teach or to demonstrate, Hunter compares the concentration needed for his work with that of an athlete in training. He holds a degree in fire science from Santa Monica College and a BA in sociology, concentrating in twentieth-century thought, from California State University, Dominguez Hills.
Selected Public Collections: American Craft Museum, New York; Arizona State University Art Museum, Tempe; The Art Institute of Chicago; The Contemporary Museum, Honolulu; Craft and Folk Art Museum, Los Angeles; The Detroit Institute of Arts; Fine Arts Museums of San Francisco; High Museum of Art, Atlanta; Los Angeles County Museum of Art; Mint Museum of Craft and Design, Charlotte, N.C.; Mobile Museum of Art, Ala.; Museum of Fine Arts, Boston; Oakland Museum of California; Renwick Gallery of the Smithsonian American Art Museum, Washington, D.C.; Wood Turning Center, Philadelphia; Yale University Art Gallery, New Haven

Carl Huskey (1911–1979) was born in Sugarlands, in the mountains near Gatlinburg, Tennessee. His grandfather, father, and brother were woodworkers, and Carl passed the craft on to his sons and grandsons. For many years Huskey made furniture and small items for O. J. Mattil's shop, Woodcrafters and Carvers, in Gatlinburg. He later opened his own business, The Village Craft Shop, which his son Charles Ray still operates. Huskey marketed his lathe-turned wares to the growing tourist trade when the Great Smoky Mountains National Park opened in 1934. He also taught woodworking for twenty-three years at the Settlement School, which is now Arrowmont School of Arts and Crafts. In 1937 he helped to organize a craft cooperative that was incorporated in 1968 as the Great Smoky Arts and Crafts Community and now numbers more than 100 craftsmen. During his lifetime he exhibited his wares at local county and craft fairs.
Selected Public Collections: Southern Highland Handicraft Guild, Asheville, N.C.

C. R. (Skip) Johnson (1928–) was born in Painted Post, New York. Introduced to the lathe as an eighth grader, Johnson became more acquainted with the tool in 1942 while making small scale models of World War II airplanes for the military. In 1957 he earned a BS from State University of New York, Oswego, and later received his MFA in furniture design under the tutelage of Tage Frid at the School for American Craftsmen, Rochester Institute of Technology. Johnson currently resides in Stoughton, Wisconsin, and is retired from a lifetime of teaching. He holds the position Professor Emeritus of Art at the University of Wisconsin, Madison, and continues to teach at Penland School of Crafts during the summers, as he has done for more than thirty-five years. He is the recipient of grants from the National Endowment for the Arts.
Selected Public Collections: Arrowmont School of Arts and Crafts, Gatlinburg, Tenn.; Wood Turning Center, Philadelphia

John Jordan (1950–) a native of Nashville, Tennessee, is a self-taught wood turner. Teaching is a significant part of his life. He conducts one class a month in his studio in Antioch, Tennessee, and travels extensively for almost half the year, teaching and demonstrating wood turning around the world. Jordan creates one-of-a-kind objects and is dedicated to using green wood to produce refined, elegant work that demonstrates attention to detail, purity of form, and emphasis on surface textures.

Selected Public Collections: American Craft Museum, New York; The Arkansas Arts Center Decorative Arts Museum, Little Rock; Arrowmont School of Arts and Crafts, Gatlinburg, Tenn.; The Contemporary Museum, Honolulu; The Detroit Institute of Arts; High Museum of Art, Atlanta; Hunter Museum of American Art, Chattanooga, Tenn.; Los Angeles County Museum of Art; Mint Museum of Craft and Design, Charlotte, N.C.; Mobile Museum of Art, Ala.; Renwick Gallery of the Smithsonian American Art Museum, Washington, D.C.; The White House; Wood Turning Center, Philadelphia

Ron Kent (1931–) was born in Chicago and received his BS in mechanical engineering from the University of California at Los Angeles in 1957. He first experienced turning in his forties when his wife gave him a small, basic lathe for Christmas. Although he is a self-taught artist who prefers figuring things out for himself, he gets his greatest satisfaction from teaching and mentoring others. Kent recently retired from his career as a stockbroker and now focuses full-time on creating turned art. He resides in Kailua, Hawaii. His work has been published extensively, and special presentations have been made to Dr. Thomas Klestil, President, Republic of Austria; Emperor Akihito of Japan; Presidents William Jefferson Clinton, George Bush, and Ronald Reagan; and Pope John Paul II, among others.
Selected Public Collections: American Craft Museum, New York; Arizona State University Art Museum, Tempe; The Contemporary Museum, Honolulu; Cooper-Hewitt, National Design Museum, Smithsonian Institution, New York; Craft and Folk Art Museum, Los Angeles; The Detroit Institute of Arts; Hawaii State Foundation on Culture and the Arts, Honolulu; High Museum of Art, Atlanta; Honolulu Academy of Arts; Los Angeles County Museum of Art; The Metropolitan Museum of Art, New York; Mint Museum of Craft and Design, Charlotte, N.C.; Mobile Museum of Art, Ala.; Musée des Arts Decoratifs, Paris; Museum of Fine Arts, Boston; The Newark Museum, N.J.; Oakland Museum of California; Renwick Gallery of the Smithsonian American Art Museum, Washington, D.C.; The White House; Yale University Art Gallery, New Haven

Frank Knox (1902–1990) was an ornamental turner who lived in New York City. A management consultant by profession, he was an authority on business forms, controlling paperwork in a bureaucracy, and integrated cost control. In 1963 he bought a Holtzapffel lathe built in London in 1853. Over time he became an expert in ornamental turning. His 1986 publication, *Ornamental Turnery: A Practical and Historical Approach to a Centuries-Old Craft,* was the first book written on the topic in over a hundred years. Knox was a member of the Society of Ornamental Turners and served as president of the International Wood Collectors Society.
Selected Public Collections: Wood Turning Center, Philadelphia

Max Krimmel (1948–) was a successful, self-employed luthier before he became interested in lathe work. Like many woodworkers, he first experienced turning as a junior high school student. Until he showed some of his own pieces (made by putting scraps of wood together and "fooling around" with an old lathe) to Dale Nish, he never thought about lathe art. Since 1986 Krimmel has concentrated on turning alabaster. He studied design at the University of Denver, industrial arts at Colorado State University, and fine art at the University of Colorado, Boulder. Born in Belefonte, Pennsylvania, the artist currently resides in Nederland, Colorado.
Selected Public Collections: Arrowmont School of Arts and Crafts, Gatlinburg, Tenn.; The Denver Art Museum; The Hoyt Institute of Fine Arts, New Castle, Pa.; Los Angeles County Museum of Art; Wood Turning Center, Philadelphia

Dan Kvitka (1958–), a native of Los Angeles, California, is a full-time wood turner living in Portland, Oregon. His father taught him to turn spindles at a young age, and his skills in wood carving and tool making became obvious during his junior high school shop classes. Workshops in Provo, Utah, with Dale Nish and the 1985 Arrowmont symposium were significant to his education as a turner. Kvitka holds a BS in industrial design from the Art Center College of Design in Pasadena, California. He has taught at Arrowmont School of Arts and Crafts, Southern California Woodturning Conferences, and the Woodworking West Woodturning Symposium at Brigham Young University. From 1986 to 1988 he was editor-in-chief of *The American Woodturner.*
Selected Public Collections: American Craft Museum, New York; American Institute in Taiwan, Taipei; Arrowmont School of Arts and Crafts, Gatlinburg, Tenn.; The Contemporary Museum, Honolulu; The Detroit Institute of Arts; Fine Arts Museums of San Francisco; Los Angeles County Museum of Art; Mint Museum of Craft and Design, Charlotte, N.C.; Museums of Fine Arts, Boston; The Museum of Modern Art, New York; Renwick Gallery of the Smithsonian American Art Museum, Washington, D.C.

Stoney Lamar (1951–), originally from Alexandria, Louisiana, received his BS in woodworking in 1979 from Appalachian State University in Boone, North Carolina. Shortly afterwards he and his wife started a woodworking shop in Saluda, North Carolina. He had planned to design and build furniture, but after borrowing a friend's lathe, he found the spontaneity of sculptured wood turning more satisfying. Summer workshops with Mark and Melvin Lindquist and David Ellsworth profoundly affected his approach to turning. In 1984 he accepted the one-year assistant's position in the Lindquists' New Hampshire studio. Lamar has lectured and conducted workshops in wood turning. He was a founding member of the American Association of Woodturners and has served on the board of directors and as president for the Southern Highland Handicraft Guild.
Selected Public Collections: American Craft Museum, New York; The Arkansas Arts Center Decorative Arts Museum, Little Rock; The Detroit Institute of Arts; High Museum of Art, Atlanta; Huntsville Museum of Art, Ala.; Mint Museum of Craft and Design, Charlotte, N.C.; Mobile Museum of Art, Ala.; Renwick Gallery of the Smithsonian American Art Museum, Washington, D.C.; Wood Turning Center, Philadelphia

Bud Latven (1949–) is a native of Philadelphia. He attended Delaware County Community College in Media, Pennsylvania, and the University of New Mexico in Albuquerque. He made custom furniture for ten years before using a lathe. Although he had no formal training on the lathe, in 1982 he accepted a job making several hundred stemmed goblets. This led to turning small bowls for enjoyment and his first show of turned objects in 1983, which was a sellout. According to the artist, his furnituremaking experience set the stage for his later constructed wood turnings. For the past several years he has had an employee/apprentice, Ann Adams, who helps construct his forms. Latven is a full-time wood turner living in Tajique, New Mexico.
Selected Public Collections: The Albuquerque Museum; Arkansas Arts Center Decorative Arts Museum, Little Rock; The Contemporary Museum, Honolulu; High Museum of Art, Atlanta; Hunter Museum of American Art, Chattanooga, Tenn.; Los Angeles County Museum of Art; Mint Museum of Craft and Design, Charlotte, N.C.; Mobile Museum of Art, Ala.; Renwick Gallery of the Smithsonian American Art Museum, Washington, D.C.; Wood Turning Center, Philadelphia

Mark Lindquist (1949–) was born in Oakland, California, and remembers watching his father, Mel Lindquist, use the lathe in his workshop in San Jose in the early fifties. They moved to Schenectady, New York, in 1954, and when Mark was ten, his father built him his own small shop. Mark received his BA in art from New England College in 1971, took graduate courses at Pratt Institute, and later earned his MFA from Florida State University. Beginning in the early 1970s, Mark actively lectured and taught through apprenticeships. He revived the wood turning program at Haystack Mountain School of Crafts in Maine during the summer of 1979 and two years later, along with his father, started a wood turning program at Arrowmont School of Arts and Crafts in Gatlinburg, Tennessee. During 1984 and 1985 he helped to organize the first National Woodturning Conference and the American Association of Woodturners. Mark currently works intermittently in his studio in Quincy, Florida. He is the author of *Sculpting Wood: Contemporary Tools and Techniques.* Recognition for his work includes receiving a Southern Arts Federation/National Endowment for the Arts Fellowship in 1989 and being an honorary board member of the James Renwick Alliance in 1996.

Selected Public Collections: American Craft Museum, New York; Arrowmont School of Arts and Crafts, Gatlinburg, Tenn.; The Art Institute of Chicago; Dallas Museum of Art; The Detroit Institute of Arts; Fine Arts Museums of San Francisco; Fuller Museum of Art, Brockton, Mass.; Greenville County Museum of Art, Greenville, S.C.; High Museum of Art, Atlanta; The Metropolitan Museum of Art, New York; Mint Museum of Craft and Design, Charlotte, N.C.; Mobile Museum of Art, Ala.; Philadelphia Museum of Art; Renwick Gallery of the Smithsonian American Art Museum, Washington, D.C.; Schenectady Museum, N.Y.; Virginia Museum of Fine Arts, Richmond; The White House; Wood Turning Center, Philadelphia

Melvin Lindquist (1911–2000), born in Kingsburg, California, was first exposed to wood turning in high school in 1928. He recalled that after several attempts he produced a spindle-turned object, a bowl, and a plate for a B+ grade. After earning his BS at Oakland Polytechnic College of Engineering, Lindquist operated a vertical turret lathe and became a master machinist at General Electric. These skills served him well when he began wood turning as a hobby in the forties and started to design his own tools. He retired from GE in 1964 and started showing his work at craft fairs. Melvin and his son Mark started the wood turning program at Arrowmont School of Arts and Crafts in 1981. That same year they moved their studio from Schenectady, New York, to New Hampshire. Melvin was a member of the American Craft Council, an Honorary Lifetime Member of the American Association of Woodturners, and a Fellow of the American Society of Quality Control. In 1983 the University of Massachusetts at Amherst named him a New England Living Art Treasure, and in 1985 he won the first National Woodturning Conference Award for outstanding achievements in studio wood turning at Arrowmont School of Arts and Crafts.
Selected Public Collections: The Detroit Institute of Arts; Fine Arts Museums of San Francisco; The Metropolitan Museum of Art, New York; Mint Museum of Craft and Design, Charlotte, N.C.; Mobile Museum of Art, Ala.; Renwick Gallery of the Smithsonian American Art Museum, Washington, D.C.; Schenectady Museum, N.Y.; Wood Turning Center, Philadelphia

Steve Loar (1949–) was first bitten by the wood bug when he turned a lamp base as a seventh grader in shop class. While studying for his BS in studio art at Murray State University in Kentucky, he was enthralled with an experimental course in wood turning. As an undergraduate and graduate student Loar assisted his design instructor, Bobby Falwell, who had recently studied with Wendell

Castle at Rochester Institute of Technology. Together they often used solid stack lamination to make one-of-a-kind furniture, cabinetry, and crafts. After receiving his MA in design studio from Northern Illinois University in DeKalb in 1976, Loar taught design and wood technology for three years at State University of New York, Oswego. Since 1982 he has dedicated himself to teaching and education administration at Rochester Institute of Technology. Being an extrovert, he prefers this lifestyle and actually turns very little. Loar was one of fifteen turners to receive a Mentor Award from the American Association of Woodturners in 1996, and he received the Excellence in Leadership award from RIT in 1994. The artist was born in Hamilton, Ohio, and currently resides in Warsaw, New York.
Selected Public Collections: The Arkansas Arts Center Decorative Arts Museum, Little Rock; Arrowmont School of Arts and Crafts, Gatlinburg, Tenn.; Los Angeles County Museum of Art; Wood Turning Center, Philadelphia

John (Jake) May (1908–1989), a native of Duxbury, Massachusetts, attended Boston Architectural Center at night from 1927 to 1931 and worked for architects and builders during the day. In the early 1930s the Civilian Conservation Corps employed him first as a foreman, then as a landscape architect. He later worked as a furnituremaker, cabinetmaker, and turner. Around 1958, while living in Portsmouth, New Hampshire, May abandoned turning for a ceramic firepot business. Just a few years before his death he returned to wood turning. He was a member of the League of New Hampshire Craftsmen and an active participant in the American Craftsmen's Educational Council. He taught at Haystack Mountain School of Crafts in Liberty, Maine, from 1952 through 1955, and in 1957 was a panelist at Asilomar Conference of American Craftsmen.

Hugh E. McKay (1951–) was born in Long Beach, California, and at the age of fifteen moved with his grandparents to the southern coast of Oregon. Throughout high school he produced objects for the tourist trade in their myrtlewood turning shop. He became interested in art while attending Southern Oregon State College. In the 1970s, the turned, covered containers and sculpture in Dona Meilach's *Contemporary Woodwork,* as well as the jewelry of René Lalique and Albert Paley, influenced his work. He wanted to emulate Lalique and Paley's use of different materials in his own sculptural pieces. He has become a master of multi-axis turning and now incorporates cast glass in many of his pieces. A resident of Gold Beach, Oregon, McKay has received numerous awards for his work and was chosen in 1996 to be an artist-in-residence for the Wood Turning Center's International Wood Turning Exchange, Newtown, Pennsylvania.
Selected Public Collections: The Detroit Institute of Arts; Los Angeles County Museum of Art; Wood Turning Center, Philadelphia

Connie Mississippi (1941–) was born in Greenwood, Mississippi, and earned her BFA at Memphis College of Art and her MFA at Pratt Institute in Brooklyn. Already an established painter, she became interested in the lathe after seeing a demonstration at a local street fair. She immediately saw its potential for making sculptural forms and elements for use in collages, which were a major focus of her work at the time. Mississippi works full-time in her studio in Topanga, California, writes for wood turning publications, and lectures occasionally. She served on the board of American Oceans Campaign in Santa Monica, California, for nine years and is currently a board member of the Wood Turning Center, Philadelphia.
Selected Public Collections: The Detroit Institute of Arts; Rockefeller University, New York; The White House; Wood Turning Center, Philadelphia

Bruce Mitchell (1949–) was born in San Rafael, California, and received his formal education from Laney Junior College in Oakland, De Anza Junior College in Cupertino, and the University of California, Santa Barbara. In 1976 he traveled for six months in Central and South America studying pre-Columbian pottery, stone carving, metalsmithing, and textiles. After working as technical assistant to wood sculptor J. B. Blunk from 1969 to 1977, he began his career as a self-taught wood turner. Mitchell currently resides in Point Reyes, California.
Selected Public Collections: Arizona State University Art Museum, Tempe; The Arkansas Arts Center Decorative Arts Museum, Little Rock; The Detroit Institute of Arts; High Museum of Art, Atlanta; Mint Museum of Craft and Design, Charlotte, N.C.; Renwick Gallery of the Smithsonian American Art Museum, Washington, D.C.; Wood Turning Center, Philadelphia

Ed Moulthrop (1916–) received his undergraduate degree from Case Western Reserve University and his MFA from Princeton University. He taught architecture and physics at Georgia Institute of Technology and for years had a thriving architectural practice before devoting himself full-time to wood turning in 1976. Moulthrop first exhibited his work in 1963, but his love of turning was established early in life. While in his teens, his interest in turning drove him to purchase a $16.95 lathe with money he earned delivering magazines. From 1954 to 1965 he was chairman of the Georgia State Arts Commission. He was honored as a Fellow of the American Craft Council in 1987 and is listed in *Who's Who in America.* He is an Honorary Lifetime Member of the American Association of Woodturners. The artist currently resides in Atlanta, Georgia.

Selected Public Collections: American Craft Museum, New York; Arizona State University Art Museum, Tempe; The Arkansas Arts Center Decorative Arts Museum, Little Rock; The Art Institute of Chicago; Atlanta Historical Society, Inc.; The Detroit Institute of Arts; Fine Arts Museums of San Francisco; High Museum of Art, Atlanta; Hunter Museum of American Art, Chattanooga, Tenn.; Kresge Art Museum, East Lansing, Mich.; Marietta/Cobb Museum of Art, Marietta, Ga.; The Metropolitan Museum of Art, New York; Mint Museum of Craft and Design, Charlotte, N.C.; Museum of Fine Arts, Boston; Museum of Fine Arts, Houston; The Museum of Modern Art, New York; Renwick Gallery of the Smithsonian American Art Museum, Washington, D.C.

Philip C. Moulthrop (1947–) was born in Atlanta, Georgia. He attended West Georgia College as an undergraduate and earned a law degree from Woodrow Wilson College of Law in 1978. He grew up watching his father, Ed Moulthrop, turn wood and gleaned from him a basic knowledge of turning, curing, and finishing green wood. Philip always enjoyed working with his hands; he had previously worked with clay and spent about twelve years doing photography and developing in his own darkroom. He started wood turning about twenty years ago and now makes his living as a full-time turner in Marietta, Georgia.
Selected Public Collections: American Craft Museum, New York; Arizona State University Art Museum, Tempe; The Contemporary Museum, Honolulu; The Detroit Institute of Arts; High Museum of Art, Atlanta; Huntsville Museum of Art, Ala.; Kresge Art Museum, East Lansing, Mich.; Los Angeles County Museum of Art; Marietta/Cobb Museum of Art, Marietta, Ga.; Mint Museum of Craft and Design, Charlotte, N.C.; Mobile Museum of Art, Ala.; The Olympic Museum, Lausanne, Switzerland; Renwick Gallery of the Smithsonian American Art Museum, Washington, D.C.; The White House; Yeiser Art Center, Paducah, Ky.

Thomas Nicosia (1899–1978) was an amateur turner who made laminated, polychromatic pieces at his Philadelphia shop from 1946 until his death. He was born in Misilmeri, Province of Palermo, Italy, and began his apprenticeship in woodworking at age ten. After immigrating to America in 1923, he repaired and reproduced antique furniture in New York City. From 1925 to 1946, Nicosia worked at Bellanca Aircraft Company in New Castle, Delaware, where he was responsible for most of the interior of the airplane Admiral Byrd flew to the South Pole. From 1946 onward he worked as a cabinetmaker, made frames for a Philadelphia art gallery, and repaired wood pieces for the Philadelphia Museum of Art and other museums, collectors, and dealers. Using a metal lathe, he started experimenting with wood turning in his spare time. Nicosia's oeuvre comprises over 200 pieces fashioned from woods from almost every continent, each incorporating an original design or variation of a classic shape.
Selected Public Collections: Wood Turning Center, Philadelphia

Dale L. Nish (1932–) was born in Cardston, Alberta, Canada. He holds a BS and MS in industrial education from Brigham Young University and an EdD from Washington State University. In college he studied woodworking, which had been an interest during junior high and high school, as well as drawing, art and design, and other crafts. He taught industrial arts in Alberta from 1958 to 1965 and in 1967 became a professor of industrial education at Brigham Young University in Provo, Utah, where he currently lives in retirement. Professional development leaves included travel and study in Denmark, Norway, Sweden, and Great Britain, as well as extensive travel in America. Nish has also lectured at many universities and several of the leading arts and crafts schools. His publications include *Creative Woodturning* (1975), *Artistic Woodturning* (1980), and *Master Woodturners* (1985). The American Association of Woodturners gave him the Outstanding Contributor Award in 1985 and Honorary Lifetime Membership in 1987.
Selected Public Collections: Arizona State University Art Museum, Tempe; Arrowmont School of Arts and Crafts, Gatlinburg, Tenn.; The Detroit Institute of Arts; High Museum of Art, Atlanta; Mint Museum of Craft and Design, Charlotte, N.C.; Mobile Museum of Art, Ala.

Harry Nohr (1896–1977) was born in Waupaca, Wisconsin, to Scandinavian parents. When he volunteered for duty in World War I, he was rejected for being too scrawny. A sergeant suggested that he return home, fatten up a bit, then try again. He took the advice, but having already been rejected as Harry I. Nohr, he signed up as Harry "E." Nohr and continued to be known by that name. After the war he had numerous jobs including owning a creamery. Nohr took up turning in 1959 and started turning full-time in 1966 when he retired as postmaster of Mineral Point, Wisconsin. He was also an avid hunter, fisherman, and conservationist. The University of Wisconsin at Platteville now has his woodworking tools, which they use to teach the craft to others. The University also named an art gallery in his honor. In 1970 Nohr was featured in an ABC television special, "With These Hands."
Selected Public Collections: Elvehjem Museum of Art, Madison, Wis.

Craig Nutt (1950–) was born in Belmond, Iowa, and currently resides in Kingston Springs, Tennessee. He holds a BA in religious studies from the University of Alabama and has been a self-employed artist since 1979. A college elective provided him with his introduction to woodworking, but access to tools and machinery was severely limited. Any meaningful experience had to wait until he got a job in an antique restoration shop where he had access to a lathe. This also led, through his boss's encouragement, to Nutt's love of gardening. Much of his work successfully melds these interests. In addition to his studio work, Nutt teaches each summer, participates in a number of conferences and lectures, and writes for *American Craft* and other publications. He is currently on the board of trustees for the Furniture Society and for a number of years served on the board of directors for the American Craft Council/Southeastern Regional Assembly. He has won many awards, including a fellowship from the National Endowment for the Arts/Southern Arts Federation in 1989.
Selected Public Collections: Birmingham Museum of Art, Ala.; The Columbus Museum, Ga.; Hawaii State Foundation on Culture and the Arts, Honolulu; High Museum of Art, Atlanta; Huntsville Museum of Art, Ala.; Mobile Museum of Art, Ala.; Renwick Gallery of the Smithsonian American Art Museum, Washington, D.C.

Rude Osolnik (1915–), born in Dawson, New Mexico, lives in Berea, Kentucky, where for forty years he taught in the Industrial Arts Department at Berea College. He received an undergraduate degree and an MFA in industrial arts from Bradley University in Peoria, Illinois. He has given workshops and demonstrated wood turning throughout the United States, including Alaska, as well as in New Zealand. In addition to being a teacher and wood artist, he is known for his production work, which included creating wooden alphabet letters for Childcraft Education Corporation, makers of educational toys, and making thousands of his signature candlesticks for major department stores in the 1950s and '60s. In 1950 Osolnik received a National Award for Contemporary Design from the International Wood Manufacturers. Between 1961 and 1987 he repeatedly served on the board of directors of the Southern Highland Handicraft Guild, which honored him with a Lifetime Achievement Award in 1997. He is a founder, Lifetime Member, and Fellow of the Kentucky Guild of Artists and Craftsmen and a Fellow of the American Craft Council. In 1992 he received the Kentucky Governor's Award for Lifetime Achievement in the Arts. He is an Honorary Lifetime Member of the American Association of Woodturners.
Selected Public Collections: Arizona State University Art Museum, Tempe; Arrowmont School of Arts and Crafts, Gatlinburg, Tenn.; Cooper-Hewitt, National Design Museum, Smithsonian Institution, New York; The Detroit Institute of Arts; High Museum of Art, Atlanta; Huntsville Museum of Art, Ala.; J. B. Speed Art Museum, Louisville, Ky.; Mint Museum of Craft and Design, Charlotte, N.C.; Mobile Museum of Art, Ala.; Museum of Fine Arts, Boston; Museum of Science and Industry, Chicago; Renwick Gallery of the Smithsonian American Art Museum, Washington, D.C.; Southern Highland Handicraft Guild, Asheville, N.C.; Wood Turning Center, Philadelphia; Yale University Art Gallery, New Haven

Stephen Mark Paulsen (1947–), the son of an expert woodworker, began painting, sculpting, and woodworking at an early age. In 1963, at the age of fifteen, he had his first gallery showing of wood sculpture and woodcuts in Palo Alto, California. He studied art, drama, and literature at the University of California at Santa Barbara from 1965 to 1971, supporting himself through the manufacture and sale of carved and inlaid musical instruments. After a brief stint in the Pacific Northwest learning logging, millwork, and the manufacture of lumber, Paulsen worked as an in-house cabinetmaker for a large industrial firm and later joined with a fellow woodworker to produce custom boxes, furnishings, and elements for classic and custom automobiles. He opened Paulsen Fine Art Woodworks in 1980 and continues to work as an independent artist in Redway, California.
Selected Public Collections: The Detroit Institute of Arts; Renwick Gallery of the Smithsonian American Art Museum, Washington, D.C.; Wood Turning Center, Philadelphia

Gord Peteran (1956–) was born in Toronto and graduated with honors from the Ontario College of Art and Design, where he worked extensively in the furniture and wood program. At that time the lathe was introduced as a secondary machine like a drill press or sander, so Peteran never received formal training on the lathe and does not consider himself a lathe artist. He teaches part-time at Sheridan College School of Art and Design, Ontario College of Art and Design, and Rhode Island School of Design in Providence. He resides in Toronto and creates most of his work for site- or situation-specific commissions.
Selected Public Collections: Canadian Craft Museum, Vancouver; Metro Toronto City Hall; The National Library of Canada; Wood Turning Center, Philadelphia

Michael James Peterson (1952–) is a native of Wichita Falls, Texas, and currently resides on Lopez Island, Washington. While earning his associate of arts and science degree from Edmonds Community College in Lynnwood, Washington, Peterson saw Ed Moulthrop's work on the cover of *American Craft.* This inspired him to try his hand at the lathe, which at that time was only occasionally used for maintenance at the college. Peterson makes his living as a woodworker and teaches for conferences, including those held by Arrowmont School of Arts and Crafts, the American Association of Woodturners, and Brigham Young University. He is a founding member of the American Association of Woodturners.
Selected Public Collections: American Craft Museum, New York; Arrowmont School of Arts and Crafts, Gatlinburg, Tenn.; The Contemporary Museum, Honolulu; The Detroit Institute of Arts; Edmonds Arts

Festival Museum, Edmonds, Wash.; Fine Arts Museums of San Francisco; Los Angeles County Museum of Art; Mint Museum of Craft and Design, Charlotte, N.C.; Mobile Museum of Art, Ala.; Museum of Fine Arts, Boston; Renwick Gallery of the Smithsonian American Art Museum, Washington, D.C.; Wood Turning Center, Philadelphia

James Prestini (1908–1993) was born to Italian immigrant parents in Waterford, Connecticut, and later moved to Westerly, Rhode Island, where he was apprenticed to a machinist. He completed his BS in mechanical engineering at Yale University in 1930. Prestini concentrated on wood turning between 1933 and 1953 while living in Chicago, where he taught design and was an assistant research engineer at Illinois Institute of Technology. He then traveled to Italy to train as a sculptor. Upon returning to America he began creating works made of stainless steel. From 1956 to 1975 he was first lecturer in design, then professor of design at the University of California, Berkeley. After retiring in 1975, Prestini devoted his time to Creators Equity Foundation, which he and his friend Jesse Reichek established to help young artists. Prestini first exhibited his work at the Museum of Modern Art in 1939 and continued to show at major venues throughout his life.
Selected Public Collections: Albright-Knox Art Gallery, Buffalo, N.Y.; American Craft Museum, New York; The Art Institute of Chicago; Berlin Bauhaus-Archiv; Brooklyn Museum of Art; Chicago Historical Society; The Cleveland Museum of Art; Cooper-Hewitt, National Design Museum, Smithsonian Institution, New York; The Detroit Institute of Arts; The Metropolitan Museum of Art, New York; Mint Museum of Craft and Design, Charlotte, N.C.; Musée des Arts Decoratifs, Montreal; Museum of Fine Arts, Boston; The Museum of Modern Art, New York; Philadelphia Museum of Art; Renwick Gallery of the Smithsonian American Art Museum, Washington, D.C.; San Francisco Museum of Modern Art; Walker Art Center, Minneapolis

H. Wayne Raab (1946–) was born in Buffalo, New York, and received his BS in art education at State University of New York at Buffalo. He also holds an MFA in woodworking and furniture design with a minor in painting from Rochester Institute of Technology. Raab was introduced to the lathe in 1965 as an undergraduate and a decade later was paying the rent with lathe-turned production work. The 1985 Arrowmont Conference inspired him to approach wood turning as an art form. His painted turned work is usually created in collaboration with his wife, Belinda, who is a weaver. The Raabs reside in Canton, North Carolina. Since 1976 Wayne has been a full-time instructor in woodworking and furniture design at Haywood Community College in Clyde.
Selected Public Collections: High Museum of Art, Atlanta; Mobile Museum of Art, Ala.; Southern Highland Handicraft Guild, Asheville, N.C.; Wood Turning Center, Philadelphia

Hap Sakwa (1950–), a native of Los Angeles, attended Hershey Industrial School and the University of Maryland, where he became interested in the craft movement and began working in leather. He moved back to California in 1972 and started working in wood a few years later. Sakwa is now a commercial photographer in Sebastopol, California. Although many of his clients are wood turners, he is no longer actively involved with the craft.
Selected Public Collections: American Craft Museum, New York; Arrowmont School of Arts and Crafts, Gatlinburg, Tenn.; Fine Arts Museums of San Francisco; Mint Museum of Craft and Design, Charlotte, N.C.; The Museum of Modern Art, New York; Oakland Museum of California; The Society for Contemporary Crafts, Pittsburgh; Wood Turning Center, Philadelphia

Norm Sartorius (1947–) was born in Pocomoke City on the Eastern Shore of Maryland. After receiving his BA in psychology in 1969 at Western Maryland College in Westminster and spending several years as a "disenchanted social worker," he became a woodworking apprentice at a Baltimore studio. This experience introduced him to creative expression as a way of life. Seeking a simple, subsistence lifestyle, Sartorius moved to West Virginia in the mid-1970s and began selling treenware at craft fairs. In 1980–81 he spent a year and a half working with one of Wendell Castle's former students, Bobby Falwell, who first suggested that his carved spoons were sculpture. Sartorius did his first real turning after this during a visit to Fred Williamson's shop in West Virginia. He later started using the lathe as a cutting tool to form his unique spoons, which since 1989 have been created as decorative art, not functional utensils. The artist lives in Parkersburg, West Virginia.
Selected Public Collections: The Detroit Institute of Arts; Renwick Gallery of the Smithsonian American Art Museum, Washington, D.C.; West Virginia State Museum, Charleston; Wood Turning Center, Philadelphia

Jon Sauer (1949–) was born in San Francisco. He was first exposed to turning as a seven-year-old when his grandfather gave his father a lathe. Sauer learned to turn on this machine and also used a metal lathe in high school. He became seriously interested in wood turning in 1978 after being inspired by exotic woods. Now he uses an 1868 Holtzapffel lathe to create his ornamental turned objects, which are often inspired by architectural elements. He maintains a studio at his home in Pacifica, California.
Selected Public Collections: Los Angeles County Museum of Art; Royal Cultural Center, Jedda, Saudi Arabia; Wood Turning Center, Philadelphia

Merryll Saylan (1936–), a native of New York City, lives and maintains a studio in San Rafael, California. She received a BA in design from University of California, Los Angeles, in 1973 and an MA in art, concentrating in woodworking, from California State University, Northridge, in 1979. She has been active in professional arts organizations helping to promote fine craft and has served on the boards of both the American Association of Woodturners and the Wood Turning Center. For a number of years she has taught design and woodworking courses and has given demonstrations and lectures about her work. Saylan has also written articles for woodworking publications including *American Woodturner* and *Woodturning.* Honors for her work include being chosen as artist-in-residence for both Grizedale Sculpture Park, Cumbria, England (1990–91), and the Wood Turning Center's International Turning Exchange in Newtown, Pennsylvania (1997).
Selected Public Collections: Arizona State University Art Museum, Tempe; Barrow-in-Furness Town Council, Cumbria, England; Cleveland Crafts Centre, Middlesbrough, England; The Detroit Institute of Arts; Mint Museum of Craft and Design, Charlotte, N.C.; Renwick Gallery of the Smithsonian American Art Museum, Washington, D.C.; Wood Turning Center, Philadelphia

Betty J. Scarpino (1949–) was born in Wenatchee, Washington, and now resides in Indianapolis, Indiana. At the age of twenty-five, while working as a computer operator and learning to be a programmer, she signed up for an evening woodworking class at the University of Missouri-Columbia. This experience prompted her to enroll full-time at the university, where she majored in industrial arts with an emphasis on woodworking. Today Scarpino combines her passion for sculpture with the knowledge and technical skill gained while producing furniture to meet her objective of turning wood vessels in nontraditional forms. From 1990 to 1993 she served as editor-in-chief of *American Woodturner,* and she has been part of the editorial team for *Turning Points.* Awards and recognition include being chosen as resident artist for the Wood Turning Center's 1999 International Turning Exchange in Newtown, Pennsylvania, and winning the Excellence in Craftsmanship Award at the Arrowmont School of Arts and Crafts in 1999.
Selected Public Collections: The Contemporary Museum, Honolulu; The Detroit Institute of Arts; Mint Museum of Craft and Design, Charlotte, N.C.; Renwick Gallery of the Smithsonian American Art Museum, Washington, D.C.; Wood Turning Center, Philadelphia

Lincoln Seitzman (1923–) first pursued wood turning as an avocation in 1984, four years after retiring as vice-president of design and production from his family's clothing manufacturing business. He taught himself to turn on a Shopsmith that had been stored in his basement for thirty years. His degree in mechanical engineering, earned from Rensselaer Polytechnic Institute in 1943, prepared him for using segmented laminations to create forms inspired by Native American baskets. For every piece, he first makes a full-size drawing and lists the required operations in sequence. According to Seitzman, because of this methodical approach to his art, he never lost a piece during production. The artist was born in New York City and currently resides in West Long Branch, New Jersey. He is a founding member and former president of the New York Woodturners Association. He served on the Wood Turning Center's board of trustees for five years.

Selected Public Collections: Arrowmont School of Arts and Crafts, Gatlinburg, Tenn.; The Detroit Institute of Arts; High Museum of Art, Atlanta; Mobile Museum of Art, Ala.; The White House; Wood Turning Center, Philadelphia

David Sengel (1951–) attended Davidson College in Davidson, North Carolina, and Hollins College in Roanoke, Virginia. After completing his undergraduate study in music in 1973, he began repairing and restoring pianos. Woodworking gradually played a more significant roll in his life until he became a full-time studio wood turner in 1987. Being primarily self-taught until that time, he started attending the Arrowmont workshops to improve his technique. Sengel was born in Radford, Virginia, and currently lives in Boone, North Carolina.

Selected Public Collections: The Arkansas Arts Center Decorative Arts Museum, Little Rock; The Contemporary Museum, Honolulu; Wood Turning Center, Philadelphia

Mark Sfirri (1952–), born in Chester, Pennsylvania, first encountered the lathe at Rhode Island School of Design (BA 1974, MFA 1978) where his instructor, Tage Frid, encouraged his efforts. Sfirri initially saw the lathe as a tool for carving, but he began to use it more creatively around 1976, making furniture parts and other forms and experimenting with multi-axis turnings. During this time he also taught at Rhode Island School of Design. Sfirri set up his own woodworking shop after moving to New Hope, Pennsylvania, where he currently resides. He teaches at Bucks County Community College, travels internationally giving lectures and demonstrations, and writes for wood turning publications.

Selected Public Collections: Arrowmont School of Arts and Crafts, Gatlinburg, Tenn.; The Detroit Institute of Arts; Los Angeles County Museum of Art; Mint Museum of Craft and Design, Charlotte, N.C.; Renwick Gallery of the Smithsonian American Art Museum, Washington, D.C.; Wood Turning Center, Philadelphia

Michael Shuler (1950–), born in Trenton, New Jersey, is a self-taught artist currently living in Santa Cruz, California. In 1964, at the age of fourteen, he was fascinated by the round elements of furniture and soon learned to turn miniature birch goblets, marbles, light bulbs—anything round. Since that time he has used the lathe extensively for furniture parts, antique reproduction and restoration, architectural components, and art objects. Much of Shuler's work falls into two categories he describes as either "segmented" wood or "organica." The first involves the use of many species of wood to create polychromatic turnings; the second is a genre of vessels created from natural forms such as pinecones, thistles, and artichokes.

Selected Public Collections: American Craft Museum, New York; The Contemporary Museum, Honolulu; Fine Arts Museums of San Francisco; High Museum of Art, Atlanta; Mint Museum of Craft and Design, Charlotte, N.C.; Mobile Museum of Art, Ala.; Museum of Fine Arts, Boston; The White House; Wood Turning Center, Philadelphia

Alan Stirt (1946–), born in Brooklyn, New York, is a self-taught wood turner living in Enosburg, Vermont. He has lectured and given demonstrations on wood turning in the United States, England, Ireland, and New Zealand, where he traveled as a Fulbright Scholar in 1993. For more than ten years he has been an instructor at Arrowmont School of Arts and Crafts. The fluted bowls for which he is best known were inspired by Sung Dynasty fluted bowls in Bernard Leach's book, *The Potter's Challenge,* and by Leach's own interpretation of these bowls. In 1997 the American Association of Woodturners gave Stirt an Honorary Lifetime Membership for his dedication and contribution to the field of wood turning.

Selected Public Collections: American Craft Museum, New York; Arizona State University Art Museum, Tempe; The Detroit Institute of Arts; High Museum of Art, Atlanta; Los Angeles County Museum of Art; Mint Museum of Craft and Design, Charlotte, N.C.; Mobile Museum of Art, Ala.; Renwick Gallery of the Smithsonian American Art Museum, Washington, D.C.; Robert Hull Fleming Museum, Burlington, Vt.; The Society for Contemporary Crafts, Pittsburgh; The White House; Wood Turning Center, Philadelphia

Bob Stocksdale (1913–) was born in Warren, Indiana, and grew up on a farm outside of Huntingdon, Indiana. As a young man he learned to do spindle turning and produced table legs. A conscientious objector during World War II, he was stationed at a camp in Valhalla, Michigan, where he had access to a lathe and started making bowls. In 1946 he set up his own shop in Berkeley, California, where he still resides. He made his living turning bowls, becoming a true master of the form. Stocksdale has been a guest instructor for numerous institutions and craft programs. He taught from 1964 to 1972 at Berkeley Adult School and from 1965 to 1986 at San Francisco Community College. He is an Honorary Member of the Baulines Craft Guild, became an American Craft Council Fellow in 1978, and was named a California Living Treasure in 1985. He is an Honorary Lifetime Member of the American Association of Woodturners. His work has been published extensively, and he has had many solo exhibitions, as well as shows with his wife, fabric artist Kay Sekimachi.
Selected Public Collections: American Craft Museum, New York; Arizona State University Art Museum, Tempe; The Contemporary Museum, Honolulu; The Detroit Institute of Arts; Fine Arts Museums of San Francisco; High Museum of Art, Atlanta; The Metropolitan Museum of Art, New York; Mint Museum of Craft and Design, Charlotte, N.C.; Mobile Museum of Art, Ala.; Museum of Fine Arts, Boston; The Newark Museum, N.J.; Oakland Museum of California; Parnham House, Dorset, England; Philadelphia Museum of Art; Renwick Gallery of the Smithsonian American Art Museum, Washington, D.C.; Royal Scottish Museum, Edinburgh; The Toledo Museum of Art; Wood Turning Center, Philadelphia

Jack Straka (1934–), born in Mahanoy City, Pennsylvania, was introduced to turning as a child. During his eighteen years with Burroughs Corporation, wood turning was just a hobby. However, seeking a major lifestyle change, he moved to Hawaii in 1975 and began to focus on wood. He studied in England with internationally known turner Peter Child, who taught Straka the cutting method of turning. Straka has turned over fifty Hawaiian-grown woods, but the majority of his bowls are made of koa. He resides in Keaau, Hawaii, and makes his living as a turner.
Selected Public Collections: The Contemporary Museum, Honolulu; Renwick Gallery of the Smithsonian American Art Museum, Washington, D.C.; Wood Turning Center, Philadelphia

Del Stubbs (1952–), born in Red Bluff, California, started turning in 1974 at the age of twenty-one. It immediately consumed his interests. After just six months he had the opportunity to spend a year in Oregon studying with Paul English. Since that time he has explored many areas of turning, including salad bowl and small item production, architectural spindles, translucent bowls, and drums and wind instruments. During the past ten years he has taught more than one hundred workshops in seven countries.
Selected Public Collections: Wood Turning Center, Philadelphia; Yale University Art Gallery, New Haven

Robert Trout (1930–) was born in Marshall-town, Iowa. He received his BA in 1960 and MA in 1961 from California State University, Long Beach. Trout was a broadly skilled craftsman who worked in clay, metal, and wood. He is now retired and lives in Garden Grove, California.

Howard Whipple (1881–1959) was born in Northfield, Minnesota, and lived in Berkeley, California. In 1903 he graduated from Williams College in Williamstown, Massachusetts. A banker by profession, Whipple taught himself to turn spindles and goblets on a lathe, which he had purchased for his sons in 1934. After receiving a band saw as a present from the California Bankers Association in 1937, he began using the intarsia technique to make intricately decorated boxes and other forms. In 1946 he retired from banking and focused on woodworking. Whipple shared his enthusiasm for his craft by lecturing to civic organizations and exhibiting his work. He preferred not to put a value on his pieces and refused to sell them.
Selected Public Collections: The Metropolitan Museum of Art, New York

Mark Lindquist

Bruce Mitchell

Harry Nohr

Melvin Lindquist

Ed Moulthrop

Craig Nutt

Steve Loar

Philip C. Moulthrop

Rude Osolnik

Hugh E. McKay

Thomas Nicosia

Stephen Mark Paulsen

Connie Mississippi

Dale L. Nish

Gord Peteran

Portraits continued from page 163

Michael James Peterson

Merryll Saylan

Michael Shuler

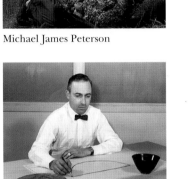

James Prestini

Betty J. Scarpino

Alan Stirt

H. Wayne Raab

Lincoln Seitzman

Bob Stocksdale

Norm Sartorius

David Sengel

Jack Straka

Jon Sauer

Mark Sfirri

Del Stubbs

A Chronological List of Selected Exhibitions

The artists in this exhibition are listed after each show in which they exhibited turned wooden objects. Exhibitions in italics were accompanied by publications.

Decorative Arts: Official Catalog, Department of Fine Arts, Division of Decorative Arts. San Francisco: Golden Gate International Exposition, 1939.
> Prestini

Useful Objects Under Ten Dollars. New York: The Museum of Modern Art, 1939.
> Prestini

Contemporary New England Handicrafts. Worcester, Mass.: Worcester Art Museum, 1943.

An Exhibition of Contemporary American Crafts. Baltimore: The Baltimore Museum of Art, 1944.
> Prestini

Good Design is Your Business. Buffalo, N.Y.: The Buffalo Fine Arts Academy, Albright Art Gallery, 1947.
> Prestini

One Hundred Useful Objects of Fine Design. New York: The Museum of Modern Art, 1947.
> Prestini

Decorative Arts Today. Newark: The Newark Museum, 1948.
> Prestini

An Exhibition for Modern Living. Detroit: The Detroit Institute of Arts, 1949.
> Carpenter, Prestini, Stocksdale

Design for Christmas. Boston: The Institute of Contemporary Art, 1949.
> Carpenter, May, Prestini

"Modern Marquetry," American Craftsmen's Educational Council, America House, New York City, 1950.
> Whipple

Los Angeles County Fair: Arts and Crafts, Painting and Sculpture. Pomona, Calif.: Los Angeles County Fair, 1950.
> Stocksdale

Design for Christmas. Boston: The Institute of Contemporary Art, 1950.
> May, Prestini

Good Design. New York: The Museum of Modern Art for the Merchandise Mart, Chicago, January and June 1951.
> Stocksdale

Los Angeles County Fair: Arts and Crafts, Painting and Sculpture. Pomona, Calif.: Los Angeles County Fair, 1951.
> Prestini

Industrie und Handwerk schaffen: neues Hausgerät in USA. Stuttgart: 1951.
> May, Prestini, Stocksdale

Design for Christmas. Boston: The Institute of Contemporary Art, 1951.
> May

"The Craftsman Loves His Kitchen," American Craftsmen's Educational Council, America House, New York City, 1952.
> Eshelman

Good Design. New York: The Museum of Modern Art for the Merchandise Mart, Chicago, January 1953.
> Carpenter

"Creations in Inlaid Wood: Intarsia by Howard Whipple, Class of 1903," Lawrence Art Museum, Williams College, Williamstown, Mass., 1953.
> Whipple

Designer-Craftsmen, U.S.A., 1953. New York: American Craftsmen's Educational Council and the Brooklyn Museum of Art, 1953; toured.
> Carpenter, Eshelman, May, Stocksdale

Design for Christmas. Boston: The Institute of Contemporary Art, 1953.
> May

New England Craft Exhibition 1955. Worcester, Mass.: Worcester Art Museum, 1955; toured.
> May

"New Jersey Designer-Craftsmen," The Montclair Art Museum, Montclair, N.J., 1956.
> Anderson

Craftsmanship in a Changing World. New York: Museum of Contemporary Crafts, 1956.
> Carpenter, Eshelman, May, Stocksdale

"Furniture by Craftsmen," Museum of Contemporary Crafts, New York City, 1957.
> Anderson

"Brussels World's Fair," Belgium, 1958.
> Eshelman, Prestini, Stocksdale

Living Today: An Exhibition of Contemporary Architecture, Furniture, Interior Decoration. Washington, D.C.: The Corcoran Gallery of Art, 1958.
> Stocksdale

20th Century Design: U.S.A. Ed. William Friedman. Buffalo, N.Y.: The Buffalo Fine Arts Academy, Albright Art Gallery, 1959; toured.
> May, Prestini, Stocksdale

Fiber Clay Metal: A National Craft Competition. St. Paul, Minn.: The Saint Paul Gallery and School of Art, 1959.
> May, Prestini, Stocksdale

California Design Eight. Pasadena: Pasadena Art Museum, 1962.
> Glaser, Stocksdale, Trout

Craftsmen of the Northeastern States. Worcester, Mass.: Worcester Art Museum, 1963; toured.
Anderson, Eshelman, E. Moulthrop, Osolnik

California Design Nine. Pasadena: Pasadena Art Museum, 1965.
Glaser, Stocksdale, Trout

Craftsmen USA 66. New York: Museum of Contemporary Crafts, 1966.
Eshelman, Glaser, E. Moulthrop

California Design Ten. Pasadena: Pasadena Art Museum, 1968.
Glaser, Stocksdale, Trout

The American Craftsmen's Invitational Exhibition. Seattle: The Henry Gallery, University of Washington, 1968.
Stocksdale

"Bob Stocksdale—Wood Turnings," American Craft Museum, New York City, 1969.
Stocksdale

Objects: USA. By Lee Nordness. New York: Viking, 1970; published in association with a 1969 exhibition organized by the S. C. Johnson Company; toured.
Nohr, Stocksdale

California Design Eleven. Pasadena: Pasadena Art Museum, 1971.
Stocksdale, Trout

Craft Multiples. Washington, D.C.: Renwick Gallery, 1975; toured.
Osolnik, Stocksdale

"California Design '76," Pacific Design Center, Los Angeles, 1976.
Saylan

American Crafts 1977. Philadelphia: Philadelphia Museum of Art, 1977.
Stocksdale

Young Americans: Fiber/Wood/Plastic/Leather. New York: Museum of Contemporary Crafts of the American Crafts Council, 1977; toured.
Mark Lindquist

Craft, Art, and Religion. Rome: The Vatican Museum, co-sponsored by the Smithsonian Institution, 1978.
E. Moulthrop

The Art of the Turned Bowl. Washington, D.C.: Renwick Gallery, 1978.
Mark Lindquist, Melvin Lindquist, E. Moulthrop, Stocksdale

"Installation of Twentieth-Century Decorative Art," The Metropolitan Museum of Art, New York City, 1978.
Mark Lindquist, Melvin Lindquist, Prestini

"Art for Use," American Craft Museum, New York City, 1980; toured.
E. Moulthrop

For the Tabletop. New York: American Craft Museum, 1980.
Mark Lindquist

A Gallery of Turned Objects. Ed. Albert LeCoff. Provo: Brigham Young University Press, 1981. Published for the exhibition "Turned Object Show," held at Bucks County Community College, Newtown, Pa.; toured.
Brolly, Brubaker, Chinn, Cummings, Diamond-Nigh, Ellsworth, Gilson, Hogbin, Holzapfel, Hosaluk, Hunter, Johnson, Melvin Lindquist, Loar, Mitchell, E. Moulthrop, Nish, Osolnik, Paulsen, Sakwa, Saylan, Stirt, Stocksdale, Straka, Stubbs

"Beyond Tradition: Twenty-fifth Anniversary Exhibition," American Craft Museum, New York City, 1981.
E. Moulthrop

Pattern: An Exhibition of the Decorated Surface. New York: American Craft Museum, 1982.
Paulsen

The Art of Woodturning. New York: American Craft Museum, 1983.
Ellsworth, Gilson, Hogbin, Hoyer, Kent, Knox, Mark Lindquist, Melvin Lindquist, E. Moulthrop, Saylan, Stocksdale, Stubbs

California Crafts XIV: Living Treasures of California. Sacramento: Crocker Art Museum, 1985.
Stocksdale

The Art of Turned-Wood Bowls: A Gallery of Contemporary Masters—And More. By Edward Jacobson. New York: E. P. Dutton, 1985; Arizona State University Art Museum, toured.
Ellsworth, Gilson, Hogbin, Hoyer, Hunter, Kent, Mark Lindquist, Melvin Lindquist, Mitchell, E. Moulthrop, P. Moulthrop, Nish, Osolnik, Prestini, Sakwa, Stirt, Stocksdale, Straka, Stubbs

"Crafts: National," Buffalo State College, Buffalo, N.Y., 1985.
Kent

Woodturning: Vision and Concept. Gatlinburg, Tenn.: Arrowmont School of Arts and Crafts, 1985.
Chinn, Cox, Cummings, Diamond-Nigh, Ellsworth, Gilson, Hogbin, Holzapfel, Hosaluk, Hunter, Johnson, Knox, Lamar, Mark Lindquist, Melvin Lindquist, Loar, Mitchell, E. Moulthrop, P. Moulthrop, Nish, Osolnik, Paulsen, Raab, Sfirri, Stirt, Stocksdale, Stubbs

Italian-American Traditions: Family and Community. Philadelphia: Balch Institute for Ethnic Studies, 1985.
Nicosia

"American Woodturners," Brookfield Crafts Center, Brookfield, Conn., 1986.
> Cox, Hoyer, Hunter, Johnson, Kent, Lamar

Craft Today: Poetry of the Physical. By Paul J. Smith and Edward Lucie-Smith. New York: American Craft Museum, 1986; toured.
> Ellsworth, Kent, Mark Lindquist, E. Moulthrop, Paulsen, Stocksdale, Stubbs

National Craft Invitational. By Townsend Wolfe, Michael Preble, and Patty Dean. Little Rock: The Arkansas Arts Center Decorative Arts Museum, 1987.
> E. Moulthrop

Works Off the Lathe: Old and New Faces. St. Louis: Craft Alliance Gallery, co-organized by the Wood Turning Center, 1987.
> Bosley, Brolly, Chase, Chinn, Cox, Cummings, Diamond-Nigh, Draper, Ellsworth, Gilson, Graham, Holzapfel, Hosaluk, Hoyer, Hunter, Johnson, Knox, Lamar, Latven, Mark Lindquist, Melvin Lindquist, Loar, Mitchell, E. Moulthrop, P. Moulthrop, Osolnik, Paulsen, Raab, Sakwa, Saylan, Sfirri, Shuler, Stirt, Stocksdale, Straka

"Turned Wood: The New Artistry," The Arkansas Arts Center Decorative Arts Museum, Little Rock, 1987.
> Kvitka, Mitchell, Peterson

Works Off the Lathe: Old and New Faces II. St. Louis: Craft Alliance Gallery, co-organized by the Wood Turning Center, 1988.
> Bosley, Brolly, Chase, Chinn, Cox, Cummings, Draper, Ellsworth, Gilson, Graham, Holzapfel, Hosaluk, Hoyer, Hunter, Johnson, Lamar, Latven, Loar, Mitchell, E. Moulthrop, P. Moulthrop, Osolnik, Paulsen, Raab, Saylan, Sfirri, Shuler, Stirt, Stocksdale, Straka, Stubbs

Lathe-Turned Objects: An International Exhibition. By Albert B. LeCoff. Philadelphia: Port of History Museum, co-organized by the Wood Turning Center, 1988; toured.
> Bosley, Brolly, Chase, Chinn, Cox, Cummings, Draper, Ellsworth, Fleming, Gilson, Graham, Hogbin, Holzapfel, Horn, Hosaluk, Hoyer, Hunter, Johnson, Kent, Knox, Krimmel, Kvitka, Lamar, Latven, Mark Lindquist, Melvin Lindquist, Loar, Mitchell, E. Moulthrop, P. Moulthrop, Nish, Osolnik, Paulsen, Peterson, Prestini, Raab, Sakwa, Saylan, Seitzman, Sfirri, Shuler, Stirt, Stocksdale, Straka, Stubbs

National Objects Invitational. By Townsend Wolfe. Little Rock: The Arkansas Arts Center Decorative Arts Museum, 1989.
> Ellsworth, Nutt

Turner's Challenge III. St. Louis: Craft Alliance Gallery, co-organized by the Wood Turning Center, 1989.
> Bosley, Brolly, Chase, Chinn, Cox, Cummings, Dotson, Draper, Ellsworth, Fleming, Gilson, Graham, Holzapfel, Horn, Hosaluk, Hoyer, Hunter, Johnson, Kent, Krimmel, Lamar, Latven, Loar, Mitchell, E. Moulthrop, P. Moulthrop, Nish, Nutt, Osolnik, Paulsen, Peterson, Raab, Saylan, Shuler, Stirt, Stocksdale, Straka

Rude Osolnik: A Retrospective. Asheville, N.C.: Southern Highland Handicraft Guild, 1989.
> Osolnik

Contemporary Works in Wood: Southern Style. Curated by Martha Stamm Connell. Huntsville, Ala.: Huntsville Museum of Art, 1990.
> Lamar, Melvin Lindquist, E. Moulthrop, P. Moulthrop, Nutt, Osolnik

Pennsylvania Lathe-Turned Objects: Trends, Transitions, Traditions 1700–1990. By Albert LeCoff and Tina Van Dyke. Philadelphia: Woodmere Art Museum, co-organized by the Wood Turning Center, 1990.
> Bosley, Brolly, Brubaker, Diamond-Nigh, Ellsworth, Eshelman, Nicosia, Sfirri

Re: Turning, 1970–1990: Works by Stephen Hogbin. Toronto: Ontario Crafts Council, 1990.
> Hogbin

Woodturning: Vision and Concept II. Gatlinburg, Tenn.: Arrowmont School of Arts and Crafts, 1990.
> Bosley, Brolly, Burchard, Chase, Chinn, Dotson, Ellsworth, Fleming, Gilson, Horn, Jordan, Kent, Krimmel, Kvitka, Lamar, E. Moulthrop, Peterson, Raab, Sauer, Seitzman, Sfirri, Stirt

International Lathe-Turned Objects: Challenge IV. Philadelphia: Port of History Museum, co-organized by the Wood Turning Center, 1991; toured.
> Brolly, Burchard, Chase, Chinn, Dotson, Draper, Ellsworth, Fleming, Gilson, Graham, Hogbin, Holzapfel, Horn, Hosaluk, Hoyer, Jordan, Lamar, Latven, Loar, E. Moulthrop, P. Moulthrop, Nutt, Paulsen, Peterson, Raab, Sauer, Seitzman, Sfirri, Stirt

National Objects Invitational. By Alan DuBois. Little Rock: The Arkansas Arts Center Decorative Arts Museum, 1991.
> Draper, Loar

Out of the Woods: Turned Wood by American Craftsmen. Mobile, Ala.: Mobile Museum of Art, 1992; toured.
> Cox, Dotson, Draper, Ellsworth, Gilson, Holzapfel, Horn, Hoyer, Hunter, Jordan, Kent, Lamar, Latven, Mark Lindquist, Melvin Lindquist, E. Moulthrop, P. Moulthrop, Nish, Osolnik, Paulsen, Peterson, Raab, Shuler, Stirt, Stocksdale

A Decade of Craft: Recent Acquisitions/Part I: Glass and Wood. New York: American Craft Museum, 1992.
    Hunter, Kent, Kvitka, Mark Lindquist, Sakwa, Shuler, Stirt, Stocksdale

"American Crafts: The Nation's Collection," Renwick Gallery, Washington, D.C., 1992.
    Hunter, Mark Lindquist, Mitchell

Redefining the Lathe-Turned Object. Tempe: Arizona State University Art Museum, 1992.
    Brolly, Burchard, Chinn, Ellsworth, Fleming, Gilson, Horn, Hoyer, Hunter, Jordan, Loar, McKay, E. Moulthrop, P. Moulthrop, Peterson, Sartorius, Sauer, Seitzman

Connected Passages: Cultural Imperative and Innovation in Contemporary African American Crafts. Philadelphia: The Afro-American Historical and Cultural Museum, 1993.
    Chinn, Cummings

Hand of a Craftsman, Eye of an Artist: A New Generation of Woodturners. Chattanooga, Tenn.: Hunter Museum of Art, 1993.
    Dotson, Holzapfel, Horn, Jordan, Lamar, Latven, P. Moulthrop, Peterson, Raab, Shuler

National Objects Invitational. Little Rock: The Arkansas Arts Center Decorative Arts Museum, 1993.
    Holzapfel, Mark Lindquist

Contemporary Crafts and the Saxe Collection. By Davira S. Taragin et al. Toledo: The Toledo Museum of Art, 1993; toured.
    Mark Lindquist, Melvin Lindquist, Stocksdale

Marriage in Form: Kay Sekimachi and Bob Stocksdale. By Signe Mayfield. Palo Alto, Calif.: Palo Alto Cultural Center, 1993.
    Stocksdale

Uncommon Beauty in Common Objects: The Legacy of African American Craft Art. Wilberforce, Ohio: National Afro-American Museum and Cultural Center, 1993.
    Cummings

Conservation by Design. Ed. Scott Landis. Easthampton, Mass. and Providence: Woodworkers Alliance for Rainforest Protection and Museum of Art, Rhode Island School of Design, 1993.
    Brolly, Ellsworth, Hogbin, Hosaluk, Sfirri, Stocksdale

Challenge V: International Lathe-Turned Objects. By Albert LeCoff. Collegeville, Pa.: Philip and Muriel Berman Museum of Art, Ursinus College, co-organized by the Wood Turning Center, 1994; toured.
    Bosley, Burchard, Chase, Cummings, Dotson, Fleming, Gilson, Hogbin, Horn, Hoyer, Hunter, Jordan, Lamar, Latven, Loar, McKay, Mississippi, E. Moulthrop, P. Moulthrop, Sartorius, Sauer, Seitzman, Sengel, Shuler, Stirt

Revivals! Diverse Traditions, 1920–1945. Ed. Janet Kardon. New York: Harry N. Abrams in association with the American Craft Museum, 1994.
    Osolnik

Turning Plus . . . Redefining the Lathe-Turned Object III. Tempe: Arizona State University Art Museum, 1994.
    Burchard, Ellsworth, Fleming, Holzapfel, Horn, Hosaluk, Hoyer, Hunter, Jordan, Kent, Krimmel, Kvitka, Lamar, Latven, McKay, Paulsen, Peterson, Raab, Sauer, Scarpino, Seitzman, Sfirri, Shuler

National Objects Invitational. Little Rock: The Arkansas Arts Center Decorative Arts Museum, 1995.
    Lamar

The White House Collection of American Crafts. By Michael W. Monroe. Washington, D.C.: National Museum of American Art, 1995; toured.
    Cox, Cummings, Dotson, Ellsworth, Fleming, Horn, Jordan, Kent, Mark Lindquist, Melvin Lindquist, E. Moulthrop, P. Moulthrop, Seitzman, Shuler, Stirt

Mark Lindquist: Revolutions in Wood. By Robert Hobbs. Richmond, Va.: Hand Workshop Art Center in association with the University of Washington Press, 1995; toured.
    Mark Lindquist

Nature Turning into Art: The Ruth and David Waterbury Collection of Turned Wood Bowls. Northfield, Minn.: Carleton College Art Gallery, 1995.
    Bencomo, Bosley, Burchard, Chase, Dotson, Ellsworth, Holzapfel, Horn, Hoyer, Hunter, Jordan, Kent, Lamar, Mitchell, E. Moulthrop, P. Moulthrop, Osolnik, Peterson, Shuler, Stirt, Straka

Craft in the Machine Age, 1920–1945. Ed. Janet Kardon. New York: Harry N. Abrams in association with the American Craft Museum, 1995.
    Prestini

Southern Arts and Crafts 1890–1940. By James Jordan III et al. Charlotte, N.C.: Mint Museum of Art, 1996.
    Huskey

Expressions in Wood: Masterworks from the Wornick Collection. Oakland: Oakland Museum of California, 1997; toured.
    Bencomo, Bosley, Burchard, Chase, Dotson, Ellsworth, Fleming, Gilson, Holzapfel, Horn, Hoyer, Hunter, Jordan, Kent, Kvitka, Latven, Mark Lindquist, Mitchell, P. Moulthrop, Peterson, Sakwa, Sartorius, Seitzman, Shuler, Stocksdale

"The Renwick at 25," Renwick Gallery, Washington, D.C., 1997.
    Bencomo, Dotson, Holzapfel

Turned for Use. San Antonio, Tex.: San Antonio Museum of Art, sponsored by the American Association of Woodturners, 1997.
    Brolly, Burchard, Ellsworth, Hosaluk, Sauer

Curators' Focus: Turning in Context. By Albert LeCoff. Collegeville, Pa.: Philip and Muriel Berman Museum of Art, Ursinus College, co-organized by the Wood Turning Center, 1997; toured.

> Burchard, Hosaluk, Hunter, Kent, Krimmel, Lamar, McKay, Mississippi, E. Moulthrop, Peteran, Saylan, Seitzman, Sfirri, Shuler, Stirt

Turned Wood Now: Redefining the Lathe-Turned Object IV. By John Perreault and Heather Sealy Lineberry. Tempe: Arizona State University Art Museum, 1997.

> Dotson, Ellsworth, Holzapfel, Horn, Hoyer, Kent, Lamar, Saylan

Moving Beyond Tradition: A Turned-Wood Invitational. By Alan DuBois. Little Rock: The Arkansas Arts Center Decorative Arts Museum, 1997.

> Brolly, Burchard, Dotson, Ellsworth, Fleming, Horn, Hosaluk, Hoyer, Hunter, Jordan, Lamar, Latven, Loar, Mississippi, Mitchell, Peterson, Raab, Sartorius, Saylan, Scarpino, Sengel, Sfirri, Stirt

Pathways. By Gene Kangas. Cleveland, Ohio: Cleveland State University Art Gallery, 1998.

> Brolly, Ellsworth, Horn, Jordan, Krimmel, Loar, McKay, Scarpino, Stirt

Celebrating the Creative Spirit: Contemporary Southeastern Furniture. By Martha Stamm Connell. Mobile, Ala.: Mobile Museum of Art, 1998.

> Nutt

East Meets West: A Showcase of Japanese and Western Turned Wood Art. Tacoma, Wa.: Handforth Gallery, sponsored by the American Association of Woodturners, 1999.

> Burchard, Ellsworth, Jordan, Krimmel, Melvin Lindquist, Nish, Osolnik, Scarpino, Stocksdale

The Art of Craft: Contemporary Works from the Saxe Collection. By Timothy Anglin Burgard. San Francisco: M. H. de Young Memorial Museum, 1999.

> Bencomo, Burchard, Ellsworth, Fleming, Hunter, Kvitka, Mark Lindquist, Melvin Lindquist, E. Moulthrop, Peterson, Shuler, Stocksdale

Living with Form: The Horn Collection of Contemporary Crafts. Little Rock: The Arkansas Arts Center Decorative Arts Museum in association with Bradley Publishing, 2000.

> Burchard, Chinn, Dotson, Draper, Ellsworth, Fleming, Hogbin, Holzapfel, Horn, Hosaluk, Hoyer, Hunter, Jordan, Kent, Lamar, Latven, Mark Lindquist, Melvin Lindquist, Loar, Mississippi, Mitchell, E. Moulthrop, Osolnik, Peterson, Raab, Sartorius, Scarpino, Sengel, Sfirri, Shuler, Stirt, Stocksdale

Turning on Furnishings 2000: Woodturning in Canada, The Turn of the Millennium. Markham, Ont.: Canadian Woodturners Association and the Wood Turning Center, 2000.

> Hogbin, Hosaluk

Turning Wood Into Art: The Jane and Arthur Mason Collection. By Suzanne Ramljak, Michael W. Monroe, and Mark Richard Leach. New York: Harry N. Abrams, in association with the Mint Museum of Craft and Design, 2000.

> Burchard, Cummings, Dotson, Ellsworth, Fleming, Gilson, Hogbin, Holzapfel, Horn, Hosaluk, Hoyer, Hunter, Jordan, Kent, Kvitka, Lamar, Latven, Mark Lindquist, Melvin Lindquist, Mitchell, E. Moulthrop, P. Moulthrop, Nish, Osolnik, Peterson, Prestini, Sakwa, Saylan, Scarpino, Sfirri, Shuler, Stirt, Stocksdale

The Fine Art of Wood: The Bohlen Collection. Detroit: The Detroit Institute of Arts, 2000.

> Bencomo, Brolly, Burchard, Dotson, Ellsworth, Fleming, Gilson, Horn, Hosaluk, Hoyer, Hunter, Jordan, Kent, Kvitka, Lamar, Mark Lindquist, Melvin Lindquist, McKay, Mississippi, Mitchell, Nish, Osolnik, Paulsen, Peterson, Sartorius, Saylan, Scarpino, Seitzman, Stirt, Stocksdale

Selected Books and Periodicals

Adamson, Glenn. "California Dreaming: The Second Generation of Studio Furniture Making in Northern California." In *Furniture Studio One: The Heart of the Functional Arts*, ed. John Kelsey and Rick Mastelli. Free Union, Va.: The Furniture Society, 1999.

—. "California Spirit: Rediscovering the Furniture of J. B. Blunk." *Woodwork* 59 (October 1999): 22–31.

Androkites, Allen. *Measured Drawings of Selected Pieces of Woodwork by Paul W. Eshelman, Craftsman and Educator*. Millersville, Pa.: by the author, 1980.

Bassett, Kendall, and Arthur Thurman. *How to Make Objects of Wood*. New York: The Museum of Modern Art, 1951.

"Bob Stocksdale Turns a Bowl." *Craft Horizons* 16, no. 6 (December 1956): 38–39.

Bowie, John. "The John Grass Wood Turning Company." In *A Sampling of Papers from the 1993 World Turning Conference*. Philadelphia: Wood Turning Center, 1997.

Brown, Sam, ed. *Getting the Most Out of Your Lathe*. Milwaukee, Wis.: Delta Manufacturing Co., 1935.

Carpenter, Arthur Espenet. "Memoirs of an Opinionated Woodie." In *Furniture Studio One: The Heart of the Functional Arts*, ed. John Kelsey and Rick Mastelli. Free Union, Va.: The Furniture Society, 1999.

Clark, Garth, and Margie Hughto. *A Century of Ceramics in the United States, 1878–1978*. New York: E. P. Dutton and the Everson Museum of Art, 1979.

A Comprehensive Handbook on Uses and Applications of the Lathe. Plainfield, N.J.: Walker-Turner Company, 1934.

Connell, Martha. "Grandmaster of Woodturning." *Turning Points* 10, no. 3 (Fall 1997).

Cooke, Edward S., Jr. "Turning and Contemporary Studio Furniture: An Uneasy Relationship." In *Papers from the 1997 World Turning Conference*. Philadelphia: Wood Turning Center, 2000.

—. "Wood in the 1980s: Expansion or Commodification?" In *Contemporary Crafts and the Saxe Collection*, ed. Davira Taragin. New York: Hudson Hills Press, 1993.

Courter, Elodie. "Wood as Fine as Porcelain." *House Beautiful* 89, no. 12 (December 1947): 132–33.

—. "Wood Shapes by James Prestini." *Arts & Architecture* 65 (August 1948): 27–29.

Crawshaw, Fred. *Problems in Wood Turning*. Peoria, Ill.: Manual Arts Press, 1909.

Draper, Addie, and Bud Latven. "Segmented Turning." *Fine Woodworking* 54 (September/October 1985): 64–67.

Duncan, Robert Bruce. "Bob Stocksdale: Still on a Roll at 75." *Woodwork* 1 (Spring 1989): 16–21.

Eaton, Alan. *Handicrafts of New England*. New York: Harper & Brothers, 1949.

Edmiston, Susan. "Fumio Yoshimura." *Craft Horizons* 31, no. 4 (August 1971): 22–25, 71.

Ellsworth, David. "Hollow Turnings." *Fine Woodworking* 16 (May/June 1979): 62–66.

Fischman, Irving. "Checkered Bowls." *Fine Woodworking* 1, no. 1 (Winter 1975): 16–19.

Frantz, Suzanne. *Contemporary Glass*. New York: Abrams, 1989.

Gelber, Steven. "Do-It-Yourself: Constructing, Repairing, and Maintaining Domestic Masculinity." *American Quarterly* 49, no. 1 (March 1997): 66–112.

Golden, Michael. *A Laboratory Course in Wood-Turning*. New York: Harper & Brothers Publishers, 1897.

Harries, Karsten. *The Bavarian Rococo Church: Between Faith and Reason*. New Haven: Yale University Press, 1983.

Hawks, Bob. "Floral Visions." *Fine Woodworking* 99 (April 1993): 54–57.

Hiort, Esbjørn. *Finn Juhl: Furniture—Architecture—Applied Art*. Copenhagen: Danish Architectural Press, 1990.

Hogbin, Stephen. *Wood Turning: The Purpose of the Object*. Sydney: John Ferguson Pty. Ltd. and Crafts Council of Australia, 1980.

Huff, Darrell. "Bowls Are His Business." *Popular Science* 169, no. 2 (August 1956): 165–68.

Industrial-Arts Magazine (1914–May 1930); changed its name to *Industrial Arts and Vocational Education* (June 1930–June 1972).

James, Gerald. *Woodturning: Design and Practice*. London: John Murray, 1958.

James Prestini, 1938–1988. Petaluma, Calif.: Creators Equity Foundation, 1990.

Karlsen, Arne. *Contemporary Danish Design*. Copenhagen: Danish Society of Arts and Crafts and Industrial Design, 1960.

Kaufmann, Edgar, Jr. "Kay Bojesen: Tableware to Toys." *Interiors* 112, no. 7 (February 1953): 64–67.

—. *Prestini's Art in Wood.* New York: Pantheon Books, 1950.

Kelsey, John. "Ornamental Turning." *Fine Woodworking* 1, no. 4 (Fall 1976): 46.

—. "The Turned Bowl: The End of Infancy for a Craft Reborn." *Fine Woodworking* 32 (January/February 1982): 54–60.

—. "Turning Conference: Notes and Information on a Recent Gathering." *Fine Woodworking* 1, no. 3 (Summer 1976): 44–45.

Kessler, Jane, and Dick Burrows. *Rude Osolnik: A Life Turning Wood.* Louisville, Ky.: Crescent Hill Books, 1997.

Klenke, William. *Art and Education in Wood Turning.* Peoria, Ill.: Manual Arts Press, 1921.

—. *The Art of Wood Turning.* Peoria, Ill.: Manual Arts Press, 1937.

—. *The Art of Woodturning.* Peoria, Ill.: Charles Bennett, 1954.

Knox, Frank M. "Ornamental Turnery: The Hobby of Kings and Princes." *Antique Trader Weekly* (October 1977): 346.

Lindquist, Mark. *Sculpting Wood: Contemporary Tools and Techniques.* Worcester, Mass.: Davis Publications, 1986.

—. "Spalted Wood." *Fine Woodworking* 2, no.1 (Summer 1977): 50–53.

—. "Turning Spalted Wood." *Fine Woodworking* 11 (Summer 1978): 54–59.

Lyon, Mary. "A Master Plays Wide Field." *Craft Horizons* 13, no. 4 (July/August 1953): 26–31.

McKinley, Donald. "The Wood-Turned Forms of Stephen Hogbin." *Craft Horizons* 34, no. 2 (April 1974): 28–32, 64.

Manual Training Magazine (1899–1903).

May, Richard. "Bowls From Green Woods." *Craft Horizons* 9, no. 2 (Summer 1949): 20–21.

Meilach, Dona. *Contemporary Art With Wood: Creative Techniques and Appreciation.* New York: Crown, 1968.

—. *Creating Modern Furniture: Trends, Techniques, Appreciation.* New York: Crown, 1975.

Milton, Archie, and Otto Wohlers. *A Course in Wood Turning.* Milwaukee: Bruce Publishing Company, 1919.

Nish, Dale. *Artistic Woodturning.* Provo: Brigham Young University Press, 1980.

—. *Creative Woodturning.* Provo: Brigham Young University Press, 1975.

—. *Master Woodturners.* Provo: Artisan Press, 1985.

Oldknow, Tina. *Pilchuck: A Glass School.* Seattle: University of Washington Press, 1996.

Pepis, Betty. "Architect-and-Wife Team Creates Furniture to Fit." *New York Times* (5 May 1956).

Perrault, John. "Turning Point." *American Craft* 47, no. 1 (February/March 1989): 30.

Popular Mechanics (January 1902—).

Popular Science (May 1872—).

Rebhorn, Eldon. *Woodturning.* Bloomington, Ind.: McKnight & McKnight, 1970.

Saylan, Merryll. "Paul Killinger." *American Woodturner* 2, no. 3 (September 1987): 18.

—. "Women's Role in Woodworking." *Woodwork* 51 (June 1998): 65–67.

Shuler, Michael. "Segmented Turning." *Fine Woodworking* 76 (May/June 1989): 72–75.

Skilled Work: American Craft in the Renwick Gallery. Washington, D.C.: National Museum of American Art, Smithsonian Institution, 1998.

Sloan, David. "Arrowmont Turning Conference: New Work, New Guild." *Fine Woodworking* 56 (January/February 1986): 64–66.

Starr, Richard. "Last Was Best." *Fine Woodworking* 32 (January/February 1982): 61.

Stocksdale, Bob. "Exotic Woods: Observations of a Master Turner." *Fine Woodworking* 1, no. 4 (Fall 1976): 28–32.

Stone, Michael. *Contemporary American Woodworkers.* Salt Lake City: Peregrine Smith, 1986.

—. "Partners in Craftsmanship." *American Craft* 43, no. 3 (June/July 1983): 6–10.

Wallance, Don. *Shaping America's Products.* New York: Reinhold, 1956.

Woodworker's Turning and Joining Manual. New York: Popular Science Publishing Company, 1934.

Zurcher, Suzette. "Prestini, A Contemporary Craftsman." *Craft Horizons* 8, no. 23 (November 1948): 25–26.

Glossary

Diagrams courtesy American Association of Woodturners

Burl: A hard woody protrusion on a tree, more or less rounded in form, usually resulting from the entwined growth of a cluster of small stalks or buds making a contorted, gnarly mass. The grain in a burl has no direction, which makes the wood stable and unlikely to split or check. Burls are highly valued by many turning artists because of their interesting designs, textures, and colors.

Chatoyence: An optical effect of some types of highly polished wood grain with an undulating, or floating luster that resembles three-dimensional satin ribbons.

Chuck: A mechanical clamping device for holding material or a tool in a lathe.

Crotch: The point on a tree where a single trunk or branch divides into two or more smaller branches. Crotch figure can be very ornate in some species.

Ebonized: A surface treatment where a deep, lustrous black stain is rubbed into the grain of a piece of wood.

Faceplate: A metal plate that screws onto the lathe for inboard or outboard turning, and onto which wood is securely attached. Faceplates are used for turning forms with bases or bottoms, like bowls or vases. (See Fig. 19, page 37).

Gouge: A hollow-bladed chisel normally made in widths from 1/4 to 2 inches, and in various radii ranging from *flat* to *fluting*. A single bevel is ground on either the outside or inside of the blade.

Headstock: The assembly containing the driving mechanism for the lathe. It is bolted to the lathe and contains the spindle for the spur or live drive.

Heartwood: The central core of wood in the trunk and branches of mature trees. At one time heartwood was sapwood, but it no longer conducts sap or has living cells. In most species of trees, the heartwood is harder and has a darker color than the rest of the wood.

Intarsia: A mosaic of small pieces of wood that are inserted and glued into hollows in a wooden support.

Lathe: A machine for working a piece of wood, metal, etc., by rotating it against a tool that shapes or cuts it. (See illustration).

Mandrel: A tapered or cylindrical axle, spindle, or arbor that is inverted into a hole in a piece of wood so as to support the wood during turning.

Metal lathe/machinist's lathe: A precision lathe for forming and shaping objects out of metal. This type of lathe has a carriage that holds the cutting tool in a chuck.

Milling machine: A machine for precisely shaping wood, metal, and other materials by rotating the tools and/or the work.

Multi-axis turning: A technique of lathe turning where more than one axis is used, in order to produce an asymmetrical object. (See illustration).

Multi-axis turning of a candlestick:

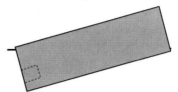

Blank mounted on first axis

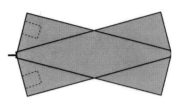

Blank spinning on first axis

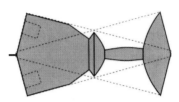

Blank turned on first axis

Blank mounted on second axis

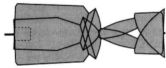

Blank spinning on second axis

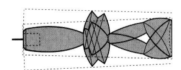

Blank turned on second axis

The completed multi-axis turned candlestick

Tailstock   Tool rest   Headstock

Ways

Lathe

Off-center turning: A technique of lathe turning where more than one center is used, in order to produce an irregularly shaped object.

Ornamental lathe: A machine used for indexed mechanical carving of an object. The cutters are in an independent chuck that rotates and moves separately from the wood. Ornamental lathes were used historically for decorative embellishment, and for making clocks and scientific instruments.

Pith: The small core of spongy cellular tissue located at the center of tree trunks, branches, and twigs.

Rose engine: A modified lathe with a special appendage invented in the eighteenth century and used for a type of ornamental turning. Precise and intricate curvilinear patterns can be engraved with this tool.

Sapwood: The physiologically active part of wood that is made up of one or more outer growth rings. Sapwood is usually lighter in color than heartwood.

Scraper: A type of chisel with a cutting edge that is made in a number of different shapes and sizes (usually rounded) and is beveled on one side. It is held differently than the skew or gouge, almost perpendicular to the work, and is used most often for finish work.

Skew (chisel): A chisel with a characteristically long blade and handle. The blade is beveled (sharpened at an angle) on both sides and can be angled or straight.

Spalting: A particular form of fungal decay of wood that produces softening and embrittlement, and irregularly shaped dark zone lines on the surface of the wood. Spalted wood is highly valued by some turning artists because of its interesting patterns and textures.

Spindle turning: Turning between centers, with the material placed on a lathe between the headstock and the tailstock. Traditionally, spindles were used for chair legs, rails, and backs, and for balusters supporting a stair handrail. (See illustration).

Split turning: A process of cutting a turned object into two or more parts. Historically, the split-turning technique was used when two identical semicircular pieces were required. The pieces were often used as decorative elements on door panels and cabinets.

Spur: A type of scrap wood normally discarded by veneer mills. Cut from the enlarged area of a tree next to its roots in order to make a more perfect cylinder for milling, the wood is gnarly and full of knots, and usually 2 to 10 inches in thickness.

Tailstock: A unit that can be moved along the ways of the lathe and clamped at a desired distance from the headstock.

Tool support base and tool rest: The tool support base is clamped to the bed and may be positioned where desired along the ways of the lathe. It contains a socket into which the tool rest fits. The tool rest may be moved up or down as required for spindle turning, or turned as needed for faceplate turning.

Veneer: Wood that has been sliced, peeled, or sawn into sheets of no more than $\frac{1}{4}$ inch thickness. Veneer is cut, fitted, and glued to the surface of wood objects such as tables and vessels to create a decorative pattern.

Ways: The longitudinal guiding surfaces on a lathe.

Spindle turning

Index

Photography